Impostors

Six Kinds of Liar

SARAH BURTON

VIKING

VIKING

Published by the Penguin Group
Penguin Books Ltd, 27 Wrights Lane, London W8 5TZ, England
Penguin Putnam Inc., 375 Hudson Street, New York, New York 10014, USA
Penguin Books Australia Ltd, Ringwood, Victoria, Australia
Penguin Books Canada Ltd, 10 Alcorn Avenue, Toronto, Ontario, Canada M4V 3B2
Penguin Books (NZ) Ltd, Private Bag 102902, NSMC, Auckland, New Zealand

Penguin Books Ltd, Registered Offices: Harmondsworth, Middlesex, England

First published 2000
1 3 5 7 9 10 8 6 4 2

Set in 12/15.5pt Monotype Bembo
Typeset by Rowland Phototypesetting Ltd,
Bury St Edmunds, Suffolk
Printed in Great Britain by Clays Ltd, St Ives plc

A CIP catalogue record for this book is available from the British Library

ISBN 0–670–87967–3

In memory of
Jane Annakin
and
Nigel Baguley

Acknowledgements

Thanks to the following people for, in various ways, helping the book on its way: Julia Boffey, Jacky Bratton, Margot Coates, Sue Ellis, Mair Fryer, Kit Harding, Harry Jackson, Ken and Marion Lazenby, Johnny Mars, Cathy Meade, Tahira Patwa, Barry and David Purves, Colin and Deborah Rogers, June Rose, Nigel Sandbrook, Donald Smith, Roy Stubbings, Sula Wolff.

Special thanks to Nick Baker, who got it going; to my editors Hannah Robson and Anya Waddington and my agent David Miller, who made it a pleasure; and to my parents Anne and Reg, my mother-in-law Mary and my husband Leslie, who made it possible.

Contents

Illustrations

Acknowledgements

Pictures 1, 2, 3, 7, 9 & 10 courtesy of Hulton Getty Picture Collection; pictures 4 & 5 courtesy of Glenbow Archives, Galgary, Canada; picture 6 courtesy of PA News; picture 8 courtesy of Popperfoto; pictures 11 & 12 courtesy of Wellcome Institute Library, London; picture 13 from *The Female Soldier; or, the Surprising Life and Adventures of Hannah Snell*, 1750; picture 14 courtesy of Kitty Oakes; picture 15 courtesy of Corbis; picture 16 from *Caraboo: A Narrative of a Singular Imposition Practiced Upon the Benevolence of a Lady Residing in the Vicinity of Bristol*, 1817

1. Introduction

Early one October morning in 1859, a Salford man was walking along the banks of the River Irwell on his way to work when he noticed a hat floating in the water. Something about this hat caught his attention. As the water swirled around it, it did not move. Closer inspection revealed that the hat was firmly lodged on the head of a dead body, standing upright in the water.

The body was conveyed to a nearby public house, where it was quickly identified as that of a well-known local character, Harry Stokes. Stokes was a master bricksetter whose special skill was in constructing chimneys and fire grates; some of the tallest chimneys in the Manchester and Salford area were Harry's work. He was locally respected, having been sworn in as a special constable during the Chartist riots, and made captain of his company. Although his brief marriage had ended in separation, he had been living for many years with a widow who, like his wife, kept a pub. Harry was a familiar, congenial figure behind the bar, and also frequented other pubs and 'ordinaries' in the area, smoking, drinking and bantering with his friends and colleagues. Perhaps it was this lifestyle which had led him into financial straits, as it was conjectured that facing destitution, he chose suicide.

The coroner's inquest would have been a mere formality, and Harry Stokes's passing have gone unremarked, had it not been the case that one of the jurors recalled a scandal at the time of his marriage. On his wedding night Harry's wife had made the complaint that her husband was 'not a man' and had immediately left him. The coroner duly directed two women to examine the body, who returned, tittering, to the courtroom, saying it was true: 'he' was a 'she'.

'Harry' Stokes's imposture was recorded in half a column in the *Manchester Weekly Advertiser* before the story sank, like Harry, almost without trace. As a journalist pointed out, but for one juror's keen memory, Stokes, as a pauper, would have been buried in her clothes, and remained for ever 'him'.

The word 'impostor' usually conjures up names such as Anastasia, the Tichborne claimant, Princess Caraboo, and other high-profile figures. Yet how many other Harry Stokeses were there? . . . or *are* there? When we talk about impostors, we are necessarily talking about impostors who have ultimately failed, simply by virtue of the fact that we *know* they were impostors: those who succeeded remain undetected. The most famous (or infamous) impostors seem to be motivated by fame and fortune – or, perhaps, these are the ones we are more likely to hear about. Yet what motivated the likes of Harry Stokes?

My research has led me into territories that I could never have foreseen at the outset. The 'real' lives impostors leave behind are almost uniformly intolerable and oppressive. The impostor is an escapologist as much as an adventurer. Endlessly creative and highly intelligent, impostors recognize the limitations of the hand life has dealt them: they cannot change the world into which they are born as losers, so they change themselves, this time, crucially, awarding themselves a sporting chance.

It is not only their ability to sustain the imposture that is impressive; once launched into the world, impostors are frequently high-achievers. Although their credentials may be faked, their abilities are often very much the real thing. Impostor doctors and academics, for example, are often at least as impressive as their qualified colleagues. Many of those who are cited in this book are, by definition, not the best – not so clever that they didn't get found out. The supreme impostors remain out there, inscrutable double-agents on a highly personal mission.

Impostors start out as almost ordinary people who consider how their lives are likely to develop, and decide that it is an unacceptable prospect. If they are only prepared to break one of society's great taboos, to lie so convincingly and consistently that they begin to believe the lies themselves, the doors of opportunity which seemed so firmly shut against them spring open. For the impostor, the strategy is entirely logical.

Although there are some factors common to most impostors, there are different kinds of impostor. There are the serial impostors who, unable ever to settle into one identity, move from one 'life' to another when the water gets too hot (or, as frequently, when they get bored). Then there are 'event' impostors, whose short-term impersonations are designed for specific occasions. These are often the most spectacular, offering the gulled parties little time to question what is going on, exploiting the element of surprise.

There are long-term impostors, such as Harry Stokes: a single gargantuan lie, a deception of such monumental proportions that it would rarely occur to anyone to question it. The women who lived their lives as men are at once the most harmless, and yet somehow the most disturbing of impostors. How did they get away with it, is the irresistible question. Get away with it they did: we will never know how many. Many, like Harry Stokes, were only discovered after death; others, like Catherine Coombes, a foreman and house painter, were discovered when, through illness or imprisonment, they lost the privacy essential to maintaining their deception. (Coombes was in her sixties when she was admitted to the workhouse following an industrial accident. Her true sex came to light because she was incapable of dressing herself unaided.) Other long-term impostors build up their second self more gradually. A sequence of small lies, sometimes established over a period of many years, are each on their own fairly innocuous, but collaborate to produce an entirely new person. This complex web of 'fibs' is often harder to unravel than deceits on a grander scale.

Impostors sometimes take on the identity of a real person (living or dead) in order to avail themselves of their qualifications, for example, or their money. These could be more exactly defined as impersonators. Others invent everything: names, dates, places; often using material from their own genuine histories, crucially adapted, embroidered, and transformed in order to lend an authentic touch to their assumed identity.

In attempting to categorize different kinds of impostors, however, there is one simple and useful division into two broad but distinct types. The first category consists of those people who use imposture to gain what could never rightfully be theirs. They may pose, for example, as an heir to an estate, or as some remarkable person in order to gain fame and fortune. Whereas this group use imposture in order to pretend to some great achievement or status, the second group use imposture to *enable* them to achieve. This group comprises genuinely and prodigiously talented people who, in their 'real' lives, would never have the opportunity to exploit their abilities and intelligence. The first group pretend they *have* achieved (or inherited); the second group pretend *in order to* achieve. They could be called, respectively, *opportunists* and *pragmatists*.

Chief Buffalo Child Long Lance and Dr James Barry, for example, were, in terms of ability and skill, streets ahead of their peers, and their lasting contributions to making the world a better place are undeniable. However, had they 'played by the rules' their palpable talents would have been entirely wasted. For *pragmatists* Barry and Long Lance, the imposture was a means by which they could fulfil their potential. For *opportunists* Louis de Rougemont and the Tichborne claimant, the imposture itself was the achievement: in each case the 'life' was a masterpiece, out of which money could be made. Whereas Barry and Long Lance worked to improve the lot of the sick, the dispossessed, the 'little people', de Rougemont and the Tichborne claimant helped only themselves.

This book is about impostors who sought more than mere financial gain from their assumed personae: some did not profit at all from their imposture while others undoubtedly did, but money was not their primary concern. These impostors didn't simply want money to which they weren't entitled: they wanted lives which could never, in the normal course of events, have been theirs.

While this book concerns itself principally with pragmatist impostors, it also draws on the histories of their baser cousins, the opportunists, in order to illustrate the means by which imposture can succeed. Both types share a common pool of strategies, although their aims are rather different. As we shall see, impostors depend not only on their ability to play a part convincingly, but on our predisposition to believe in it.

Although parallels can be drawn which connect their lives, each impostor is an original, a 'one off', an entirely singular and unique individual. The crucial moments at which they cross the line from an authentic to an assumed identity are likewise unique, when the apparently insignificant event transforms the ordinary person into a work of art.

Early in the nineteenth century a little girl found herself tramping a dusty lane into the village of Whitby, near Doncaster. Eight years old, she had run away from home, where life had become intolerable. Neglected and abused by her parents, as soon as she could walk she had been made to assist her violent father in his arduous work as a bricklayer. Having no other skill, arriving in Whitby she immediately sought out the local bricklayer and offered her services. The bricklayer looked on approvingly as the ragged little creature demonstrated his considerable skill and strength – for all the circumstances dictated that this child was a boy. Harriet Stokes, crucially, did not correct his mistake, but gave her name as Harry.

2. Louis de Rougemont:
'A Sort of Wizard'

Sir, I invite your Highness, and your train,
To my poor cell, where you shall take your rest
For this one night, which – part of it – I'll waste
With such discourse as, I not doubt, shall make it
Go quick away; the story of my life,
And the particular accidents gone by
Since I came to this isle.

– The Tempest V.i

Although this lord of weak remembrance, this,
Who shall be of as little memory
When he is earthed, hath here almost persuaded –
For he's a spirit of persuasion, only
Professes to persuade . . .

– The Tempest II.i

'The adventures of Louis de Rougemont – as told by himself' was the publishing phenomenon of the 1890s. In his autobiography, which was serialized in *Wide World* magazine, de Rougemont described his incredible adventures, spanning thirty years, during which he had been lost in the vast, and then largely unexplored wastes of the Australian outback. He owed his survival in large part to an original imposture: he posed not as another person, but as a god. *Wide World*'s circulation rocketed as de Rougemont's amazing story was lapped up by avid readers around the globe.

The motto of the magazine, 'Truth is Stranger than Fiction', seemed utterly endorsed by de Rougemont's account. He told how, as a young French gentleman living with his mother (estranged from her well-born but impoverished husband) in Switzerland, he had set out to seek his fortune and wound up on a pearling expedition to New Guinea. After several weeks at sea a terrific storm blew up: the ship was wrecked, and the crew and captain were drowned. De Rougemont's life was saved by the only other survivor of the wreck:

I am sure I should have been drowned had not my brave dog come to my rescue and seized me by my hair . . . [He] tugged and tugged at me until he had got me half-way through the breakers . . . I then exerted myself sufficiently to allow of his letting go my hair, whilst I took the end of his tail between my teeth, and let him help me ashore in this peculiar way.

However, de Rougemont's relief at getting on to dry land soon evaporated. 'Thank God,' he later reflected, 'I did not realize at that moment that I was doomed to spend a soul-killing *two and a half years* on that desolate, microscopical strip of sand!' He estimated his desert island to be less than a hundred yards long and ten yards wide.

De Rougemont was fortunate in being able to rescue a number of useful tools and supplies from the wreck of the *Veielland* and demonstrated considerable resourcefulness in constructing a hut out of shells and planting crops with which to vary his diet of turtle eggs and sea birds. However, his mental stamina was severely tested during the long months ahead, as every day he scrutinized the horizon, hoping against hope for the sight of a sail. He warded off depression 'and manias generally' by taking up gymnastics, becoming 'a most proficient tumbler and acrobat', and also entertained himself by taking rides on the backs of giant sea turtles. Bruno, the wonder dog, also proved an invaluable and cheering companion, and was the first to see a boat when it finally came.

However, de Rougemont was not to be saved; it was he who was to turn rescuer. Having beaten off sharks in order to reach the catamaran, he discovered on it the prostrate bodies of a family of aborigines. The man, woman and two boys were pitifully thin and dehydrated, apparently more dead than alive. De Rougemont nursed the family with great care, and they, once restored to consciousness, gradually overcame their terror of this strange white creature, whom they clearly believed to be 'a kind of Supreme Spirit from another world'. De Rougemont, crucially, did not enlighten them on this point, and later actively encouraged and exploited this misapprehension. The woman of the family, Yamba, seemed to him the most intelligent, and he was soon able to communicate with her. She explained that they had been on a local turtling expedition when a terrific storm had blown them far out to sea. This convinced de Rougemont that mainland Australia could not be far away. Before the arrival of his companions, de Rougemont had constructed a large boat, using materials he had salvaged from the *Veielland*, which, to his great frustration, he found impossible to launch alone. As soon as his visitors were fit, they helped him get it afloat, and set sail for their home.

When they finally arrived, to be greeted by a welcoming party, de Rougemont's worries were far from over: 'I viewed their approach with mixed sensations of alarm and hope. I was in the power of these people, I thought. They could tear me limb from limb, torture me, kill and eat me, if they so pleased.' From the long conversations he had by this time had with Yamba, he knew her people were cannibals.

Fortunately, the natives were not unfriendly, although the sight of this *white* man initially terrified them. During the days that followed the natives were increasingly impressed with de Rougemont and invited him to remain with them as long as he wished. He was offered a wife, and negotiated a swap with Yamba's obliging husband.

Yamba. Ah! noble and devoted creature! The bare mention of her name stirs every fibre of my being with love and wonder. Greater love than hers no creature ever knew, and not once but a thousand times did she save my wretched life at the risk of her own . . . By this time she could speak a little English, and was so marvellously intelligent that she seemed to discover things by sheer intuition or instinct. I think she never let a day go by without favourably impressing the chiefs concerning me, my prowess and my powers; and without her help I simply could not have lived through the long and weary years, nor should I ever have returned to civilisation.

Yamba had early on grasped that although de Rougemont was indeed an extraordinary man, he was no magician, or white spirit. But she also perceived the usefulness of her tribespeople thinking him so:

Almost every evening the blacks would hold a stately *corroboree*, singing and chanting; the burden of their song being almost invariably myself, my belongings, and my prowess – which latter, I fear, was magnified in the most extravagant manner.

In order to maintain this mythical image of himself, de Rougemont took great care never to fail at anything he undertook:

Once the mysterious white stranger was found to be full of the frailties of the ordinary man, his prestige would be gone, and then life would probably become intolerable. Thus everything I did I had to excel in, and it was absolutely necessary that I should be perpetually 'astonishing the natives', in the most literal sense of the phrase.

As well as engineering situations in which he might impress the aborigines – here greatly aided by his tomahawk, stiletto and his bow and arrows (the aborigines had no metal blades and archery was unknown to them) – de Rougemont also learned to exploit random events. One day, when out in a boat hunting dugongs with Yamba he accidentally harpooned a baby whale. The whale's mother appeared, smashed up de Rougemont's boat and pursued the baby to land, beaching herself. The aborigines assumed that de Rougemont had single-handedly killed and brought ashore both whales, 'and in the *corroborees* that ensued, the poets went almost delirious in trying to find suitable eulogisms to bestow upon the mighty white hunter'. Learning of this great feat from smoke signals, aborigines from hundreds of miles around came to witness de Rougemont's catch. With the loss of his boat escape by sea now seemed impossible, so, anticipating an overland journey, de Rougemont took the opportunity to acquaint himself with the chiefs of neighbouring tribes.

In the mean time Yamba had made a little canoe for local expeditions, and on one of these excursions, to a nearby island, de Rougemont found another opportunity to augment his public image:

I had not gone many yards down this track, when I was horrified to see, right in front of me, an enormous alligator! This great reptile was shuffling along down the path towards me, evidently making for the water, and it not only blocked my advance, but also necessitated my immediate retreat. The moment the brute caught sight of me he stopped, and began snapping his jaws viciously. I confess I was quite nonplussed for the moment as to how best to commence the attack upon this unexpected visitor. It was impossible for me to get round him in any way, on account of the dense bush on either side of the narrow forest track. I decided, however, to make a bold dash for victory, having always in mind the prestige that was so necessary to my existence among the blacks.

I therefore walked straight up to the evil-looking monster; then, taking a short run, I leaped high into the air, shot over his head, and landed on his scaly back, at the same time giving a tremendous yell in order to attract Yamba, whom I had left in charge of the boat. The moment I landed on his back I struck the alligator with all my force with my tomahawk, on what I considered the most vulnerable part of his head. So powerful was my stroke, that I found to my dismay that I could not get the weapon out of his head again.

While I was in this extraordinary situation – standing on the back of an enormous alligator, and tugging at my tomahawk, embedded in its head – Yamba came rushing up the path, carrying one of the paddles, which, without a moment's hesitation, she thrust down the alligator's throat as he turned to snap at her. She immediately let go her hold and retreated. The alligator tried to follow her, but the shaft of the paddle caught among some tree trunks and stuck. In this way the monster was prevented from moving his head, either backwards or forwards, and then, drawing my stiletto, I blinded him in both eyes, afterwards finishing him leisurely with my tomahawk, when at length I managed to release it.

Yamba was immensely proud of me after this achievement, and when we returned to the mainland she gave her tribesmen a graphic account of my gallantry and bravery. But she always did this. She was my advance agent and bill-poster, so to say. I found in going in a new country that my fame had preceded me; and I must say this was most convenient and useful in obtaining hospitality, concessions and assistance generally.

Good old Yamba, of course, kept quiet about her own part in the battle with the alligator. Without Yamba, de Rougemont later freely admitted, his imposture would have been impossible to carry off.

After a year and a half with Yamba's tribe, de Rougemont, accompanied by his devoted wife, set off overland for white society. Yamba's astonishing abilities to provide food, water and shelter in the most unpromising circumstances sustained them through fever, drought, and flood. During the latter they constructed a raft, and proceeded on their journey by skirting the coast. After several months, they came unexpectedly upon a ship at anchor. The crew, Malayan fishermen, were only too willing to take de Rougemont on board, and back to 'civilization':

They even offered Yamba a passage along with me; but, to my amazement and bitter disappointment, she said she did not wish to go with them. She trembled as though with fear. She was afraid that when once we were on board, the Malays would kill me and keep her. One other reason for this fear I knew, but it in no way mitigated my acute grief at being obliged to decline what would probably be my only chance of returning to civilisation. For this I had pined day and night for four or five years, and now that escape was within my grasp I was obliged to throw it away. For let me emphatically state, that even if civilisation had been but a mile away, I would not have gone a yard towards it without that devoted creature who had been my salvation, not on one occasion only, but practically every moment of my existence.

To add insult to injury, after eighteen months away, bad weather drove the devoted couple back to Yamba's people. (Many years later, after his return to white society, de Rougemont recalled that his knowledge of Australia's geography was lamentable, and he was usually entirely mistaken about where he was. At this time, however, even armed with the maps that did exist – which themselves contained large areas of unmarked terrain – a number of white explorers had disappeared, never to be seen again.) Yamba and de Rougemont decided it would not be in their interests to inform the tribe they had not come back of their own free will, and instead intimated that the great white spirit had chosen to return to his people. As it happened, he arrived at a moment when they were particularly glad to see him:

Human nature is, as I found, the same the world over, and one reason for my warm welcome was that my blacks had just been severely thrashed by a neighbouring tribe, and were convinced that if I would help them to retaliate, they could not fail to inflict tremendous punishment upon their enemies.

De Rougemont, who was becoming reconciled to the strong

possibility that he might never be able to return home, decided he had better make the best of the situation he found himself in, and agreed. He trained his troops daily, and planned an attack along the lines of an important medieval battle (the Swiss encounter at Grandson) he had learned about at school:

I ought here to describe my personal appearance on this important day, when, for the first time, I posed as a great chief, and led my people into battle, filled with the same enthusiasm that animated them. My hair was built up on strips of whalebone to a height of nearly two feet from my head, and was decorated with black and white cockatoo feathers. Around my middle I wore a kind of double apron of emu skin, with feathers.

His face and body were painted yellow, white, black and red, 'so that altogether you may imagine I presented a terrifying appearance'. Despite the precautions he had taken, which included a personal bodyguard of two top warriors, de Rougemont knew that his supernatural powers were being put to a crucial test:

Just before the battle commenced I had a real inspiration which practically decided the affair without any fighting at all. It occurred to me that if I mounted myself on stilts, some eighteen inches high, and shot an arrow or two from my bow, the enemy would turn tail and bolt. And so it turned out.

His image as a mighty warrior enhanced, far from resting on his laurels, de Rougemont worked hard to maintain the illusion of his supernatural abilities, exploiting the aborigines' terror of departed spirits by making himself 'a huge hideous mask out of a kangaroo skin' in which he prowled the perimeter of the camp after dark, making strange noises. 'On these occasions,' he explained, 'the blacks thought I was in my natural element as a spirit.' Despite his privileged position in the tribe, de Rougemont still hankered for home, and his disgust for his people's customs (their cannibalism and barbaric treatment of women he found most appalling) increased rather than faded as time passed. He determined, if he could not escape, at least to explore a little. He and Yamba duly set off. Whenever they approached a new tribe's territory, Yamba, his navigator, scout and public-relations manager, as well as his dearest friend and comfort, went in as before, ahead of the white god. By the time de Rougemont arrived 'Yamba had been as busy as a showman out West,' spreading reports of his supernatural prowess and magical attributes. Seen as 'a sort of wizard', de Rougemont was accordingly treated with great respect wherever he went.

While staying with one of the friendly tribes they had encountered, de Rougemont learned of a neighbouring chief who had *two white wives*. Greatly intrigued, de Rougemont investigated and, with Yamba's help, gained access to the young women:

Looking back now, I remember they presented a truly pitiable spectacle. They were huddled together on the sandy ground, naked, and locked in one another's arms. Before them burned a fire . . . Both looked frightfully emaciated and terrified – so much so, that as I write these words, my heart beats faster with horror as I recall the terrible impression they made upon me. As they caught sight of me, they screamed aloud in terror. I retired a little way, discomfited, remembering suddenly my own fantastic appearance. Of course, they thought I was another black fellow come to torture them.

I went back and stood before the girls, saying, reassuringly, 'Ladies, I am a white man and a friend; and if you will only trust in me I think I can save you.' Their amazement at this little speech knew no bounds, and one of the girls became quite hysterical. I called Yamba, and introduced her as my wife, and they then came forward and clasped me by the hand, crying, shudderingly, 'Oh save us! Take us away from that fearful brute!'

The first priority was to provide the girls with dresses (made out of cockatoo feathers). Although a cannibal chief, de Rougemont was a Victorian gentleman, and was deeply embarrassed in the presence of naked white women. He learned from the girls that they were Blanche and Gladys Rogers, daughters of a sea captain. Due to a combination of unfortunate circumstances they had become separated from their father, who sank with the ship, and had been kidnapped by cannibals, who barbecued the sailors accompanying them. Taken as wives by the savage chief the girls repeatedly attempted suicide, but were always restrained by the women set to guard them. De Rougemont was understandably upset by the unfolding tale, and he and Yamba determined to find a way of rescuing the unfortunate girls. He challenged the chief to a wrestling match – the victor would win the white women. The chief was 'magnificently muscular' and much bigger than his opponent; however, de Rougemont succeeded in flooring him twice before finishing him off with a deadly punch to the chest (carefully concealing from the spectators the stiletto in his fist):

As I withdrew the knife, I held it so that the blade extended up my forearm and was quite hidden. This, combined with the fact that the fatal wound bled mainly internally, caused the natives to believe I had struck my enemy dead by some supernatural means . . . You will observe that by this time I would seize every opportunity of impressing the blacks by an almost intuitive instinct; and as the huge savage lay dead on the ground, I placed my foot over the wound, folded my arms, and looked round triumphantly upon the enthusiastic crowd, like a gladiator of old.

Fortunately, the spectators were glad to see the back of their despotic chief, so there were no reprisals, and de Rougemont and Yamba soon set off with the Rogers girls. Finally they returned to Yamba's tribe, who took the presence of de Rougemont's 'new wives' as a sign that he intended to remain with them. De Rougemont derived considerable pleasure from the girls' company (he and Yamba treated them as daughters), conversing in English, singing hymns and reciting passages from Shakespeare. To the natives' amusement the girls taught de Rougemont to perform an

Irish jig; to Bruno's consternation he taught them to yodel. Yes, faithful Bruno was still at his master's side, although local and visiting aborigines often offered to 'adopt' him. De Rougemont saw, in their interest in his dog, a further opportunity to promote his special status, and informed them:

. . . that Bruno was my *brother*, whose soul and being he possessed! His bark, I pretended, was a perfectly intelligible language, and this they believed the more readily when they saw me speak to the dog and ask him to do various things, such as fetching and carrying; tumbling, walking on his hind legs, etc. etc. But even this argument did not suffice to overcome the covetousness of some tribes, and I was then obliged to assure them confidentially that he was a relative of the Sun, and therefore if I parted with him he would bring all manner of most dreadful curses down upon his new owner or owners.

With the addition of the Rogers girls to his family, de Rougemont was at his happiest since the shipwreck had altered the course of his life. The girls found in de Rougemont the father they had lost at sea: and he had the comfort of their company. But this picture of familial bliss was about to be blighted by tragedy:

I now come to what is possibly the most painful episode of my career, and one which I find it impossible to discuss, or write about, without very real pain. Even at this distance of time I cannot recall that tragic day without bitter tears coming into my eyes, and being afflicted with a gnawing remorse which can never completely die in my heart.

One day, a ship was sighted, moving slowly across the gulf. Within minutes twenty catamarans were launched, and headed after the ship; de Rougemont, Yamba and the girls – who were beside themselves with excitement, and had begged to be permitted to come – attempted to head the ship off by setting out in a different direction. As they neared the ship the people on board evidently believed they were about to be attacked by savages, and fired on the canoe, which overturned in the ensuing panic. When Yamba and de Rougemont managed to scramble back on to the canoe, they realized the girls were missing. They were never seen again. De Rougemont was devastated, and consumed with remorse: 'I blame myself for not having forbidden them to go in the canoe,' he wrote many years later. 'If I had retained one atom of my self-possession I would never have dreamed of approaching the little European vessel at the head of a whole flotilla of catamarans, filled with yelling and gesticulating savages.'

De Rougemont now had no reason to stay. Sickened and depressed, he decided to undertake the great journey home, untroubled now by the likelihood of failure and death by starvation and dehydration. On this marathon trek de Rougemont and Yamba encountered plagues of rats and locusts, and on one occasion it rained fish. They also came across significant quantities of gold, the uselessness of which, in the circumstances, rendered it uninteresting, and they left it where it lay.

Crossing an inhospitable desert, de Rougemont's spirits soared briefly when he spotted a party of white explorers – yet sank abruptly when, on approaching them, he and Yamba were shot at and obliged to keep their distance. A few days later, the intrepid couple discovered another white man, named Gibson, who had become separated from this same party and now rambled aimlessly, raving. De Rougemont naturally missed social intercourse with his own 'kind' and his morale again lifted at the prospect of a new companion. However, despite his and Yamba's best efforts, Gibson never regained his sanity, and rather than contributing to their pool of social and practical resources, he became an intolerable burden:

I remember that native chiefs frequently suggested that I should leave him, but I never listened to this advice for a moment. Perhaps I was not altogether disinterested, because already my demented companion was looked upon as a kind of minor deity by the natives . . . Indeed his strange gestures, antics, and babblings were sufficient in themselves to convince the blacks that he was a creature to be reverenced.

Poor mad Gibson died. (After his return to his own society many years later, de Rougemont was to learn that the explorers he had seen were members of the famous Giles expedition of 1874, who named the Gibson desert after their lost companion.) Gibson's death was followed by two new additions to de Rougemont and Yamba's family – a son and a daughter – again causing them to draw their travels to a halt. The proud father decided to build a house – or rather, to have one built for him:

I did not dare to do much manual labour, because it would have been undignified on my part . . . It was a source of infinite satisfaction to me to feel that I had a *home* I could call my own. I had grown very weary of living like an animal in the bush, and lying down to sleep at night on the bare ground . . . As the months glided into years, and I reviewed the whole of my strange life since the days when I went pearling with Jensen, the thought began gradually to steal into my mind, 'Why not wait until civilisation *comes to you* – as it must do in time? Why weary yourself any more with incessant struggles to get back to the world – especially when you are so comfortable here?' Gradually, then, I settled down and was made absolute chief over a tribe of perhaps five hundred souls.

Although, as a returned spirit, de Rougemont was believed to have special qualities, he was perturbed by the presence of a powerful medicine man in his tribe, and consequently he felt the continual need to reinscribe his own authority. When fine ash fell over the surrounding country (he later found out this was due to the eruption of Krakatoa), de Rougemont gave the natives to understand that he had had something to do with it. He also impressed them with the illusion of burning water, by igniting crude oil he had collected in the outback:

Now, the medicine-man belonging to the tribe in my mountain home presently found himself (or fancied himself) under a cloud, – the reason, of course, being that my display of wonders far transcended anything which he himself could do. So my rival commenced an insidious campaign against me, trying to explain away every wonderful thing that I did, and assuring the blacks that if I were a spirit at all it was certainly a spirit of evil.

De Rougemont realized that the medicine man's continual attempts to undermine his position would become serious. He had to come up with a dramatic display of his powers, which would end the challenges once and for all. As he was wandering in the bush, considering this problem, he came upon a large nest of snakes:

I marked the spot in my mind, and returned home, pondering the details of the dramatic victory I hoped to win. Day by day I returned to this spot and caught numerous black and carpet snakes. From each of these dangerous and poisonous reptiles I removed the poison fangs only; and then, after scoring it with a cross by means of my stiletto, I let it go, knowing that it would never leave a spot so ideal – from a snake's point of view. Needless to say, I might have met my own death in this extraordinary business had I not been assisted by my devoted wife.

De Rougemont was ready to issue his challenge; the medicine man, taken by surprise, accepted. The tribe, and many interested neighbours, assembled at the spot de Rougemont had chosen. He summoned the snakes with a whistle before the intrigued company:

Selecting a huge black snake, who bore unobtrusively my safety mark, I pounced down upon him and presented my bare arm. After teasing the reptile two or three times I allowed him to strike his teeth deep into my flesh, and immediately the blood began to run. I also permitted several other fangless snakes to bite me until my arms and legs, breast and back, were covered with blood. Personally I did not feel much the worse, as the bites were mere punctures, and I knew the selected reptiles to be quite innocuous. Several 'unmarked' snakes, however, manifested an eager desire to join in the fun, and I had some difficulty in escaping their deadly attentions. I had to wave them aside with a stick.

Understandably, the medicine man felt unequal to this challenge, and de Rougemont was at last able to relax. He lived out the remainder of his 'lost years' as a benevolent chief, turning his hand to more peaceable projects, such as inventing the wheel. Tragically, at only the second point in his exile when he had achieved a contented and settled existence, the objects of his affection were to be snatched away. Bruno, de Rougemont's first rescuer and loyal companion throughout his adventures, a canine of astonishing longevity, died; then his young children, who had never been strong, both faded away; and finally, Yamba, whose very name de Rougemont was always to revere, passed into the next world, leaving him – he felt – utterly alone. 'The blacks had long since put me down as a great spirit come to visit them, and they even located by common consent a certain star in the heavens which they decided was at one time my home, and to which I should eventually return.' With the death of Yamba, life among the aborigines lost its savour for de Rougemont, and he decided to return to his real home, little caring if he should perish in the attempt. After a long and arduous solitary journey he came upon the first signs that he was nearing 'civilization': after thirty years lost in the Australian bush, a trail of litter pointed the way 'home'.

A group of prospectors, who were the first white men de Rougemont encountered, clearly thought that he was mad and gave no credence to the tale he unfolded. It was not until, having worked his passage to England, he entered the offices of *Wide World* magazine that he found a receptive audience for his undeniably strange story.

No sooner did the first instalment appear in print than the

brickbats started flying. Two incidents related by de Rougemont early in his narrative instantly attracted a deluge of criticism. The first concerned his claim that, in the early days of his shipwrecked, solitary existence, he used to pass the time by riding on the backs of sea turtles, which he 'steered' by poking them in the appropriate eye with his toe. This claim was evidently ridiculous to many readers. 'An Australian' wrote to the *Daily Chronicle*, 'I have caught and handled some thousands of turtles, and I never yet saw one which when afloat and when touched anywhere on its body, did not sink almost vertically.' Other correspondents, showing no little contempt for de Rougemont's 'fable', agreed. Yet perhaps truth really is stranger than fiction . . . Admiral J. Moresby wrote expressing some surprise that de Rougemont's reports had been received with scepticism: 'I had considerable experience of turtle catching and know of a midshipman who got on a turtle's back and enjoyed a ten minutes' ride, before he brought the animal to a standstill.' T. H. Haynes was similarly mystified by the turtle controversy, asserting, 'The natives do catch turtles by riding them until they stop, and I do not doubt the possibility of even steering them on their course.'

The other early disputed claim was that, prior to de Rougemont's shipwreck, a man on the pearling expedition with him fell victim to a giant octopus, which rose out of the water, enveloping both man and boat in its monstrous tentacles, and dragged them under the surface. The following is a mere sample of the criticism this provoked:

During my 25 years' experience in Pacific seas I have never heard of an octopus weighing more than 15lbs being found in shallow waters, such as pearlers would work in. An octopus weighing 15lbs would have tentacles about 10 feet in length; but even one with tentacles of 30 feet could not take a *boat* under the surface. M de R's description of the anatomy and appearance of the creature is a revelation to me.

'No octopuses are known of the size mentioned,' affirmed another correspondent, while yet another noted that the octopus incident was 'almost identical with one current in the old Penny Magazine'. However, once again the case was not cut and dried. G. F. Link wrote:

. . . my own experience in the colder waters of Bass's Straits amply warranted my belief in the existence of monster octopii in the tropical seas on our northern shores capable of mastering a powerful swimmer. I myself encountered an octopus on the southern coast of Victoria, whose tentacles measured 6ft 2 in length, making the huge creature some 13ft across.

C. J. Whelan drew readers' attention to an account by Deny de Montford, in which:

Dens, a navigator, avowed that in the African seas, while three of his men were employed during a calm in scraping the sides of his vessel, they were attacked by a monster of this kind, which suddenly appeared, seized them in its arms, and drew two of them under water in spite of every effort to save them, and that the thickness of one of the creature's arms, which was cut off in the contest, was at its base equal to that of a foreyard, while the suckers were of the size of ladles.

We read also of another crew who were similarly attacked off the coast of Angola. A gigantic cuttlefish threw its arms across the boat and was on the point of dragging it down when the crew succeeded in cutting off its arms with swords and hatchets. In comparison with the above, M de R's octopus is a baby . . .

Having exhausted the subjects of turtles and octopuses, critics turned to other creatures, heaping scorn on de Rougemont's 'suggestion of an amount of animal life which has never hitherto been accorded to the Australian continent':

. . . As to the pelicans and sea fowl [described as frequenting the tiny island on which de Rougemont first found himself], no pelicans are known to frequent such localities, or to nest there. Gulls, or terns, or boobies are not known to nest in barren spits of sand, liable to be washed over by the sea. As to the parrots, the 'countless thousands' that arrived is a new fact in ornithological distribution.

'Pelicans are by no means uncommon off that coast,' a second correspondent asserted; 'no one ever saw a kangaroo or an emu in the northern territory,' wrote a third, provoking the ire of a fourth:

Now that is quite wrong, for in 1865 Capt G T Brown of the ship *Calliance* was one day presented with a fresh kangaroo tail, by one of the colonists, after the ship was wrecked in Camden Harbour; and I myself helped to make a soup of it, and ate some of it afterwards. We lived on the mainland by Augustus Island for three months, *and* saw pelicans about the coast as we were leaving.

At times the debate entered surreal territory, as when one reader took issue with de Rougemont's assertion that 'I knew that wombats haunted the islands in countless thousands, because I had seen them, rising in clouds every evening at sunset':

The wombat is a species of marsupial. It is about the size of a badger, being about 3 feet in length, having moderately long, very coarse fur, grey in tint, mottled with black and white. It is a burrowing animal, a root feeder, and far from active – yet M de R has seen them 'rising in clouds'. His adventures are, indeed, 'amazing'.

De Rougemont's publisher was not amused: 'wombats' was a mistake; de Rougemont of course meant 'flying squirrels'. But the pedants were not to be put off. A Professor Forbes contributed:

M de R states that he grew about half an acre of corn on his sandspit. If he will calculate the area of that interesting spot he will discover that a bank 100 yards by 10 does not contain half an acre. His straw sufficient for thatch was grown also before his first wet season spent on the spit. Even at the rate of three crops a year, this is, all things considered, an especially good record. Grass high enough to hide in, one notes with interest, grew up, after the appearance of M de R on this *barren* spit . . .

And so it went on. In order to satisfy the sceptics de Rougemont willingly subjected himself to examination by journalists and a number of experts from the Royal Geographical Society. The editor of the *Daily Chronicle* reported that:

Be his story true or false, M de R is a remarkable man. His skin is deeply browned; he has clearly lived long under burning skies. He has a most alert, vigorous and versatile mind. He speaks English with the utmost fluency. We admit that he never seemed to be concocting a reply to questions which were sprung on him, and his answers were singularly direct and explicit.

However, his answers did not satisfy his audience. The fact that he was unable to show with any degree of exactness on a map where he had been was duly mocked. He was unable to give enough examples of local vocabulary for anyone to identify the languages he had learned. Yet de Rougemont, who was now involved with a syndicate who proposed to send a party with him back to the region in order to exploit the gold reserves he had discovered, had a perfectly reasonable argument for not providing more exact particulars. He had contracted with the syndicate, in exchange for an unnamed sum, not to divulge the whereabouts of his find; similarly, to furnish the linguists with examples of local dialects would lead them to the treasure as surely as a map would.

Frustrated, his critics attacked on other fronts. How was it that de Rougemont had never encountered the numerous pearlers and diggers passing through the region? How had he not come across even one of the isolated but numerous sheep stations dotting the country? How was it that he had never met the telegraph line traversing the country from Adelaide to Port Darwin? (A record-breaking cyclist lost in the outback had recently summoned assistance by cutting the wire.) Perhaps most vehemently argued were de Rougemont's claims that he had been fired at by white explorers. A Mr Calvert wrote that the members of the Giles expedition:

. . . were noted for their inoffensive attitude towards the natives, and had he thrown down his weapons and walked open handed towards them he would most certainly have been received and accorded a hearing. Two of the four men that he met on that occasion I knew personally, and can unhesitatingly answer for.

Another correspondent agreed: 'Anyone who knew that intrepid explorer Ernest Giles knows full well that he never once attacked a black camp' (adding, disconcertingly, 'unless for punitive measures'). David Carnegie, himself an explorer, went further: 'it is not the custom of any white man,' he declared, 'explorers or prospectors, to fire upon unoffending blacks, as if they were rabbits.' (While those intimately connected with explorers and exploring rushed to attack de Rougemont on this point, significantly this detail did not strike other readers as implausible.)

De Rougemont's defenders continued to speak out in numbers, citing convincing precedents for his fantastic claims. James Morrill, of Maldon in Essex, spent seventeen years with the natives of North-eastern Australia; and William Buckley of Macclesfield lived for thirty-two years with an aboriginal community in the most southerly part of Australia. (Both men had written autobiographies.) The accounts of other explorers and their extraordinary findings and experiences had provided sport for the mocking wit of columnists and cartoonists alike – just as de Rougemont's exploits were now – and had later been acknowledged as not only authentic, but landmark discoveries. As 'X' wrote to the *Daily Chronicle*:

Sir, Will you permit me to point out that when M du Chaillu wrote his celebrated book on Equatorial Africa, giving the details of what he had seen with respect to cannibalism, and also with respect to the existence and habits of the gorilla, by many educated men the whole narrative was treated with derision, contempt and openly expressed disbelief? Later information duly confirmed the general truth of the statements that were made by M du Chaillu, and today the gorilla occupies a distinct and fully recognised position in natural history.

An 'Anglo-Australian', among other correspondents, detected a note of chauvinistic arrogance in the scorn being heaped upon de Rougemont by the British scientific establishment, and reasonably warned readers:

. . . not to take too seriously anything that has been written to discredit this most interesting and remarkable man, or to impugn the truthfulness of his statements. Australia is a big country, and if one or two of your correspondents know anything worth telling, from personal observation, it will refer only to a very limited area, and in no sense to the portions visited by M de R, which still remain almost unexplored. Just one word as to the matter of taste. I trust many an Englishman's cheeks have tingled, as mine have, in reading the treatment this forlorn Australian adventurer has received from his critics. It reminds one that when a dog is to be beaten any stick is good enough for the purpose.

'LGR' took a particularly generous stance on the matter, suggesting that de Rougemont was not deluding, but deluded:

I was struck by sundry passages and events which seemed to reflect – possibly unconsciously – the experiences or inventions of previous writers. It seems quite possible that during the long period of his isolation and subsequent sojourn among the savages, much that M de R has read in his boyhood in 'Robinson Crusoe', 'The Swiss Family Robinson', and 'The Arabian Nights' came back to him as actual personal experiences, and by some psychological processes he honestly identified himself with the marvellous adventures he relates.

The question to which no one had a ready answer was: who were Blanche and Gladys Rogers – the shipwrecked girls de Rougemont and Yamba had rescued from the savage chief? All attempts to trace the existence of a Captain Rogers, his ship, or his daughters, foundered.

The correspondence-war raging in the pages of the *Daily Chronicle* made fascinating reading – almost as fascinating as de Rougemont's tale itself. For a brief month the controversy dominated tea tables and club rooms, dividing public opinion into those for and those against de Rougemont. Attacks on him became more personal; cartoons and poems appeared depicting him as frankly ridiculous. The man himself was an object of great interest on the rare occasions he appeared in public. A fellow diner at a London restaurant, disappointed at the adventurer's appearance, expressed the view that it was 'no wonder the cannibals didn't eat him.' However, the whole debate was about to shift into a higher gear.

The *Daily Chronicle* suddenly announced a halt to the publication of all correspondence on the matter. The editor had received 'some important communications in regard to M de Rougemont' which required investigation. A few days later the *Chronicle* printed the following letter from an F. W. Solomon:

During May last a man called at our office, introducing himself to be Mr Green, a Swiss. I had a long conversation with him in reference to a wonderful diving apparatus he had invented, but which unfortunately had been lost in a shipwreck on its way from Australia to this country, he having come by another vessel. He was now compelled to remain in London until a duplicate set of papers arrived from Australia, but asked for the address of a firm whom I thought would be able to make a costume of a certain material which might be used for this particular purpose.

I then took him to a prominent member of our firm, to whom he explained that he was in rather distressing circumstances. Finding repeated applications for assistance on the strength of the diving costume were useless, he then represented himself as an artist, offering to make a large black and white drawing of myself or any member of my family. He was given a pencil and paper and asked to make a sketch on the spot, but he cleverly dodged this by various excuses.

I may say he showed several letters of recommendation, one being from a clergyman of prominent position in Australia, besides mentioning gentlemen of high social standing in London who were going to assist him.

I have not seen him from the end of May until one night about a fortnight ago I met him accidentally in the Earl's Court Exhibition. After having shaken hands and passed the usual compliments, to my utter astonishment, and, I may say, disgust, he walked away, and this after having spent several hours at various times with me at the office.

The fact of having seen his photograph in the 'Strand Magazine' has brought all this vividly to my mind, and there is not the slightest doubt but that Mr Green and M. L de Rougemont are *one and the same person.*

The *Daily Chronicle* now had the bit firmly between its teeth, and reporters were dispatched to investigate not only de Rougemont's story, but de Rougemont himself and his former incarnations as Green, Grien or Grin. Their collective findings made interesting reading to those who had been following the debate. The feature began:

Nothing is more true than that truth is stranger than fiction. The travellers' tales which are appearing in the 'Wide World Magazine' are curious and interesting, and they have deservedly attained a wide popularity. Yet it is open to doubt whether the plain unvarnished truth concerning M

Louis de Rougemont, alias Henri Louis Grin, is not on the whole more curious and interesting than the ingenious tissue of lies which he has palmed upon the public.

The true story uncovered by the dogged investigative journalists of the *Daily Chronicle* sent the paper's circulation rocketing. It transpired that the young Louis had left home not as an independent gentleman, but as a travelling servant. His employers had included the actress Fanny Kemble:

In or soon after 1870, Louis Grin entered the service of a Swiss banker in London, M de Mieville. Owing to his overbearing and superior ways Louis was by no means popular with the other servants, but being a clever, astute, and exceedingly useful man, M de Mieville appreciated his services. At the same time, he did not like the man, on account of his overbearing ways. In fact, the old gentleman used to say 'It is Louis who is the master, and I the servant!'

The de Mieville family credited Louis in particular with a devouring taste for reading, and were under the impression that even at that time he was filling his mind with books of travel, and nursing a secret taste for adventures. Just as he was losing his place in the de Mieville household he heard from a friend that there was a chance of a position in the family of Sir William Robinson, who was going out to Western Australia to take up the post of Governor. In about a year he again lost his place. By that time, however, he had saved a modest sum of money, and drifted from Sydney to Western Australia.

Now styling himself Grin, Grien or Green he did indeed embark on pearling expeditions, and was in fact shipwrecked. However, he was lost to view for – at the longest – three years. As the *Chronicle*'s journalist observed, 'M de Rougemont has, in fact, merely added a zero to the truth.' The *Chronicle* outlined a sequence of failed entrepreneurial projects attached to de Rougemont's (or Grin's) name, and the paper had also located a wife de Rougemont abandoned, living in poverty in Sydney with several children. His own family was also tracked down. They laughed at the idea that he had been lost to the world for thirty years, having had frequent letters from him during his absence, and neighbours also rejected as risible the idea that Louis's father had been some kind of nobleman:

His father, Antoine Samuel Emmanuel Grin, was known from Yverdon to Suchy as a notorious drunkard and ne'er-do-well. He obtained a situation at Yverdon as carter, but was discharged because of his irregular and dissolute habits. For a long time his other son, François Grin, Protestant pastor of Suchy, allowed him enough to live on, but the day on which the allowance was paid he expended it all on drink. He then became a tramp about the country. He was arrested time after time, and slept more often in the police cell than anywhere.

His son François having refused to increase the monthly allowance, the father determined to disgrace his clergyman son. With that intention he indulged freely at Yverdon, and went towards his son's house. For his riotous conduct he was imprisoned, and at seven o'clock in the morning of the 17th of May, 1885, hanged himself in his prison cell at Vallorbes.

The editors of the *Chronicle* were also beside themselves with glee on another account. Having failed to find any evidence that the shipwrecked English girls 'de Rougemont' claimed to have rescued ever existed, they were intrigued to learn that Grin's own daughters, still living poverty-stricken in Sydney, were also named Blanche and Gladys. The 'monstrous fraud' which Grin had perpetrated on an unsuspecting readership had been concocted in the Reading Room of the British Library, where he had spent several weeks assiduously collecting material in order to lend authenticity to his tale. And now, the publicity-courting Louis had disappeared without trace.

De Rougemont, or Grin, had remained elusive since the first positive proof of his imposture had been published. He now resorted to a final and desperate ploy to rescue his name – or one of them.

The *Daily Chronicle* received a letter from a Louis Grin, whose details dovetailed exactly with the facts uncovered by that paper, who objected in the strongest possible terms to being confused with the Louis de Rougemont currently hitting headlines in London. The *Daily Chronicle* was only too delighted to pass this information on to its readers. Meanwhile, the *Wide World* magazine, far from being chastened by the revelations, was busy preparing a special double issue of the magazine for Christmas, to capitalize on the rocketing sales of the magazine – now 400,000 per issue. The *Daily Chronicle* reported this fact with po-faced indignation, although, as Mr Fitzgerald, editor of *Wide World* remarked, the *Chronicle*'s own sales were doing very-nicely-thank-you on the strength of the de Rougemont story. The focus of their righteous indignation was now, subtly, to shift. Under a headline 'Not Wholly Responsible' the *Daily Chronicle* informed its readers:

We have been from an early period of this investigation inclined to believe that the adventurer who posed before the British association was sinned against as well as sinning. Lately we have seen reason to believe that his health has suffered by reason of some sort of brain injury. We have now learned from an unimpeachable source connected with the Mieville family that during his early years of domestic service he suffered a severe accident by falling a considerable height from a window, and sustained an injury to his skull. He was long ill, and it appears to be the opinion of some of those who knew him before and after that mishap that the accident to some extent affected his brain. We mention this incident as some sort of apology, so far as he is concerned, of the transactions in which he has taken part.

The *Chronicle*'s editor suggested that Grin had been aided and abetted – and possibly initially encouraged – in embroidering his tales by the editor of *Wide World* magazine himself. This view was vindicated when the *Daily Chronicle* learned that Fitzgerald had referred in a letter to a M. de Rougemont 'who for two years was a castaway among the cannibal blacks'. The letter had been sent in July – a month *before* Fitzgerald's magazine had begun to publish de Rougemont's story.

It had all been a vastly entertaining fuss over nothing. In one sense, both the *Daily Chronicle* and *Wide World* magazine emerged as winners (sales, after all, were what mattered); poor old Henri Grin was exposed not only as the loser but as a serial failure. As more details emerged, it appeared that as well as his careers as footman and pearler, he had also been, at various times, a 'doctor', a photographer, an artist and an inventor. A sequence of failed entrepreneurial schemes designed to make his fortune only drew him deeper into debt. His potato-digger was declared 'quite useless', but harmless, unlike the diving suit he attempted to patent, which killed the unfortunate man charged with testing it.

While his 'life story' certainly made him some serious money, it also transformed him in a different way. In 'The Adventures of Louis de Rougemont' Henri Grin reinvented his failed life as a success story: the wife he deserted was replaced by the loyal Yamba; his hopeless lack of business acumen was transformed, in his hands, into the heroic initiative of a survivor; washed-up in the real world, he shipwrecked himself on an island of imagined adventure. In the age of the pioneering self-made man, the footman made himself a king.

This 'exceedingly useful man' remained out of the public eye for several years. However, in July 1906 he was to be found at the London Hippodrome. With the aid of a huge tank of water he was preparing a public demonstration of his turtle-riding skills. He succeeded.

He emerged again, briefly, during the Great War, as the inventor of a meat substitute. His 'tall bearded figure, lank and stooping' was last seen selling matches in Shaftesbury Avenue. 'This ghost of the streets was dressed in an old ragged overcoat, over the top of which the thin hair fell, and showed above it a calm, philosophical, curiously intelligent face.' The self-styled explorer and cannibal chief died a pauper in 1920.

3. VIPs; or
'Guess Who's Coming to Dinner?'

The uniform – our fetish! It is a disgraceful comment on all those high-sounding words like public spirit, civil courage before the mighty, rule of the law and so on; the fact is that the uniform is the supreme power in Prussia. They all lie on their bellies before a uniform.

– A Berlin newspaper on the Köpernick incident, 1906

Harry Domela has rendered us an invaluable service. No satire could have shown up better the ridiculousness of sycophancy, no sociological and philosophical thesis could have revealed so well the true character of German monarchism. Unfortunately, we must fear that the judges, hurt in their most sacred feelings, will understand neither the humour nor the political significance of this affair. But all the more does Prince Harry deserve the gratitude of those whose sympathies he has gained more quickly and completely than any real prince.

– *Tagebuch*, January 1927

Everyone likes to feel special, and many people enjoy being the centre of attention, although few would go to the lengths to which Henri Grin resorted in order to gain public recognition. There are those who legitimately derive power, or a position of importance, from their jobs or from an accident of birth; others, leading otherwise quiet lives, enjoy only a few brief moments of the limelight: the student receiving an award, the amateur actor in a play, or the bride on her wedding day. A particular category of impostor seeks this kind of attention on a more regular basis; they have a desire to be perceived and treated as Very Important Persons. They do not, like Henri Grin, claim to have had an extraordinary adventure, or to have performed a great exploit; they claim, more simply, status for its own sake.

Ironically, the celebration and protection of the individual, of selfhood and identity, which is at the core of VIP status, is only accessible to such people by their pretending to be someone they are not. This may seem to be an empty achievement, one from which no real satisfaction could be derived, yet there are hundreds of cases of dedicated VIP impostors, some devoting much of their lives to a particular claim to fame, others becoming 'serial' VIPs, which suggests that this kind of imposture fulfils a function that is less obvious than some other categories. While it is true that the VIP impostor may gain financially, or even politically, from his deception, it is also apparent that he is often in search of other 'perks'. What he sometimes appears to seek is simply respect: a public acknowledgement that he is *somebody*.

Many of these cases also amply illustrate the extent to which the impostor's victims are ripe for this kind of deceit. The experience of Wilhelm Voigt demonstrates how other parties may unknowingly be drawn into the imposture, and not merely accommodate, but actively assist, the impostor.

In October 1906 the Mayor of Köpernick found himself in a spot of trouble. A captain and ten grenadiers in the Prussian Guards marched into the town hall and promptly arrested both him and his treasurer. The baffled mayor learned that it was believed that someone had been cooking the municipal books, and the accounts plus 4,000 marks (a significant though not vast sum) were confiscated as evidence. Two carriages were summarily commandeered to convey the mayor and treasurer under military guard to General Moltke in Berlin for further interrogation.

They need not have been unduly concerned, however, for

General Moltke was equally mystified as to why the two local worthies had been sent to him. In fact, both mayor and treasurer were innocent; the villain of the piece was the arresting captain, who was no captain, but a cobbler from Berlin, at this moment on the train home, 4,000 marks richer.

Wilhelm Voigt, like many impostors, had a background in petty crime and, by the age of fifty-seven, had spent nearly half his life in prison. As one biographer has it: 'Apart from rampant recidivism, Voigt had absolutely no claim to fame.' He had begun his imposture modestly, merely walking about the streets of Berlin in the second-hand uniform of a captain in the Prussian Guards. Soldiers, programmed to react to the uniform, would jump to attention as the captain passed, and Voigt felt emboldened to go a little further. On the day of the Köpernick incident he had entered a local army barracks, barked at a group of grenadiers to form a squad, marched them down to the railway station and boarded the train for Köpernick. So ingrained in the troops was the unquestioning obedience of orders from a superior officer that none hesitated.

The case of the 'Captain of Köpernick' received much public attention, and opinion was sharply divided between those who were outraged by this criminal abuse of the authorities – both military and municipal – and the majority, who were amused and even impressed by the cobbler's initiative and daring. In the genre of popular contemporary humour, Voigt had delivered a custard pie to the pompous face of the establishment. Even the Kaiser was said to have viewed Voigt as a 'lovable scoundrel', and it may have been his influence that led to Voigt serving only two of the four years to which he was sentenced for the crime. A wealthy admirer, considering him a 'national treasure', also gave him a generous pension. He toured America with a cabaret act based on his experience, and the story was made into a play and a film.

It seems doubtful that Voigt had his audacious stunt in mind when he first began wearing the uniform; the idea probably developed over a period of time, when he realized that people unquestioningly accepted the identity the uniform declared. He may even have improvised the whole thing as he went along. If his aim, in first donning his disguise, was to gain a degree of respect and admiration from his fellow citizens, the end result far outstripped anything he could have hoped for.

Stephane Otto also liked to appear in uniform, and had indeed been a hero of the Great War, joining the Belgian army in 1914 at the age of fifteen and receiving several decorations for bravery. However, he emerged from the war a drug addict, and began a sequence of impersonations and impostures, posing as the young relation of a succession of high-profile figures. He also promoted himself to the Belgian General Staff, gatecrashed a US army awards ceremony at Koblenz, reviewed the troops and pinned a medal on the proud chest of the commander of the US forces, Major-General H. T. Allen. He was in and out of prison for various minor swindles, frauds and impostures for the rest of his short life, appearing in court for the last time in England, in the uniform of a French naval officer. At the age of only thirty he jumped to his death from a third-floor window.

This sobering tale illuminates the fine line dividing the functional from the dysfunctional impostor. Otto was probably psychologically damaged by the war, and careered from one identity to the next, both, according to the *Daily Express* 'to assuage his thirst for glory', and to relieve his financial difficulties. He seems not to have cut the charming or charismatic figure that many impostors project, and probably appeared desperate and pathetic, as the circumstances of his death certainly were.

Those who specialize in 'one-off' imposture, such as Voigt and Otto perpetrated, may be termed 'event' impostors. The acknowledged master of event imposture was an American. On 26 July 1921 *The New York Times* printed the following item, received from Washington the previous day:

Princess Fatima, Sultana of Afghanistan, who has attracted unusual attention during her visit to this country because of a white sapphire set in the right side of her nose, was formally received at the White House today by President Harding.

The princess and her two sons were dressed in native costumes for the occasion and accompanied by an American naval officer specially detailed as interpreter. Mr Harding's military and naval aids were present for the ceremony, which was carried out with all the formality customarily attending the visit here of a distinguished foreigner.

It is not, as might be thought, the interesting figure of Princess Fatima who should be the object of suspicion here, but the naval officer accompanying her. Needless to say, he was not a naval officer. He was Stanley Clifford Weyman, also often known as Stephen Weinberg, and by at least ten other names, who was once described in court as having a penchant for 'attaching himself to persons in the limelight'. Weyman was, however, much more than a hanger-on of the rich and famous: his string of short-term impostures was frequently spectacular and inventive, and often it was he who was the star.

Weyman had been a bright boy from Brooklyn, who wanted to go to college and medical school, but his parents couldn't afford it. Consequently, he had a succession of lowly administrative and menial jobs but, like a superhero in a children's comic, he led a secret double life as a VIP. As is often the case with impostors' early adventures, they initially lacked subtlety. His first alter ego was US consul representative to Morocco, replete with purple uniform. This diplomat patronized the best establishments in New York and yet could never be traced when the bills came in. The consul soon found his way to prison.

During this period of serious reflection, Weyman made an imaginative leap which was to stand him in very good stead in the future. What renders the impostor vulnerable, he reasoned, is the fact that he has no referees, no one to vouch for him. What he needed was a partner, conveniently placed. So Weyman became not one, but two people: a military attaché from Serbia and a lieutenant in the US Navy. The two men were acquainted, each able to refer third parties, should they require any kind of confirmation, to the other. Unfortunately, both these interesting characters were apprehended at the same time, at least affording company for each other in prison.

Following his release in 1915, Weyman became Lt Commander Ethan Allen Weinberg (Consul General for Romania). Like Voigt and Otto, Weyman was a natural military officer, and had perfected an exacting and critical style which kept everyone on their toes and gave them no time – or reason – to question his authority. When, resplendent in a 'dazzling blue uniform with gold braid and red epaulets', he inspected the company of the USS *Wyoming*, as the ship's captain later admitted, 'the little guy put on one hell of a tour.' At the time, the captain, like everyone else, had suspected nothing, and had been as pleased as the rest of his officers to accept the consul's unexpected offer to treat them all to dinner at the Astor Hotel. (The bill for the dinner would of course be taken care of by the Romanian consulate.) The proposed party received advance attention in *The New York Times*, alerting the FBI – which was now well acquainted with Weyman – to the event. Weyman was unceremoniously arrested at the party and was perhaps understandably upset, being heard to remark as he was led away: 'You could have waited until after dessert.' History does not record whether the *Wyoming*'s officers ever got their pudding.

None of this put Weyman off his inspecting: as Royal St Cyr, a lieutenant in the Aviation Service, he was arrested in 1917 while conducting a rigorous tour of inspection of an armoury in Brooklyn. Again the authorities were bamboozled; it was a military tailor who thought there was something 'queer' about the lieutenant and alerted detectives. However, it was the Princess Fatima affair that was probably his masterpiece. He had not merely tagged along, but personally orchestrated the entire event, when he discovered that the princess was being virtually ignored by the State Department during her visit to the US. He took it upon himself to visit her at her hotel as the State Department Naval Liaison Officer (a title he had dreamed up himself), apologizing profusely for the oversight. He, personally, would take her to Washington to meet the President. Weyman also gave the princess to understand that it was quite usual for visiting dignitaries to offer cash in order to purchase gifts for various state department officials: $10,000 should take care of things. The princess gladly complied.

Although Weyman often succeeded in receiving money by such dubious means, he hardly ever profited by it, but reinvested it in his current scheme. In this instance he laid out the money on a private railway carriage to convey the princess to Washington in appropriate style, and on a luxurious hotel suite for her when she arrived. His next task was to set up the meeting. Once again, a uniform speaks for itself, and it was as a lieutenant commander in the Navy that he visited the State Department and mentioned the names of some important senators who were, he said, anxious to promote the meeting. And so it was that Stanley Clifford Weyman introduced Princess Fatima of Afghanistan to Secretary Charles Evans Hughes and President Warren G. Harding. Mild discomfort (was it yet suspicion?) was felt when Weyman broke with protocol, and chatted informally with his (theoretical) commander-in-chief, but it was not until a news editor saw the photographs taken on the White House lawn of the princess, the President, the secretary and the irrepressible Weyman that the impostor was exposed.

Weyman enjoyed his relationship with the newspapers, to whom he frequently issued press releases. Earlier in his career several papers had dutifully passed on to their readers his announcement of his recent marriage to a celebrated child actress and the couple's sub-sequent decision to divorce and instead adopt each other. During his trial for the Fatima caper a deadpan newsman wrote:

Stephen Weinberg, known as the 'Great Impostor', indicted for impersonating a navy officer in presenting Princess Fatima to President Harding, was sent to Raymond Street Jail because, he said, Bellevue alienists made him late for trial yesterday and the court wanted him to be on time today.

Although it was a journalist who had blown the whistle on him, in court it was once more a tailor who provided the damning evidence. Despite the fact that Weyman had forked out the sultana's money for a private railroad coach and a sumptuous hotel suite, Morris Jacobs testified that Weyman had neglected to pay him for making his naval uniform. Jacobs had then tried to track down his errant customer by looking him up in the naval register and discovered, inevitably, that he did not exist. Weyman's defence at the trial was insanity. The judge, unmoved, sentenced him to three years.

If the life of the impostor can seem, at times, a sequence of high-spirited japes, the courtroom scene described in *The New York Times* provides a sobering reminder of its pathetic aspect:

Weinberg made a plea for clemency on his own behalf and promised to be good in the future. Morris Weinberg, father of the accused, also asked mercy for his son, as did Mrs. Weinberg, wife of the defendant. She broke down when she concluded her plea and was led out of the courtroom.

The sentence was reduced to two years.

Although the press was often duped by Weyman, on one occasion they made use of his particular talents. The official visit of the beautiful and powerful Queen Marie of Romania to America was exciting great interest, although no journalist had yet managed to penetrate her zealously protective entourage to gain an interview. Then, at the offices of the *Evening Graphic*, the inspired cry 'Get Weyman!' went up. Within hours the paper was printing a full interview with Queen Marie, with material provided by Weyman, whom she had entertained, believing him to be a Secretary of State.

Subsequent impostures included hospital official, lawyer, visiting lecturer and doctor. It was as the actress Pola Negri's personal physician that Weyman again had a moment of national fame. Negri, as one writer has observed, 'was a woman who enjoyed ill-health', and when her lover Rudolph Valentino died, Weyman issued regular press releases on her condition, and at Valentino's funeral shepherded her through the record-breaking crowds, even pausing to administer relief to a woman who had fainted in the crush.

Weyman subsequently established a faith-healing clinic at the dead star's house. Judge Gerald Sparrow, who included Weyman in his survey of impostors, believed that Weyman may actually have possessed healing powers, 'for a study of the career of this truly remarkable man suggests he was no mean mesmerist at a time when the healing properties of mesmerism and auto-suggestion were still in their infancy.' It was also as a doctor that Weyman received a seven-year prison sentence for offering advice to young men on how to dodge the draft during the Second World War by feigning various medical conditions.

In 1948 Weyman turned journalist, worming his way into the United Nations at Lake Success with bogus credentials. He was soon on first-name terms with the principal American and Russian delegates, Warren Austin and Andrei Gromyko. According to one source, Austin and Gromyko both regarded Weyman, not mistakenly, as 'a highly intelligent and shrewd observer of the international scene'. Weyman was elsewhere reported to be 'prolific in offering suggestions about the way the United States delegation should handle its affairs'. A 'real' job here would probably have suited Weyman down to the ground: he was at the centre of things, rubbing shoulders with the men who were making history. The Thai delegation was so impressed with him that he was invited to become their press officer. This was the moment at which the poacher could have turned gamekeeper, but Weyman seems to have courted his own destruction by contacting the State Department with an inquiry about whether the post, which came with full diplomatic accreditation, would affect his US citizenship. His name immediately rang bells, and that was the end of his UN connection.

It has been observed that impostors sometimes seem to pursue unnecessarily risky strategies, as Weyman did by drawing the State Department's attention to him in this way. Whether or not Weyman did have a deep-seated perverse desire to be exposed, he was, repeatedly. His last brush with the law occurred in 1954 when he attempted to defraud a bank of $5,000 for a home-improvement loan for a home that did not exist. At the trial Weyman again failed to convince the judge that he was insane.

Judge Gerald Sparrow has observed that 'in the end . . . Stanley Weyman became almost an American institution. The public gasped with a kind of outraged admiration at each new exploit.' As to Weyman's motivation, Sparrow believed that 'his whole career derived from his early obsession, his great passion to enter the world of the professional and upper class. When that ambition was thwarted, he devised means of obtaining his goal without human sanction.' However, the fact that Weyman never set out to carve a niche for himself in which he could settle, never planning long-term impostures, seems to argue against this. Brief periods of fame – often lasting only a day – were all he sought, suggesting that he never intended an enduring transformation. He seems, rather, like those people who cannot resist a 'dare': once an imposture occurred to him, perhaps he found it an irresistible challenge. He may well, also, have thrived on his notoriety, on the 'outraged admiration' of the American public. Imposture often demands great courage, a quality Weyman did not lack – fatally, as it turned out. One night in 1960, carrying out his legitimate job as a night porter at a New York hotel, he tackled a masked gunman attempting to rob the safe. Weyman was shot dead. The gunman escaped with $200.

Weyman shared with several other impostors an interest in mental illness, and in one of his personae gave a lecture at the University of Middlesex in a subject on which he was, at least, expert: 'Insanity: its defence in crime'. One of the observations he made to the students was that prison psychiatrists should be 'subjected to a searching mental examination'. As to his capacity for insight into his own situation, there is little to go on. The most a journalist could coax from him was the simple observation: 'One man's life is a boring thing. I lived many lives. I'm never bored.'

Just as Voigt, Otto and Weyman all discovered the power of a uniform, and Weyman experimented with various professional titles, impostors have also explored the very top end of the VIP range, fully exploiting the extraordinary attractiveness of hereditary titles and aristocratic connections. As one impostor-watcher observed in 1974:

The feudally minded British are inordinately impressed with anyone who appears to spring from the upper ranks of society. Even in these egalitarian times a man who claims to be an Eton and Oxford educated nobleman commands immediate deference. If he can hint at an ancient title, a medieval country seat and connections with royalty all defences are down.

It may well be argued that the British are no longer 'feudally minded', yet old cultural habits die hard, and it would be disingenuous to deny that a title – for many people – carries a mystical aura. It is certainly the case that part of the legacy of more élitist times is that people are unlikely to question a title, or demand it be proven. Such was the successful assumption of Lt Col Allen – also Commander Coxon, Captain Hurst, Professor Hoskins, and Lords Antrim, Harrington, Hamilton, Moyne and Vernay, as he was otherwise known. In his book *The Gullibility Gap* Derek Cooper relates one of Allen's beautifully simple ploys. In June 1967 he telephoned a West End jeweller and announced himself as one of the Queen's equerries:

Her Majesty wanted to present someone with a platinum and diamond brooch. Could the jeweller hasten to the Palace to discuss designs? He suggested a rendezvous in the Royal Mews to avoid the crowds watching the Changing of the Guard. The jeweller arrived at the Mews only too delighted to execute so regal a commission. He asked a policeman for the Colonel and an aristocratic figure in tweeds stepped forward and introduced himself. The jeweller gave him a £600 necklace on approval. Which is the end of the story.

The British are not alone in their capacity for going weak-kneed at the merest sniff of blue blood; the Germans, it seems, used to be at least as easily impressed by a title, as Harry Domela proved. Domela's background, rootless and directionless, gave him the classic psychological profile of an impostor-in-waiting. Born in 1903 to a wealthy German family settled in the Baltic region, he was persecuted as an outsider by his Russian classmates. His aliena-tion from the local youths was compounded when he joined the German Freikorps, which had recently suppressed a revolution in the Baltic. Moving to Germany, he was too young to join the regular army and had a series of menial jobs, one of which was as a gardener to a baroness; the aristocratic manners and deportment he observed while working here were to be of use to him later. At the end of the Great War he found himself homeless and unemployed in an economically depressed Berlin, having lost his father and brothers in the fighting. He had nothing, and nothing to lose. He experi-mented with various titles, soon learning that the same doors which had been slammed in the face of Harry Domela quickly opened to admit, for example, the young Baron Korff. However, like Weyman's, his early forays were inexpert, not to say clumsy, and he ended up in prison several times. This threatened to become a pattern. What Harry Domela needed was a really Big Idea.

It is not clear whether luck played a part in what happened next, or whether Domela had finally hatched a brilliant plan. The Weimar Republic had abolished titles of nobility, and Heidelberg, for which

Domela now headed, remained a haven for ex-aristocrats who still kept up the old ways. Posing as Prince Lieven of Latvia, Domela began to frequent the clubs, where the young privileged circle – usually with military connections – who befriended him soon suspected there was more to Prince Lieven than met the eye. How was it that he was so ignorant of military matters? And so reticent – or inconsistent – about his past? There was only one explanation: this man was not Prince Lieven. He was, they agreed, merely using this identity to conceal a greater secret: that he was in fact Prince Wilhelm of Hohenzollern, the Kaiser's grandson.

This interpretation of the situation was aided by the fact that Domela bore more than a passing resemblance to the young prince. It also explained his spectacular ignorance of all things martial: members of the ex-royal family were prohibited from using their titles if they retained connections with the army, so this was obviously a deliberate ploy to allay suspicion. And so it was that Harry Domela became the heir to the throne in the event of a restoration of the monarchy. His 'true' identity became an open secret.

When he visited the regions of Thuringia and Prussia, therefore, it was with rather more confidence. Word was out that Prince Lieven was merely an identity assumed by Prince Wilhelm who, being a modest young man, did not wish to draw attention to himself during his stay. The prince was royally entertained by those who retained an allegiance to – or even merely respect for – the crown, and was never embarrassed by the presentation of a bill at a hotel or restaurant; on the contrary, proprietors saw his patronage as a compliment to their establishments. However, as the press drew attention to his activities, it was becoming an increasingly risky game.

Like most impostors, Domela was always alert to any sign that the game was up. He knew he was being watched by detectives, and when he heard that Herr von Berg had arrived at his hotel, he immediately recognized it as the name of the chief administrator of the royal estates, and fled. He spent a day on a drunken binge with his old Weimar friends before heading for the infamous institution which is traditionally the last refuge of those wishing to leave the past behind: the French Foreign Legion.

Had Harry in his haste paused to inquire, he would have discovered that Herr von Berg was an innocent banker from Frankfurt, but his paranoia got the better of him. In any case, as it turned out, his number was up. As he boarded the train for France, he felt the long arm of the law heavy on his shoulder. He spent seven months in prison in Cologne awaiting his trial, putting the time to good use writing his life story. When he came to trial all the witnesses affirmed that Domela's imposture had been harmless, and he was freed.

Domela's book became a bestseller, and he also made money from the film rights. Two plays about his life were staged. In a typical twist to the life of the impostor, Domela played himself in one of the productions, and tried to sue the actor who played him in the other. Despite his fame, by 1930 Domela had 'disappeared from view', a phrase which often appears at the end of impostors' biographies, but which irresistibly suggests an invisibility only accessible to the inveterate impostor.

Some impostors have gone to great lengths to press their claims to royalty, manufacturing convoluted and often improbable histories and mountains of paperwork in order to support their story, whereas others, like Domela, have been content to play out the charade only for as long as it was profitable, avoiding any detailed investigation of their claim. Olive Wilmot Serres (1772–1834) followed the former route, inventing a chain of events which made her the daughter of Henry Frederick, Duke of Cumberland (George III's youngest brother). Among the seventy-odd documents she assembled in order to 'prove' her case were included a marriage certificate relating to her mother's marriage to the Duke, and a second marriage certificate showing that George III himself had married one Hannah Lightfoot before bigamously marrying Queen Charlotte, thus conveniently destroying the succession.

Olive's attempts to appear royal seemed clumsy and vulgar to some. One diarist who attended a City of London dinner in 1820 at which the 'splendid object' was present leaves this barbed portrait:

No one can have any doubt of the royalty of *her* birth. She is the very image of our Royal family. Her person is upon the model of the Princess Elizabeth only at least three times her size. She wore the most brilliant rose-coloured satin gown you ever saw, with fancy shawls (more than one) flung in different forms over her shoulders, after the manner of the late Lady Hamilton. Then she had diamonds in profusion hung from every part of her head, but her nose, and the whole was covered with feathers that would have done credit to any hearse. It turned out that Princess Olivia of Cumberland had made her claim as Princess of the Blood to sit at the right hand of my Lord Mayor. The worthy magistrate, however, with great spirit resisted these pretensions, and after much altercation she was compelled to retreat to another table.

The newspapers were similarly scornful of the tenacious princess, who now dressed her footmen in royal liveries. The *Leeds Mercury* observed sarcastically: 'The Lady of whom we speak was famed for dealing in documental evidence; but, unfortunately for herself, the writers of all her documents always happen to die before their letters and certificates are produced.'

When, after Olive's death, her daughter Lavinia Ryves took the case to court, claiming her right to the title Duchess of Lancaster and a legacy of £15,000, *The Times* noted disparagingly:

No less than eighty-three documents were produced at the trial, and besides these there are about fifty more which have been referred to at different times. These, for the most part, consist of declarations and protestations of all the great personages introduced into the story, who would seem to have thought it the best means of keeping their secret by constantly committing it to little bits of paper. They are written, for the most part, on mere scraps, and the petitioner attempted to account for their size by alleging that they had been cut smaller . . . that they might be the easier kept.

The case was thrown out by the Lord Chief Justice.

Olive Wilmot was reputed even as a schoolchild to have 'displayed the first fruits of a very vivid imagination', and she was certainly a woman of no little talent as an artist, having exhibited at the Royal Academy and been appointed landscape painter to the Prince of Wales. Her obsession with becoming a 'royal' is believed by some to have been an illness, her delusions of grandeur a psychiatric condition.

Stella Chiappini, later Lady Newborough (1773–1843), invented a variant on Olive Wilmot's complex fiction, this time grafted on to the French royal family, although hers had a distinctly fairy-tale flavour about it. On his deathbed, she reported, her father, a policeman named Lorenzo Chiappini, revealed to her that she was not his daughter but had been born to an aristocratic couple travelling through the region of Tuscany where the Chiappinis lived on the same day that his own wife had given birth to a son. The traveller, desperate for a male heir, had pleaded with Chiappini to exchange the children. Chiappini, rendered vulnerable by poverty, and having several children already, acceded to the swap, and came away the richer by it.

As it happened, years before Stella was to learn of her exalted rank she began to move rapidly up the social scale. By the age of thirteen and a half she had become an actress and married her first husband, a fifty-year-old Englishman, Thomas Wynn, First Lord Newborough, who eventually returned with her to his substantial estates in Wales. Three years after Newborough's death in 1807, Stella married a landed Russian baron, Edward von Ungern-Sternberg. She was therefore a woman of considerable wealth and social standing when she began to pursue her claim.

Her real parents, she calculated, were Philippe Joseph, Duke of Orleans, and his wife Adélaide de Bourbon-Penthièvre, and their changeling 'son' – who Stella maintained was actually the child of Chiappini the policeman and his wife – was about to become King of France. Stella went to great lengths to enlist support for her case, finding allies in the 'Elder Bourbon' royal line, who in any case perceived the Orleans family as usurpers and regicides. However, she failed, and more recent historical inquiry has proven the impossibility of either the Duke and his wife Adélaide, or even the Duke and a mistress, having been anywhere near Tuscany at the time of Stella's birth.

It is observable that both Olive Wilmot and Stella Chiappini were girls born into ordinary circumstances (Olive's father was a house-painter), whose lives touched the edges of royal circles: Olive as an artist by royal appointment, and Stella as a European aristocrat by both her marriages. The third in this trio of queenlings was also of low birth but royal connection.

When Princess Susanna Carolina Matilda, sister of Queen Charlotte, visited America in the 1770s she became an instant favourite. Society hostesses all over Virginia and North and South Carolina competed to offer the entertaining and engaging princess hospitality. It was therefore a shock when one day, as the princess was holding court at a friend's house, a man arrived claiming she was an escaped convict, and escorted her off the premises at gunpoint.

Sarah Wilson (her real name) had quit her Staffordshire village home in 1771, and found a post soon after arriving in London as servant to Caroline Vernon, one of Queen Charlotte's ladies-in-waiting. Unfortunately Wilson proved a thief, was convicted of stealing items from the royal apartments and sentenced to death. As a result of intervention on Caroline Vernon's part, her sentence was commuted to transportation to the colonies.

After landing in Baltimore, Maryland, Wilson was sold into the service of a planter named William Devall, of Bush Creek, Frederick County, which was still under British jurisdiction. As soon as the opportunity presented itself she ran away and headed south, over the border. By some astonishing oversight, throughout her trial and voyage Wilson had retained possession of the items she had stolen from the English court: some jewels, a fine dress, and a portrait of the queen. These she now employed to confirm herself in her new identity as Princess Susanna Caroline Matilda, the sister of Queen Charlotte. Wilson, it has been observed, was skilled at embroidery 'in more senses than one', and she carefully stitched a crown with her monogram into all her linen. (In matters of authenticity, the smallest details often prove the most persuasive evidence.)

Virginian society was enchanted by the princess. She had come to America, it was whispered, as the result of a court scandal. The inside information Wilson had picked up as a servant in the royal household made her seem a convincing intimate of the queen, and news of the old country – especially spicy gossip – was welcome to the settlers, who had not been home for many years. Silencing the murmurs of surprise that the princess, who like her sister Charlotte originally hailed from Germany, did not converse in that language, Princess Susanna explained that she had vowed never to let her mother tongue pass her lips until she was reconciled to her sister's favour. The aristocratic emigrée was passed from household to household, as her hosts vied to win her special notice. The princess had of course let it be known that she was still not lacking in influence in England and many prestigious appointments remained in her gift: hopeful candidates therefore proved ever willing to relieve the princess's financial embarrassments.

Wilson's imposture lasted for about eighteen months until, as is so often the case with impostors, her fame proved her downfall, and her master William Devall, learning of the exiled princess, quickly put two and two together. He dispatched one Michael Dalton to recapture her, which led to the dramatic scene at the house in South Carolina described above.

Wilson stoically buckled down to servant life for two years before a happy coincidence sent another English slave girl named Sarah Wilson to the colony. Swapping places with her, our Sarah Wilson disappeared once more. She later married a British army officer named William Talbot, whom she set up in business with the capital saved from her period as princess – which she had again, extraordinarily, managed to preserve. They moved to New York, had a large family, and are believed to have lived happily ever after.

It is striking that Sarah Wilson's off-the-cuff impersonation was significantly more successful, and certainly more fun, than the dogged attempts of Olive Wilmot and Stella Newborough to 'prove' their entitlements. Both Wilmot and Newborough seem obsessive, driven by something so powerful that their claims came to dominate their whole lives, to the extent that Newborough's family deserted her in her 'mania' and went back to Russia, and Wilmot was considered 'mad'.

There seems to be an issue of control here. Sarah Wilson was more of an opportunist in the mould of the entrepreneur: always ready to take the maximum advantage of any situation which presented itself; crucially, Wilson did not for a moment believe herself to be a real princess. On the other hand, both Newborough and Wilmot made their cases concrete, by building up an archive of papers and becoming embroiled in legal battles, which gave a tangible reality to the fantasy, making retreat from it less and less possible. Wilson was able to put on and take off her fake identity as easily as the dress she had stolen; Newborough and Wilmot became so obsessed with their invented identities that they became alienated from their own real selves. The actress and the artist fell for their own creations; only Sarah Wilson, the servant girl from the country, retained the sense of perspective essential in achieving the happy ending.

It is and was always obvious that not Harry Domela, purported grandson of the Kaiser, nor any of these three women presented any remotely serious threat to any monarchy, or succession, and they seem to have sought merely the status and wealth which went with the royal terrain, rather than the real power. However, history is littered with royal impostors who set their sights considerably higher. Lambert Simnel and Perkin Warbeck are perhaps the two most famous examples from English history. Briefly, the political background against which their claims were set was this: After many years of bloodshed between the two factions, the House of Lancaster had succeeded in establishing Henry VII on the throne, despite the estimation that 'he had the worst claim of any English king since William of Normandy. When Richard III lay dead there were . . . 29 people still alive with a better claim than Henry's.' The House of York (the Plantagenets) were beaten, but continued to look for a way back to power. However, they were without a leader, or even a figurehead, to provide a focus point around which support could be rallied.

Richard Simons, a priest and tutor at Oxford, took it upon himself to provide the needed figurehead. For his instrument he selected one of his students, the fifteen-year-old Lambert Simnel, whose features fitted the general look of the House of York. Simons set about a programme of intensive coaching on everything he knew, or could find out, about the public and private lives of the York dynasty. He decided to make Simnel the sole surviving Plantagenet heir: Edward, Earl of Warwick. Simons and his cohorts began their campaign in Ireland, where opposition to the current incumbent in England was guaranteed. And so it was that the son of a baker was crowned King of England and Ireland in Christ Church Cathedral in May 1487. The improvised flavour of the coronation of this bogus king is reflected in the detail that the crown used was hastily borrowed from a statue of the Virgin Mary.

Back in England, the real king produced the real Earl of Warwick, who had been imprisoned in the Tower of London since the age of ten. Richard Simons, however, had cause to feel optimistic. His protégé enjoyed the support of Lord Lovel, John de la Pole, Earl of Lincoln, and perhaps most importantly, Warwick's own aunt, Margaret, Dowager Duchess of Burgundy, who furnished the cause with two thousand German mercenaries. They would invade England on two fronts: the Germans from the east, and the Irish from the west. Once in England they would join forces, their strength augmented by thousands of Englishmen who were, Simons maintained, only waiting for the opportunity to oust Henry from the throne. The invasion went ahead, but the expected support did not materialize. After a long and bloody battle against Henry's forces at Stoke, the pretender and the priest were captured and their allies killed.

Execution was the usual punishment for treason, but Henry seems to have decided that the usurpers should learn, and should be seen to learn, their proper place. The priest Richard Simons he banished to a monastery. Lambert Simnel, the man who would be king, was made a scullion in the royal kitchen. Historian Jeremy Potter has noted that although Simnel was in one sense forgiven by Henry, he was never forgotten:

He was spared to be mocked and, by his example, to discredit other pretenders. At a banquet in the king's palace at Greenwich he was employed as a cup-bearer when Henry entertained some Irish lords and wished to take the opportunity of insulting them. The Irish, he remarked, would be crowning apes next.

Margaret, Duchess of Burgundy, who had provided such welcome support for Lambert Simnel, had good reason to wish to see Henry Tudor ousted, as he had confiscated most of the estates granted to her by her brother Edward IV. When Simnel failed, she began to look about for a new challenger. Perkin Warbeck was from a merchant-class family in Flanders and seemed to fit the bill well. Margaret helped cast him in the role of Richard Plantagenet, Duke of York, the youngest of the two child princes whom it was believed Richard III had infamously murdered in the Tower. For some time rumours had been circulating that the princes had in fact escaped their uncle's clutches, providing the perfect opportunity to pass Warbeck off as one of them. Just as the priest had coached

Lambert Simnel, the Duchess now set about schooling Perkin Warbeck:

with such diligence [she] instructed [him] both of the secrets and common affairs of the realm of England, and of the lineage, descent and order of the house of York, that he like a good scholar not forgetting his lesson could tell all that was taught him promptly without any difficulty or sign of any subornation: and besides he kept such a princely countenance, and so counterfeit a majesty royal, that all men in all manner did firmly believe that he was extracted of the noble house and family of the dukes of York.

The Irish, predictably enough, loved him, and he was recognized by the Emperor Maximilian and the Duke of Saxony, as well as the kings of Scotland, Denmark, Portugal and France; the latter, Charles VIII, giving him the freedom of the French court. Warbeck provided a convenient stick with which Henry's European enemies could beat him, and as such he could only be in favour when the English king was out. During a thaw in Anglo-French relations, the 'Duke' was sent back to the Duchess, who was concerned that friendliness between the English and French courts was likely to lead to a slackening in support for the usurper Warbeck, which would also reflect badly on herself. A neat public-relations exercise was in order.

She disowned Warbeck. She had, she said, made a fatal misjudgement in the case of Lambert Simnel and did not intend to go down the same road with Perkin Warbeck. Following the frantic efforts of her advisers the Duchess reluctantly agreed to a final interview with the young pretender. She would question him closely, in front of witnesses, to give him a final chance to prove his identity. Of course the Duchess, having taught Warbeck everything he knew, appeared to give him a thorough grilling. He passed with flying colours, and was embraced by the Duchess as the true Duke of York. The news of the test, as Margaret had intended, spread.

As a soldier, Perkin Warbeck had less luck. His first invasion of England ended before he and most of his men had even disembarked; the 150 men who landed first were captured and executed for treason. He then attempted a land invasion from Scotland. King James, no friend of Henry Tudor, covered every eventuality with becoming caution: he married a kinswoman, Lady Catherine Gordon, to Warbeck, as insurance against Warbeck succeeding in gaining the English crown, but held back from committing many of his resources to the planned invasion, in case it failed. Determined opposition and appalling weather ensured that it failed: over three days the invading force covered less than four English miles before retreating back over the Scottish border. James, at least, had saved face.

Warbeck's European allies grew increasingly reluctant to antagonize Henry, and following the Scottish débâcle his most influential supporters abandoned his cause, leaving him as his principal counsellors a motley crew consisting of a grocer, a tailor and a scrivener. Young Warbeck, nothing daunted, now headed for his 'least unpromising destination', Ireland, from which he led his final assault, landing in Cornwall and proclaiming himself Richard IV of England. Against all odds, he had chosen his moment well, as Cornishmen were already involved in an anti-tax rebellion, and thousands of them rallied to his cause. Nevertheless, loyalist forces won the day, and although Perkin Warbeck escaped, he eventually surrendered.

King Henry paraded the now self-confessed impostor through the streets of London, where curious crowds thronged to gawp at Warbeck 'as if he were a monster'. Yet as in the case of the previous pretender, Henry Tudor proved lenient to his enemies, and had Warbeck committed to the Tower rather than executed. The ingrate however continued to make a nuisance of himself, escaping, and after his capture plotting to escape again, this time drawing into his scheme a fellow prisoner, the Earl of Warwick, ironically the very man Lambert Simnel had posed as. An incriminating letter was intercepted and both Warwick and Warbeck were tried for treason and executed in 1499.

Like many instances of imposture, those of Simnel and Warbeck were unique products of their time and place. The absence of a mass media bringing images of the rich and famous into every home certainly made this kind of imposture more feasible than it would be today. However, there was another important sociohistoric factor operating in these cases. Because the authority of the monarchy depended on the concept of the divine right of kings, there was no route into power other than by birth; the Plantagenet rebels could not have been led by anyone, however brilliant a military commander or politician he might be: he had to be a Plantagenet. Yet at the same time, these instances show that divine right could be cheerfully ignored by the likes of Margaret, Duchess of Burgundy, herself a 'royal', if expediency demanded. The idea that those of royal blood had been ordained by God to rule seems to be revealed by these impostures as a known fiction which was useful in defending the monarchy from the masses, but did not necessarily carry such great weight with the nobility itself.

Both Lambert Simnel and Perkin Warbeck, it seems, began to believe in their claims as rightful. Unlike most impostors, who operate solo, or those who have – at most – one accessory, Simnel and Warbeck were under terrific pressure from other people. Firstly, they each had a dedicated and manipulative mentor who had raised them from obscurity to a position of tremendous importance. Secondly, they were surrounded by powerful and skilled politicians all of whom either truly believed, or had powerful reasons for pretending to believe, in their claims. Thirdly, they were regularly reminded that invested in them were the hopes and dreams of thousands of ordinary people. In this atmosphere it is perhaps easier to understand why the young men began to accept their destiny.

Simnel and Warbeck were at an advantage over some royal pretenders, who have found themselves competing with other impostors for their crowns. For example, over a period of sixty years at least forty people claimed to be the 'lost Dauphin', the son and heir of King Louis XVI and Queen Marie-Antoinette. It was only because the circumstances under which the real Dauphin died seemed so mysterious that such claims were possible. The French royal family, including Louis Charles, the eight-year-old Dauphin, had been arrested and imprisoned in the Temple in Paris in 1792 by revolutionaries. The following year, the king, then the queen and the Dauphin's aunt were executed. His sister Marie-Thérèse was taken away (and later exchanged for prisoners of war and exiled), leaving only the Dauphin. The boy was at first put in the care of a cobbler and his wife, who were charged with re-educating him, but after January 1794 he lived alone in a small cell, getting little exercise or attention and only visited occasionally by commissioners who came to report on his condition to the government.

The commissioners observed that after nearly a year of solitary confinement the child suddenly deteriorated, developed swelling in his limbs and became so introverted that he lost the power of speech. One M. Harmand reported that the child made no response to the commissioners' questions: 'His features did not change for a single moment; there was not the least apparent emotion, nor the least astonishment in his eyes, as though we had not been there.' As the child became more and more obviously ill doctors were called in, one of whom died suddenly a few days later. More doctors followed, but the Dauphin continued to sink, and on 8 June 1795 he died. Doctors (two of whom did not see the patient) established the cause of death as scrofula (tuberculosis of the lymphatic system). The child was buried in an unmarked grave at the Church of Sainte Marguerite. The anonymous grave fed suspicions that the Dauphin had been poisoned, or that he had been smuggled out of the city and another child substituted.

It was not long before the first 'lost Dauphin' was found. Jean Marie Hervagault explained that he had been spirited out of the Temple in a basket of laundry and swapped with the son of a tailor, who had brought him up (in the manner of Lady Newborough). He was arrested several times for spreading this sedition and eventually locked up in a lunatic asylum. The tailor's son, Hervagault, was followed by a shoemaker, an old soldier and a bricklayer before a more worthy successor appeared in the shape of Henri Hébert, self-styled Baron de Richemont, whose tale knocked Hervagault's laundry basket into a cocked hat. One day, he explained, while he was languishing in his cell, a cardboard horse arrived, apparently a toy from a well-wisher. However, the horse, which was hollow, contained another little boy who exchanged places with the Dauphin. The cardboard horse's presence in the Temple was objected to – as its senders had known it would be – and sent out. If listeners to this tale were not yet gasping and stretching their eyes, the best was yet to come:

Once outside, the boy was transferred to a similar but larger animal, which was covered with a real horse's skin, and was so lifelike that it was almost impossible to tell it from a real one. When night fell it was harnessed to a cart and two live horses were placed in front. The legs of the sham horse were flexible, and the driver by pulling some strings was able to create the illusion of three trotting horses. The inside of the horse was padded, and under the tail was a large air-hole, and so, in comparative comfort, Richemont made his escape from Paris.

Astonishingly, this incredible tale was widely believed. Hébert proved as much of a nuisance to the authorities as the others, and was also sent to prison. This time, presumably, no mechanical horses came to the rescue.

Yet Hébert's tale was not the most far-fetched. The most unlikely and convoluted web of events was described by a later recovered Dauphin, Karl Wilhelm Naundorff, a watchmaker from Spandau, and it was his fantastical yarn that was to convince the most people. Naundorff explained that he had been somehow drugged and removed to another, unused, part of the Temple while a wooden figure was placed in his bed. When the model was discovered, the matter was hushed up and a deaf-mute child was installed in the Dauphin's place – thus explaining his silence when interviewed by the commissioners. An attempt to poison this child failed; the expert physician called in to treat him realized there was foul play and was in turn poisoned. Yet another sick child became the Dauphin, and it was when this child died that Naundorff was smuggled out of the building in the coffin intended for his 'double'. The dead child was hidden in the attic, the doctors signed what they were told to, and Naundorff was taken to the royalist province of the Vendée.

Thereafter Naundorff lived in Italy, Germany, England and Holland, maintaining his campaign to prove his identity. His applications to the Dauphin's surviving sister, Marie-Thérèse, and more distant relations were ignored, but he found support from several prominent figures, including court officials and an ex-governess of the Dauphin, who pleaded with Marie-Thérèse to give him an interview. She steadfastly refused all such requests. Naundorff shared several physical anomalies with the Dauphin, and knew many intimate family details. On the one hand the cobbler's wife who had looked after the Dauphin recognized him at once; on the other, the Temple guards swore they had seen the real Dauphin die. Naundorff himself died in 1845 in Holland and his descendants continued the campaign for recognition, but in vain.

Numbered among the remaining thirty-five-odd 'found' Dauphins were two Americans: the then famous naturalist and ornithological artist John James Audubon, and the missionary and Iroquois chieftain, the Revd Eleazor Williams, who rejected the crown he believed was his due in the belief that God had brought him 'so low from such a height' in order to minister the 'poor Indian people'. The British, also, provided a Dauphin, Augustus Meves, whose story was as amazing as any yet heard. Unfortunately, he 'became so confused by questions of identity that, on meeting Naundorff, he mistook him for himself, and was shortly afterwards certified as insane'.

Few impostor monarchs have actually gained power, as did the character known as the False Dimitry during the Time of Troubles (1598–1613) in Russia. In fact, he was soon known as the First False Dimitry, as he was followed by the Second and Third False Dimitrys. A little historical context is in order: Ivan IV, Tsar of Muscovy, who reigned from 1533 to 1584 was known as Ivan the Terrible. During his reign hundreds of thousands of people were hanged, strangled, beaten to death, impaled and disembowelled, while many others were merely tortured. Quite aside from his political reputation, he seems to have deserved the titles of Ivan the Terrible Husband and Ivan the Terrible Father. In all, he worked his way through seven wives in the relentless pursuit of sons; only the first and last wives produced boys who lived: Ivan and Fyodor from his first marriage, and Dimitry from his last. Despite having wanted sons so badly, Ivan was careless enough to kill his eldest son in a quarrel. When Ivan the father died, Fyodor therefore succeeded as Tsar, and his brother-in-law Boris Godunov ruled as regent. Godunov sent the baby Dimitry and his mother to live outside Moscow, accusing her of plotting to make her son Tsar.

Dimitry, who was epileptic, seems to have inherited his father's carelessness: at the age of eight, playing in the open air with other children, he accidentally stabbed himself to death during a fit. The incredible circumstances of his demise bred rumours: it was Godunov's doing, one story ran; the boy had survived, went another. Twelve years on, in 1603, the 'able but completely unscrupulous' Godunov was Tsar when Dimitry apparently resurfaced in Poland in the shape of a young valet. The returned Dimitry gained Polish and Cossack support, and began to convert to Catholicism, winning him further friends, yet he wisely concealed this from his Russian orthodox allies. Although Godunov was certain Dimitry was a fake, he could hardly prove it by admitting that he'd killed the real one, so he sent assassins to dispose of the upstart. In this Godunov inadvertently helped the man he intended to eliminate: the men were caught, causing those who had doubts about Dimitry to be finally convinced that Godunov perceived him as a real threat, and therefore the real Dimitry.

In September 1604 Dimitry began his advance on Moscow, leading 1,500 men, and entered the city the following June, by which time both Godunov and his son Fyodor II were dead. This was to be his most glorious hour, because from the moment he arrived at the Kremlin he began to make fatal errors. These ranged from small but telling *faux pas*, such as failing to kiss an icon when it was offered to him, to serious misjudgements, such as taking a Catholic wife and bestowing the titles Caesar and Invincible on himself.

The ambitious Prince Shuisky who, like Ivan the Terrible, could trace his lineage back to Rurik the Viking, cried impostor, and ordained a horrible death for the False Dimitry:

After being stabbed repeatedly he was tied by the testicles and thrown to the courtyard seventy-five feet below. His body was left for three days so that all might walk by and curse it, then it was burnt. The ashes were placed in a cannon pointing to the West – toward Poland – and fired off in that direction.

Prince Shuisky was crowned Tsar. The false Dimitry, it emerged, was a monk, Youri Otrepyev, who had escaped from the Chudov monastery in the Kremlin. Ironically Otrepyev had proved an excellent ruler: generous, intelligent and progressive (he even considered emancipating the serfs, which would have altered the whole course of Russian history), and opposed to cruelty and violence. To the xenophobic, religiously intolerant and generally bloody-minded Muscovites of the time it was perhaps this even disposition which spoke most forcefully against him being the son of one of history's most barbaric autocrats.

All of these pretenders – whether English, French or Russian – were able to thrive (for a time, at least) not only because there were powerful political factions behind them, but also because popular hopes of the restoration of a rightful line of succession were invested in them. Indeed, their miraculous 'reappearances' represented a reincarnation of hope itself. And just as in other cases of impersonation, powerful motives for belief in these claimants seems to have blinded their supporters to fairly fundamental inconsistencies in their impersonations. If there is a fine line between fervent patriotism and mass hysteria, it is demonstrated nowhere more clearly than in the multiple 'reappearances' of King Sebastian of Portugal.

When he was crowned, aged fourteen, in 1568, King Sebastian was dubbed 'another Alexander', and he indeed turned out to be everything a romantic hero should be: bold, devout, universally adored – and blond. However, both his martial and religious enthusiasm bordered on mania, causing a contemporary to note: 'he rides and prays too much for the good of the nation.' Obsessed with the idea of forging an African empire, Sebastian declared he would win Morocco for Portugal, and against all sensible advice the headstrong young monarch set sail from the Algarve at the head of a fleet of 800 ships. On landing in North Africa the Portuguese had no campaign plan, drifted south, and at Alcácer-Quibir, hopelessly outnumbered, were annihilated by the Moors. A third of Sebastian's men were killed in the battle, and most of those remaining were captured and sold as slaves. Fewer than a hundred men escaped to Argila or Tangier. The heroic Sebastian was numbered among the dead.

Or was he? No body was found after the battle, and the corpse which the Moors sent to Portugal some time afterwards was regarded with suspicion. These circumstances of course left the door open to the possibility that dashing King Sebastian was not dead, but had somehow escaped the battlefield. Possibility became transformed to hope when, in 1580, Portugal fell under Spanish power: as one writer succinctly summarizes the transition of attitude, at this point 'the lost king became a symbol of lost sovereignty.' Patriots believed that the lost king would return and free his people.

Lost kings duly began to appear. In the first decade after 1584 three Sebastians came forward. The first, a handsome but decidedly dark-haired youth, was exposed and consigned to the galleys before he knew what had hit him, but regained his wits sufficiently to re-emerge some time later as an impostor Duke of Normandy. The second, 'a failed monk', fared rather better, at least having, as an auspicious starting point, the reddish fair hair of the young king. He took care to be 'discovered' doing penance for his role in the downfall of Portugal, and would retell the tale of the battle in suitably anguished tones, punctuated with groans of guilt and sighs of regret. This calculated display of grief and contrition was sufficient to convince many people, and attracted enough support for the impostor to raise an army. Eventually he was arrested by the Spanish, at which point he declared that his plan had been to expel the Spanish from Lisbon, admit his imposture, and then leave it to the people to choose their king. This admirable plan was thwarted by the Spanish, who had him hanged, drawn and quartered.

The third would-be Sebastian was a pastry cook who, at sixty years of age, was far too old to fit the part and was summarily executed. It was not until 1598 – twenty years after Sebastian's disappearance – that a serious contender emerged.

This Sebastian explained that he had languished in a monastery until, one night, he had a dream which instructed him to return to his proper vocation. He duly presented himself before the governors of Venice and invited interrogation to verify his claim. Although he answered the questions put to him to everyone's satisfaction, the case was far from cut and dried. To name but one anomaly among many, this King of Portugal spoke no Portuguese. This was accounted for by him having taken a vow not to speak the language for a number of years. A further discrepancy lay in his appearance: like the first impostor Sebastian, the fourth was 'a swarthy individual'. He wisely made no attempt to explain this, instead choosing to join in the general astonishment, occasionally exclaiming in surprise: 'What has become of my fairness?'

The Portuguese took little interest in him until the Venetian authorities, under pressure from Spain, locked him up, which they took for a sign that Spain took him seriously, and began to believe that they should too. When he was released from prison in 1600 he had at least learned Portuguese, but too late: on being taken to Naples by his supporters, he was recognized as Marco Tullio Catizzone from Calabria; the wife he had abandoned helpfully confirmed the identification. Catizzone was condemned to the galleys, and was later executed.

As time passed, the belief that Sebastian would return gained rather than lost its power. As Portuguese historian A. H. de Oliveira Marques explains this extraordinary phenomenon:

Far from dying, the rumor acquired more and more adherents and became increasingly complex in its formulation. The prophecies of a certain Bandarra, a shoemaker who lived in John III's times and who heralded the future coming of a hidden (*encoberto*) king, redeemer of mankind, were now interpreted as referring to Sebastian and his fate.

Sebastianism became a kind of Portuguese messianism: like King Arthur or Jesus Christ, Sebastian would defy mortality and come again to save his people. Sebastianism remained in the background of Portuguese culture for nearly 300 years, 'intensifying especially when a sense of decline or desperation made a prophesied return to greatness a consolation'. In 1807, for example, it was foretold that Napoleon would be defeated by Sebastian. The last *Sebastianista* appeared in 1813 when a 'madman' dressed as a Moor, claiming to be Sebastian's envoy, pitched up in Lisbon. Centuries earlier he would have been sent to the galleys; now he became the subject of prints and figurines.

As the history of Sebastianism illustrates, the success of VIP impostors of course depends on a particular social group's appetite for and susceptibility to them, whether that social group is a band of soldiers, accustomed to unquestioning obedience, a collection of people anxious to ingratiate themselves with their social 'betters' or a political faction badly in need of an icon. But when that social group consists of wised-up, not to say cynical, wealthy, late-twentieth-century New Yorkers, for example, how would the impostor fare? David Hampton, who posed as the son of actor Sidney Poitier (who has no sons), managed to dupe Osborn Elliott, dean of the Columbia University Graduate School of Journalism, and John Jay Iselin, president of New York's public television station WNET, among other worldly-wise media luminaries.

One ruse Hampton used was to contact a wealthy individual or couple, claiming to be a friend of their son or daughter. He was in a spot, he would explain; he had been mugged and was stranded in the city with no money and nowhere to stay. Mention of his well-known 'father's' name dispelled any latent doubt: he would be offered a room for the night and some cash to tide him over. The stolen address book of a student at Connecticut College furnished him with his targets. Although theft seems to have been a motive, usually only relatively small amounts of cash were 'loaned' (anything between $20 and $350), and it has been noted that 'it seemed to have been equally important to Mr Hampton that others acknowledge his chosen identity.' It was indeed the deception that had been practised on them, rather than the financial loss, which was resented by his victims. John Jay Iselin remarked, 'I didn't consider him a calculated criminal. He defrauded more of the spirit than the flesh.'

In a future age, historians reading the newspaper reports of the case might be unaware of the important nuance provided by Poitier's racial identity: the black actor is so well known that for a journalist to spell out his colour would be as *de trop* as describing Monroe as a 'female star'. The 'black' element of his identity is emphasized in the way contemporaries think of Poitier by his association with many film roles in which he played individuals confronting racial bigotry. In films such as *In the Heat of the Night* and *Guess Who's Coming to Dinner* (both 1967) Poitier played an intelligent, educated, liberal, middle-class, urban professional black, a characterization which Poitier himself came to personify. Should a young black person, therefore, wish to claim an impressive show-business-family connection, he could light on no one better in order to ingratiate himself with intelligent, educated, liberal, middle-class, urban professional whites.

It was perhaps this largely undiscussed (at least by the New York press) aspect of Hampton's imposture which was possibly the source of most pain to his victims: they may have felt ashamed of their motives in believing Hampton's story. What kind of heel would turn away Sidney Poitier's son in his hour of need? And, crucially, how would it look? Hampton's selection of fake identity can therefore be appreciated as uniquely well chosen. His choice of personal relationship to his victims was also psychologically powerful. When a friend of your child calls on you for help, vested in your reason for obliging them is your hope that – were your own son or daughter in a similar fix – their friends' parents would reciprocate. Hampton therefore capitalized on another emotional weak spot: how could they resist?

Hampton served two years for impersonating Sidney Poitier's non-existent son. Following his release from prison he got into further trouble in the States before drifting around Europe for three years. In 1991 the story was revived in the public memory when John Guare's play *Six Degrees of Separation*, which was based on Hampton's scam, became a Broadway hit. Hampton himself resurfaced, allegedly making death threats to the playwright and later attempting to sue Guare for a share of the show's proceeds; elsewhere he claimed to have written the play himself.

John Guare's choice of title for his work referred to the notion that any two people in the world are connected in some way by a maximum of 'six degrees of separation' – i.e. a path through this number of people who are in some way connected can be traced to link any two strangers. The theory demonstrates that this is, indeed, a small world, within which even smaller worlds may encompass many shorter paths between strangers, with fewer degrees of separation. Within the theatre world, for example, it is not uncommon for two actors on first meeting to discover that they share many mutual acquaintances. John Guare recalls that during the final previews of *Six Degrees of Separation* the cast was visited backstage by the French film-star Michel Piccoli.

Evan Handler, an actor in the play, greeted Piccoli particularly warmly. 'I met your son when I was in Paris,' he told him.

Piccoli looked blank. 'I have no son,' he said.

4. Ferdinand Waldo Demara
and Other Professional Types

> Flash photography nor fingerprinting nor videotape brings
> impostors full stop. In a world of proliferant degrees and
> diplomas, impostors have more room than ever to move on
> from one half-life to the next. These days embossed papers
> substitute for personhood, identification cards for identity,
> licenses for learning . . .
>
> – Hillel Schwarz, *The Culture of the Copy*, 1996

One of the most disconcerting types of impostor is the man or
woman who impersonates the academic, the doctor, the priest,
and so on: the impostor 'professional'. Our confidence in such
professionals derives wholly from our belief that they are qualified
to teach, heal and advise us. Consequently we allow them intimate
access to the workings of our minds, bodies and souls, which we
would otherwise reveal only to those we know best, and most trust.
We allow – indeed expect – them to chide us, advise us and
otherwise 'parent' us. If we discover that the basis for this faith in
them is non-existent – that they are impostors – we may justifiably
feel abused. If their behaviour towards us has been satisfactory, it
may even be the case that we would prefer, in retrospect, that their
secret had not been revealed to us. It is often the traumatization of
trust, rather than potential incompetence, which is disturbing.

It is not only we as consumers of their services who stand to
suffer from the impostor's crime: the professions they infiltrate also
lose credibility, and it is primarily against these institutions that the
public directs its anger – the 'fault' is theirs for failing to spot the

interloper. The institutions recognize and capitalize on the fact that, provided no damage has been done, consumers would 'rather not know' they have been deceived. In these cases it seems in no one's interest dramatically and publicly to unmask the impostor. It is preferable quietly to spirit him away, with stern injunctions never to try the like again. The impostor vanishes and public confidence is intact. Ironically, of course, in this way institutions and professions effectively collaborate with the impostor; their desire to avoid publicity serves his interest. At another university, another hospital, another parish, he lives to lie another day.

When the associate professor of physics at the University of New Hampshire, Dr Kenneth D. Yates, was revealed in 1954 to be Marvin Hewitt, a highschool drop-out with no qualifications at all, he was in his fifth teaching job in seven years. At least two other colleges had discovered his deception, but apart from removing him from the faculty had taken no action. Indeed, the university authorities in New Hampshire had intended to let him go quietly, and only went to the press when the details leaked out.

It was not only concern for the university's prestige that influenced these decisions; Hewitt, like many impostor professionals, was outstanding at his job and admired by his fellow academics, who had no wish to humiliate him or, possibly, damage his prospects for employment elsewhere. Dr Robert F. Chandler, the president of the university, described Hewitt to the press as a 'brilliant physicist', and said his teaching was 'very satisfactory'; he was fired not for his inability to do the job, but because he had misrepresented his qualifications.

When his imposture became public, Hewitt received widespread support from colleagues, past and present, who recognized an exceptional mind when they saw one, while establishments as diverse as the US Atomic Energy Commission and the British Admiralty Office expressed interest in his work. He subsequently chose to 'fade from sight', and was never – as far as we know – heard from again.

Impostor academics can fake only their credentials; their actual abilities are daily and publicly put to the test, and provided that they 'do the business' in the classroom their backgrounds may never be questioned. On the other side of the world – and of the political divide – David Chakhvashvili, a Moscow caretaker, moonlit successfully as a science professor during the 1960s and 1970s. Although he had received no formal science education, he taught courses on atomic physics and the technological revolution without arousing suspicion. Following his eventual arrest by Soviet police, Chakhvashvili 'disappeared'. It is not known whether this signified a sudden and sinister end to him altogether or whether his talents had been recognized, and were being more privately utilized, by the state.

Marvin Hewitt had described himself as having a 'compulsion' to teach. An unwavering sense of purpose, or destiny, motivates many impostor professionals. A particularly worrying example is evident in a fairly recent case in which Brian MacKinnon, a Scot in his early thirties, posed as Brandon Lee, a Canadian teenager, to satisfy his overwhelming desire to become a doctor. MacKinnon, a medical student at Glasgow University, had repeatedly failed his exams and eventually been excluded from the course, but he believed he was born to be a doctor and could not accept rejection. He therefore began his elaborate imposture in order to re-enter university by a route which circumvented his past academic record: he went back to school and retook his 'A' levels under a different identity.

Exposure rarely lessens the impostor's desire to succeed in his planned course; it just makes it more difficult. Just as Hewitt spoke of his 'compulsion' to teach, after his deception was discovered, MacKinnon, interviewed in 1997, said of medicine, 'It's my purpose,' 'I'm just driven by that one idea,' and, more chillingly, 'I'll go to any lengths – any imaginative lengths – to ensure that by 1999 I'm back at medical school. I'll be there, and no one will know I'm there, and no one will find me.'

Impostor lawyers, although there have been many, are not included here, as their principal interest is almost always money, rendering them creative crooks rather than intriguing impostors. Impostor doctors and academics, however, are evidently in pursuit of other, less quantifiable gains, and they are joined in this category by impostor priests. Examples of these range from the Revd Wilfred Ellis, rector of a Suffolk parish for twenty-five years before he was revealed in 1883 to be no church minister but an ex-pork-butcher, to Roberto Coppola, a nineteen-year-old who was arrested in Rome in 1975 after impersonating a priest for over two years. In both cases the most serious consequence of the impostures was an administrative rather than a moral panic, as hundreds of couples discovered that they were not officially married: in the earlier case Parliament had to intervene to ensure the legitimacy of the children of these unsuspecting sinners.

The chameleon-like qualities of the impostor usually render him or her invisible to history, and even among those who are known, few 'lives' have been chronicled in detail. Their own views of what they are doing and why appear even more rarely. One oasis in this desert of inside information covers a sequence of impostures in the 1940s and 1950s in North America. The cases described in an article by Joe McCarthy for *Life* magazine, and also in a book written in 1959 by Robert Crichton, led to a tightening-up of procedures for checking credentials and verifying references in many institutions, and these writings serve to illustrate both the phenomenon of the complicit institution, and a variety of factors which emerge as common themes in many cases of imposture.

This 'rash' of impostures occurred across a broad spectrum of professions, and its numerous manifestations included Dr Robert Linton French (doctor of psychology); Jefferson Baird Thorne and Martin Godgart (both schoolteachers); Dr Cecil Boyce Hamann (a biologist) and Dr Joseph Cyr (a surgeon); Anthony Ingolia (law student) and Ben W. Jones (maximum-security-prison warden). None of these men was qualified to be doing what he was doing

– Ben W. Jones even had a criminal record himself. In fact, they all did. For all these men were one man: Ferdinand Waldo Demara, who deservedly became known as 'the great impostor'. Demara also had a strong leaning towards the Church, and his Trappist and Benedictine incarnations included Brothers Mary Jerome, John Berchmans, Robert Copernicus and John Payne. Demara was nothing if not versatile.

When Demara was apprehended as Martin Godgart, school-teacher, one of the arresting detectives was already familiar with his story. He explained what it was that put Demara in a class of his own: 'This guy didn't just assume the name or the titles like most impostors. He lives the lives and does the jobs.' And he did them well, often spectacularly so. As a naval surgeon he never lost a patient, and certainly saved lives, in one case operating to remove a bullet lodged in the tissue surrounding the heart. Governor Ellis of Huntsville Prison, Texas (known as the Alcatraz of the South), was also impressed by Demara's skill in handling dangerous and psychologically unstable prisoners: on at least one occasion he had disarmed a violent and unbalanced man by the power of gentle reasoning alone; he also single-handedly defused a potential riot situation, which in the past had ended in fatalities. Ellis said that Demara:

. . . was one of the best prospects ever to serve in this prison system. His future was bright, if not almost unlimited. I can say this – if he could only appear again with some legitimate credentials, and somehow this past was wiped out, I'd be proud to hire the man again.

Demara's abilities as a schoolteacher were such that when he was unmasked and arrested a delegation of parents pleaded not only for his release but for his reinstatement at the school. He was the best teacher, they claimed, their kids had ever had. Yet when this same man was operating in his own, legitimate persona, he was a consistent failure.

Demara was exceptional in undertaking such a wide variety of professional impostures, but as the previous examples of impostor professionals show, there are many instances of impostors who in more modest ways 'lived the lives and did the jobs'. These were not conmen who posed for a short time as someone in an official capacity in order to defraud; their only financial reward was the enhanced salary of their technically undeserved status. The reward which was of most value to them was arguably the experience itself, as is illustrated in the life and careers of Ferdinand Waldo Demara.

From a very early age Demara had wanted to devote himself to the Catholic Church. To this end, in 1935 at the age of fourteen he ran away from home and asked to be admitted to a Trappist monastery in Valley Falls, Rhode Island. Despite his extreme youth, faced with his equally extreme tenacity, the monks and his parents agreed to let him stay. Taking into account the Trappists' spartan diet, rigorous regime and vow of silence, they believed that the young man would be home in no time. As it turned out, Demara stayed for two years, earned his habit and hood, and was named Frater Mary Jerome. He loved the life, and was stung to the core when the monks told him that he didn't have 'the right stuff'. True, by night he dreamed of bread and gravy; true, by day he found it increasingly difficult to keep quiet: he was sixteen and had joined one of the most demanding religious orders in the world. Nevertheless, he was heartbroken and later said of his rejection: 'I think it was the greatest hurt in my life.'

Demara went home, feeling cheated and determined somehow to prove the Trappists wrong. The unshakeable resolution to pursue a chosen career, by hook or by crook, was no less powerful in Demara. (Much later in his life, after repeated exposure, a dozen Catholic institutions, and a variety of identities, he continued to maintain that 'I am only waiting to feel a true call again before once again trying to find my meaning in the service of the Catholic Church.') He went on to work for the Brothers of Charity, was renamed Brother John Berchmans, and was assigned as bottle-washer and kitchen boy to 'aged, sick and disciplined priests' at the Retreat St Benoît outside Montreal. This was to prove an education indeed. Here were men well acquainted with the seamier side of the Church, and its more mysterious movements. Demara soon lost a sense of awe regarding his superiors in the Church: 'After what I learned and saw there, I never felt uneasy in the presence of a bishop. I felt he was probably no better than me but just disguised it better and had better connections.' After falling out with the brothers in charge, Demara ran away, pinching a small amount of cash from the office as he went.

The Brothers of Charity sent him next to a children's home in West Newbury. Despite its name, 'Boyhaven', the home exuded a rather sombre and loveless atmosphere which Demara, put in charge of the fourth grade, set about changing. He replaced traditional teaching with trips, games and story-telling. While the boys lapped up this attention, Demara's methods were not appreciated by the Brother Superior. Demara left, this time taking a car with him, and headed for Boston. It was now 1941.

A disturbing pattern was emerging. Despite his undoubtedly good intentions, Demara's career in the Church was going nowhere. After three false starts he had now become a thief as well. He decided on a complete change of direction and enlisted in the United States Army. Almost immediately he realized he had made a terrible mistake. He survived by becoming, in his words, a 'real wise guy', and devoted himself to the diligent study of every scam possible to render military life tolerable. Robert Crichton was able to interview his subject at length, and drew the following pertinent observation:

Somewhere along the way he had . . . developed a highly personal version of Thomas Locke's social contract philosophy which, for those who have forgotten it, goes, roughly: If the individual in a society can't go along with the rules of that society then the individual reserves for himself the right to withdraw from that society. He is a part of society as a result of his freely made contract with it, and he can at any time declare the contract null and void.

This rationale can also be observed operating in the lives of many other impostors, who often see their actions as entirely justifiable – under the circumstances. Brian MacKinnon *knew* he deserved to be a doctor and perceived the obstacles in his way as the result of irrational ill will towards him. He did not fail; he was conspired against. Unfairly persecuted, as he saw it, he was justified in compensating for his disadvantage by bending the rules. Demara's contract with the world was also rapidly deteriorating. Since the authorities had failed to be impressed by him, he was no longer obliged to be impressed by them. He had to get out of the Army, and it didn't matter how.

Anthony Ingolia, his tent-mate at Keesler Field Air Force Base in Biloxi, Mississippi, was to provide the way out. One weekend Ingolia took Demara home with him. To the young man's embarrassment, his mother's idea of entertainment for their guest was to trawl through a box of photos, cuttings, mementoes and records relating to her son's history. Ingolia need not have been embarrassed: Demara was fascinated, and pored over the personal archive for ages. 'What do you see in those things?' a bored Ingolia asked him. 'Life,' Demara replied. 'I see a whole life ahead of me.'

A few weeks later Demara made an excuse to return to Ingolia's home, and stole that life. He was wanted for car theft, Ingolia was not; Demara had a poor record of service in the Church, to which he still wished to return, Ingolia had no record; the military police would soon be looking for Demara, but not for Ingolia. Crichton explains why the theft was, in Demara's view, a reasonable act:

Since his aim was to do good, anything he did to do it was justified. With Demara the end *always* justifies the means. Stealing Ingolia's papers was not in itself a bad act if he didn't do bad things with them. It was, in fact, a good act.

Although the use of Ingolia's papers constituted Demara's first imposture, it is worth bearing in mind that at this point Demara had already had three names quite legitimately. So far he had been F. W. Demara, Frater Mary Jerome and Brother John Berchmans. The liberating possibilities of a new start, and a new identity, which the Church traditionally offered – twice in Demara's case – perhaps even sowed in his mind the notion that when one life disappointed, one was entitled to try another.

After fleeing the Army, brief and unsatisfactory stays in two more Trappist monasteries followed. Demara again decided he needed a change. This time, using his own name, he enlisted in the Navy. He should have known better, as he was no more suited to the Navy than he had been to the Army. He campaigned to be accepted into hospital school and proved an excellent student. Yet once more his ambitions were thwarted. Although he passed the basic course, he was refused advanced training, because he did not have the appropriate educational background. He was again beset by feelings of hurt and injustice: 'I went around as if someone had hit me right between the eyes. Here I scored the highest on all the tests and because someone had a couple of years in college they picked him and kicked me out.' But Demara was not about to give up. 'The thing to do,' he realized, 'was to *get* the proper background.'

Demara was to become adept at borrowing identities, forging official certificates, and composing bogus references. He so impressed himself on this first occasion with the package of papers he produced to back his application to medical school that he decided to pass it over and go straight for an officer's commission. But Demara had overstretched himself. The authorities were checking out his credentials: a showdown was inevitable; the shame would be intolerable. As the suicide note found on the quayside with his Navy uniform explained: 'I have made a fool of myself. This is the only way out. Forgive me. F. W. Demara.'

Demara's death, of course, was as fake as his forged documents. It served its purpose, however, providing a dead-end to any search for him. He then bought an honourable discharge and an officer's identification card (both forgeries), and from a collection of identities he had now assembled, chose to become Dr Robert Linton French, ex-Navy officer, doctor of psychology. His impulse to serve the Church was still as relentless as his ability to do so was lacking: after another false start with the Trappists he decided to try the Benedictines, who he'd heard were more 'intellectual', and joined the New Subiaco Abbey, in the Ozark mountains of Arkansas. The monastery ran a boys' school where Demara taught science (for which he studied at nights) while awaiting novitiate training.

Still as Dr French, he next joined up with the Clerics of St Viator in Chicago, who appointed priests with specialist knowledge to Catholic communities. This was just the ticket for a recent convert (as Demara now represented himself) with a psychology Ph.D. The Clerics – to Demara's chagrin – entered him in a crash course in theology at De Paul University. Faced with a list of subjects to study, many of which Demara couldn't initially even pronounce, he nevertheless put his shoulder to the wheel and emerged with outstanding grades: the records of the university show that he earned straight 'A's in rational psychology, metaphysics, cosmology, epistemology, ethics and natural theology.

'I knew I could do it but I had to have it proven to me,' he later said. 'That experience really changed me. No matter how I might feel I still can't work up any respect for acquired learning. I can for character but not learning. A man with a good mind who trusts it can learn anything he needs to know in a few months.' Just as Demara had early on learned (through his experience at the retreat for straying priests) that the mysteries of the Church shrouded men who were all too human, which had given him immense confidence, similarly his academic experience dispelled the awe in which he had previously held men of learning. In both cases, he felt, anyone with the will and the wit could do the same job competently.

When his novitiate training began, though, Demara had qualms.

'I mean, I was a fake, all right, but I had scruples and a sense of honor and decency. I couldn't become a priest.' Having had a legitimate interest in the Church (there was nothing fake about Demara's own Catholicism), and despite his low opinion of many priests, Demara evidently felt that this would be crossing a sacrosanct boundary. Yet this same man was prepared to allow his parents to believe he was dead (via the faked suicide) and went on to impersonate a doctor, which is arguably more dangerous to the public than impersonating a priest. However, it seems likely that Demara's decisions had nothing to do with their possibly negative effects on other people, and everything to do with his own needs. It would have been moral torture for Demara to have to sit and listen in a confessional, while people poured out their misdemeanours to him, in the absolute trust that he was capable of absolving them. It was not his flock's moral well-being he feared for, but his own.

Hesitating at the prospect of entering the priesthood under a false identity, but his confidence boosted by his success in his theology exams, Demara left the Clerics of St Viator ('I disappeared. No explanations. I just disappeared.'), this time heading for a brief stay with the Order of St Camillus in Milwaukee, before making his way to Gannon College, a small but expanding Catholic institution in Erie, Pennsylvania. Taking the initiative, he approached the college with the suggestion that he set up and run a department of psychology. The ambitious little college welcomed Dr French with open arms, and in very little time Demara found himself, as dean of the school of philosophy, more than competently teaching a variety of courses in psychology. How, it may well be asked, did he manage it?

Biographers of impostors frequently observe that their subjects have phenomenal memories. Two points arise from this. Obviously, impostors are good, or what seems as likely, become good at assimilating and retaining information which should be easily called upon by the character they are assuming. The impostor who cannot remember his borrowed or invented 'facts' will not be an impostor very long. Secondly, there is a general reluctance to admit that it may not be merely the memory of the impostor which is well above average, but his mental capacity in general which is superior. (Even Demara's strategies for covering the holes in his academic knowledge demonstrate great intellectual resourcefulness.) Crichton notes that 'during the years Demara had been passing as Dr French he had been doing a haphazard but massive amount of reading, and he had collected an undigested, uncollated, but remarkable amount of psychological information.' This understates the situation. When given the opportunity to study subjects as diverse as medicine in the Navy, and theology at De Paul University, Demara had in both cases come top of the class, starting from a knowledge base of zero. He was surely capable of teaching himself psychology to a more sophisticated degree than Crichton is willing to admit. Because the impostor is a fake, there is almost always a tendency for biographers, however affectionate, to underplay their very real achievements.

Both the impostor academics mentioned earlier, Hewitt and Chakhvashvili, possessed more than exceptional memories: they had a full and firm comprehension of their subjects, although both were entirely self taught. In Demara's case specifically, there is every reason to believe that he had an exceptional grasp of psychological principles: his whole career depended, after all, on his abilities to anticipate and manipulate people's reactions. (This was to be demonstrated most strikingly later in his life in his extraordinary abilities with so-called 'psychotic' convicts.) When asked by a journalist whether teaching psychology at an even higher level, as he later did, caused Demara any anxiety, he looked surprised. 'Why? I just kept ahead of the class. The best way to learn anything is to teach it.' It was not his professional incompetence but his beer-drinking which aroused his boss's suspicions. One thing led to another, and Demara was soon moving on.

It may have been noticed that Demara had a penchant for what sociologists term 'total institutions', environments frequently sought out by impostors. A total institution is an institution which, broadly speaking, encompasses the whole day-to-day lives of its occupants. Access to the outside world is limited and regulated; both work and leisure time are spent within the environment, with the same people. It can consist of larger or smaller units. Thus, the Navy is a total institution, but so is a submarine; the Catholic Church may be described as a total institution, but so may the individual convent or monastery. Total institutions are characterized by a closely regulated and tightly controlled regime, usually involving uniforms, rigid timetables and strict rules. They are also, in one sense or another, self-sufficient communities. The prison or the boarding-school are other examples.

The total institution insists on a uniformity of behaviour and appearance, which may account for its appeal for the impostor. Demara, for example, certainly liked to feel he 'belonged' somewhere, although conformity was never his strong point. Yet the magnetism of total institutions for Demara is the essence of his tragedy: he desires, insatiably, to 'fit in', to become indistinguishable from the group, even to become invisible; yet pulling in the opposite direction is his instinct to initiate and innovate, to excel, to stand out. It is not enough to be in the Navy, Demara must be an officer; he cannot be satisfied with teaching, he must be head of his own faculty. He seems to seek the security of the known parameters of the total institution, with the bonus of some status and authority within it.

Instances of Demara's prescient understanding of institutions and how they operate can be seen in his theory about power in such organizations, a theory he put to practical use both in the example just mentioned (his establishment of his own department at Gannon College) and in the place he went to next, the Benedictine St Martin's Abbey and College, in Olympia, Washington, where he soon set up his own Psychological Center, offering both lectures and counselling. (He was now known as Brother Robert Copernicus of the Pious Society of St Mark.) As Crichton reports it:

He had come to two beliefs. One was that in any organisation there is always a lot of loose, unused power lying about which can be picked up without alienating anyone. The second rule is, if you want power and want to expand, never encroach on anyone else's domain; open up new ones.

Demara never joined someone else's committee, for example, where power relationships already existed and territories of interest were already marked out; instead, he set up his own. He called this 'expanding into the power vacuum', and it may provide a useful tip for ambitious non-impostors. However, its twin aspects of gaining power *without making enemies* are particularly important to the impostor, who can do without rubbing people up the wrong way, giving them cause to look for reasons to discredit or undermine him. Again, this example demonstrates Demara's intelligent application of psychology (industrial psychology was one of the courses he offered), suggesting that he understood the principles sufficiently well to put them into practice.

Demara's academic career was not to last, however. The military authorities finally caught up with him and charged him with the capital crime of desertion in time of war. Demara brought the full force of his thespian and creative skills to bear on his defence. Throwing himself on the mercy of the court martial he represented himself as an idealistic young man who had entered the Navy when freshly out of a Trappist monastery but had become depressed and corrupted by the experience, eventually fleeing back to the Church. The court martial 'bought' his story, and he was sentenced to six years, of which, as a result of his good behaviour, he was required to serve only eighteen months. The Army, who had also been looking for Demara, found him already in the Navy prison and dropped charges. During his spell 'inside' he had access to all parts of the prison in his role as editor of the camp newspaper (imaginatively entitled *Tars and Bars*). 'When I left there I knew enough about it to run the place,' Demara commented, adding characteristically: 'better than it was run, I mean.'

His subsequent social status (Demara, ex-con) deeply bothered him, especially being hustled along by the police, wherever he happened to be.

As Dr. French, those cops wouldn't have treated me that way. I really hated not being French. No. What I hated most was being Demara again. Who was Demara? Anyway you looked at it, French was somebody, good or bad. Good *or* bad, Demara – that guy was a bum.

Demara was determined to sort his life out. Within the year he aimed to begin studying law, get married and start a family. His criminal record presented a rather serious impediment to the first ambition. No matter; he wouldn't be Demara. Acquiring the appropriate documents, he borrowed the identity of one Dr Cecil Boyce Hamann and entered Northeastern Law School. By night he worked as janitor in an eye hospital to pay his fees. During whatever time remained he devoted himself to the search for a wife. It wasn't easy:

I tried *very* hard. I learned to dance. I told charming stories. I spent every cent I had on women. I think they liked me. I liked them. But nothing – nothing happened at all. You know why? Love is something real and I was a fake, and all of us must have sensed that. It didn't work.

For Demara, even his love life was a carefully prepared campaign. This one was doomed to flounder, not through outside interference but self-knowledge.

Although his grades at law school were good, he was bored to distraction. 'There were times there when I thought I was losing my mind. No wonder most lawyers are so boring. It's a plot. Only one of their own beastly boring breed can suffer through those schools.' He abandoned the dreams of a legal career, wife and children, and returned to more familiar ground: the priest with a Ph.D. He joined the Brothers of Christian Instruction in Alfred,

Maine, where he – as Dr Hamann – took the name Brother John Payne. Now he was a zoologist, specializing in cancer research. Demara had come to the right place at the right moment: the arrival of an academic heavyweight like Hamann seemed a miracle to the brothers: most of their novices were young farm boys who had to be transformed into parochial schoolteachers. Demara later told *Life* magazine:

I was regarded as a windfall. They rolled out the red carpet and all the bells in the place began to ring. Now that they have read about me, I imagine the good brothers have changed their opinion. If a legitimate college graduate went there now and knocked on the door, they would probably punch him on the nose.

He immediately set about 'expanding into the power vacuum', aiming to transform the college run by the brothers into a university – in which he, of course, would play a leading role. It was at this time that he made the acquaintance of Dr Joseph Cyr, with whom he became close friends. Cyr, a Canadian medical doctor, was trying to get a licence to practise in the States. Demara, never one to pass up an opportunity, generously offered to help him, taking all his records and credentials to expedite the affair. (Later, when newspaper reports intimated that Demara had stolen Cyr's credentials, Demara categorically denied this, saying proudly, 'I didn't steal his papers. He *gave* them to me.') Meanwhile, Demara was also making enemies. When the university charter was granted, he was amazed to learn that he was not to be the new university's chancellor – nor even a head of department. He was listed as a biology instructor. He quit on the spot, and left – in one of the brothers' cars.

He presented himself at a Royal Canadian Navy recruiting office as Dr Joseph Cyr. The Korean war was under way and the Navy was frankly desperate for doctors; Demara also piled on the pressure to enlist him:

I told them that if they didn't take me in a hurry I'd join the Canadian army. That did it. Within two hours they had me on a train to Ottawa and I was commissioned there the next day. I passed the physical exam without taking off my clothes and they never even bothered to take my fingerprints. One of the admirals on the selection board told me the processing that I went through in a day usually takes ten weeks.

Only nine days after making his previous getaway, Demara was a surgeon lieutenant assigned to the RCN hospital at Halifax. At this point one cannot fail to wonder what on earth Demara thought he was doing. Had he considered how serious the consequences of medical imposture might be? Demara, as always, evidently thought he could handle it.

He had flirted with medical imposture before. Somewhere between Gannon and St Martin's he had pitched up as a medical doctor at a hospital run by the Brothers of St John of God in Los Angeles. His stay was short, as he was disappointed to find that the hospital was a home for geriatrics. Something had happened as he left which should have warned him off such a dangerous area for ever. A young brother wished to satisfy his curiosity on one matter: what advantage did the doctor derive from wearing *barber*'s white coats? Unchastened, during his stay at St Martin's Abbey for some reason Demara had also let slip that he was a medical doctor, with the consequence that members of the community began coming to him for treatment. Demara answers the inevitable question:

The seriously sick know they're sick and so do you. Those you send to a hospital. The rest are all going to get better sooner or later, and anything you do for them will seem right, and because they think you're a doctor, they'll automatically feel better.

Simple, really. However, having arrived at the hospital at Halifax, he was understandably concerned that he might miss a serious illness, and approached his superior with an enterprising project.

'I've been asked by some people to work up a rule of thumb guide for the people in lumber camps,' he reasonably explained. 'Most of them don't have doctors handy and they're pretty isolated. Could we get together a little guide that would pretty well cover the most serious situations?' The doctor obligingly produced what was to become Demara's bible.

Derek Cooper in *The Gullibility Gap* points out that we all know the doctor's script: 'Where do you get the pain . . . just slip off your top things . . . now relax . . . does that hurt . . . take this along to the chemist's and if it doesn't get any better come back in a fortnight's time . . . no, the *other* door. Next . . .' He mentions a number of cases of medical imposture, including a mental-hospital patient who picked up enough of the patter and jargon to pass as a psychiatrist at four other hospitals, and a failed medical student who was employed as a surgeon by no fewer than twelve English hospitals and carried out, *en route*, 150 operations. A brief survey of the indexes of any national newspaper reveals less ambitious but no less disturbing examples.

During the time Demara was at Halifax, the unexpected happened: now that he had given up looking for love, love came looking for him. Catherine was a nurse in the Navy, and at least as besotted with him as he was with her. He wanted to get married and settle down. He wanted to tell her that he wasn't Joe Cyr. But he didn't know how. Afraid of losing her by the truth but determined not to marry her as Cyr, Demara began to drink heavily. As usual, escape was his only solution. He pleaded with HQ to be sent as soon as possible into active service in Korea. Although Catherine was pained by this delay to their wedding plans she promised to wait for him. It was with some relief that 'Dr Cyr' reported on board His Majesty's Canadian ship *Cayuga*: now he was responsible only for the lives of 292 people.

The *Cayuga*'s mission was to patrol the east coast of the country, occasionally blasting broadsides in the direction of the North Koreans' fortifications. The voyage out had been peaceful and the most serious demand on Demara's services had been to pull a couple of the Captain's teeth. One day, however, a junk bearing a miserable cargo of badly wounded South Koreans pulled up alongside the ship. Demara's moment of truth had arrived. Aware that three of the men were extremely bad cases, requiring surgery, he dealt with the minor injuries first. As the crew looked on, absolutely trusting in the 'doc', Demara for the first time experienced the full weight of the lonely isolation of the impostor. There was no possibility of escape from the alarming scenario unfolding before him.

A bad storm had blown up by the time Demara had to begin surgery on the worst cases. The whole crew was doing its utmost to keep the ship as steady as possible to enable the doctor to work. The first patient had taken a bullet in the chest. Contemplating the scalpel, and what he knew he had to do with it, Demara left the room, drank a triple dram of rum, and returned. He prayed. He cut through the skin, the fat, the connective tissue, and found himself calling for 'clamps' and 'rib spreaders' and, more surprisingly, knowing what to do with them. He felt the bullet, lodged in the pericardial sac, a quarter-inch from the violently beating heart. New doubts assailed him. Should he take it out and risk a haemorrhage? Should he leave it in and hope the surrounding tissues would heal? Despite the crew's efforts, the ship continued to roll. Demara reached for the forceps and retrieved the bullet. Having squirted coagulant into the wound, Demara prayed hard with the chaplain for it not to bleed. It didn't. Demara sewed him up and called for the next patient. Compared with the last, it was a relatively simple, although bad, shell-splinter groin wound. The third was tricky again. Something had passed right through the man's body, and although no muscle or bone damage had occurred, the wound was infected, and one lung partially collapsed. Demara carefully cleaned the wound, and then by using a needle effected a total collapse of the left lung. Crichton describes the scene when he had finished:

They turned out the bank of emergency lights and he was dumbfounded to see in every porthole the faces of crew members pressed against them. He was also amazed to see that it was light outside. He had gone through the night and it was early morning. He knew that it was obvious, but he could not risk making the Churchillian sign of victory and the men cheered their doctor with a wild, spontaneous cheer. They weren't sure what they had witnessed but they sensed they had seen something very special and something heroic.

Demara's patients recovered, and the medical drama on the boat caught in a storm was seized on by a press information officer badly in need of good news to give the folks back home. Just as Stanley Clifford Weyman's party for the crew of the USS *Wyoming* had been undone by publicity, Demara was about to reap the dubious rewards of his fame. Back in Canada, the real Dr Cyr was amazed to read of his own heroics under the picture of his good friend Brother John Payne. He knew Brother John was a doctor – Dr Cecil B. Hamann, to be precise. The Navy in Ottawa instructed the CO of the *Cayuga* to suspend Cyr – or Hamann – immediately. Commander Plomer, however, was easily persuaded by Demara that an awful mistake had been made. Demara suddenly realized something much worse: Catherine would be aware of the whole story. He drank himself into oblivion and was transferred to the cruiser *Ceylon* in a cargo sling, only sufficiently coherent to mumble: 'Tell them I'll be back.'

Here the complicity of institutions with impostors again reveals itself. The Navy could do without Demara's kind of publicity, and emphatically did not want to be told that Cyr was not even a doctor. The authorities therefore accepted that Demara was really Hamann, a doctor who for personal reasons had fled the US and disguised himself as Cyr in order to enter the Canadian Navy. He was discharged. His medical credentials remained intact.

Demara received a letter from Catherine saying that she didn't care about anything: she loved him, not his name. Demara couldn't bear her thinking she knew his secret – that he was really Hamann – and that there was so much more that was shameful that she did not know. He kept his distance. Impostors are usually unable to maintain close personal relationships, but Demara's case does seem particularly tragic. Catherine appears to have been an exceptional woman and one wonders whether there was something perverse in Demara's refusal to at least try to become reconciled with her, to tell her the whole story and let her make her own decision. (Crichton's book details the extraordinary lengths she went to to keep him before he went to sea.) He drowned his sorrows in drink for a while, before going home to Lawrence. That Christmas he received a card from his shipmates on the *Cayuga*. Berton Braley's poem 'Loyalty' was written on the back:

> He may be six kinds of liar,
> He may be ten kinds of fool,
> He may be a wicked high flyer,
> Beyond any reason or rule.
>
> There may be a shadow above him
> Of ruin and woes to impend,
> And I may not respect, but I love him,
> Because – well, because he's my friend.

Realizing that he had never done a thing for his parents, Demara sold his story to *Life* magazine and gave them $2,000 of the $2,500 it raised. He then began his penance for, as he saw it, ruining Catherine's life: he became Demara again. He went from job to job, as he was now fairly well known, and people tended to be wary of him. He worked for a spell at a school for children with special needs, and later at a hospital for the criminally insane. This was extremely demanding – and hazardous – work, but Demara thrived on it:

I knew I was learning a great deal, a great deal that most men never even see. And I was mastering it. I could talk to those people and they could talk to me . . . I seemed to have this hypersensitive attraction to the wildly insane. The worst offenders would sense it at once and walk right up to me. I began to think that I was crazy, too. I had good reason to think that, of course.

He returned to heavy drinking and rambled through other people and places. From two significant facts – living under his own real identity, and selling his life story to *Time* – it would seem reasonable to deduce that Demara had determined to end his career as an impostor once and for all, and indeed this had probably been his intention. The problem was that there was no future, and certainly no fun, in being Ferdinand Waldo Demara, ex-impostor. Some-how he came by the credentials of a Southern gentleman by the name of Ben W. Jones. 'Jones' could make the changes which seemed somehow inaccessible to Demara. He joined Alcoholics Anonymous and worked for a short time in a hotel before, via an elaborate process of faked and tampered documents, he secured a job at Huntsville prison.

Huntsville was a huge maximum-security prison. At this time in Texas the criminally insane were not treated distinctly from other prisoners. Those who in other state penitentiaries had drawn attention to themselves by violent and even murderous actions found their way inexorably to Huntsville. Here they were treated as caged animals – and often more brutally.

Demara was first assigned to guard duty on the vast prison farm. The staff were typically inflexible hard men, willing to discharge their guns at the prisoners on any pretext. Demara quickly came up with a plan which saw him transferred back inside the prison in charge of setting up a recreation programme ('expanding into the power vacuum': he hadn't lost his touch). He quickly earned the liking and respect of the inmates and the governor, Mr O. B. Ellis, if not of the other staff. Not only did he establish study periods, games tournaments and other recreational facilities, but he seemed to have an uncanny way with the most difficult and dangerous men, and an ability to dissipate tension in the most unpromising confrontations.

Demara drew both on his own experience and on his self-taught psychology in handling delicate and highly charged situations. Instead of clubs, tear-gas and buckshot, he deployed trust, sympathy and tenderness. Recognizing that fear often caused people to lash out, he disarmed the violent with reassurance, which proved far more effective, and significantly less bloody. He also always offered the troublemaker an honourable way out: a concept which was alien to the traditional guards whose instincts were utterly to crush resistance – often leading to a subsequent backlash as humiliation and resentment once more boiled over. Thus gentle negotiation would lead to face-saving compromise whereby, for example, a prisoner would not throw down a weapon but would allow Demara to take it out of his hand. Dignity was maintained, and no one was hurt. It was, of course, a high-risk strategy. As with the insane, Demara was not afraid. As he said himself, it was rational people who most worried him.

As a result of his exceptional gifts with the most demanding prisoners Ellis invited Demara to work in maximum security, what he called 'the toughest of the tough'. Demara asked first to be shown round. 'There were people in there with eyes so wild and strange it made me wonder if people don't really get star crossed or aren't reincarnated from lynxes and wolves and those moon howlers.' Demara's guide warned him against getting too close to the bars, as these were 'psychotics'. The professor of psychology in Demara recognized the challenge and determined to meet it.

Crichton describes the conditions at Huntsville, which he visited a few years after Demara's employment there:

There is no zoo in the United States in which animals are as desperately caged as are the men in Huntsville's maximum security. The cells are low, narrow and short and never can a man extend himself. This alone is maddening enough, as maddening as the company he must keep.

Never does a prisoner come in any form of contact with a guard. The keepers of the den pack tear-gas billies, heavy truncheons which can eject a tear-gas pill on need, vomit gas, pistols, blackjacks, manacles, rifles and shot guns.

And the prisoners are equally armed no matter what the authorities do. They can't have spoons because spoons are turned into double-edged knives. They made the mistake of allowing the men plastic toothbrushes and these became murderous knives.

The worst punishment, far worse than a beating, is the 'pisser'. This is solitary confinement. The name 'pisser' stems from the fact that the sole apparatus in the cells is a small round hole, which is the end of a water pipe. It is flushed several times a day. In between then the convict has a choice of using it either as a latrine or as a drinking fountain. The diet is bread and water. The prisoner is lowered into the pisser and the longer a man endures it the greater the hero he is. The longer a man does endure the more certain he is to be mad or to be becoming madder.

Demara's strategy with the already disturbed men kept in these conditions was to treat them as a caring father would a sick child. He recognized that the prisoners became violent when they were fearful, and yet that the system was designed to keep them in a perpetual state of fear. This he counteracted by responding to outbursts of aggression with calm reassurance; just as one parent might smack a child having a tantrum while another might soothe them through it, Demara's methods were at the opposite end of the scale of anything that had been tried at Huntsville before. When a young prisoner, faced with a spell in the 'pisser', committed suicide, a prisoner in a neighbouring cell reacted so violently and extremely that the tension in the block reached a dangerous level – a major and serious incident seemed inevitable. Demara worked his magic. Governor Ellis said:

I don't know how he managed it. I don't know what he did or what he said. But he knew how to handle that man and the situation. I know I've never seen anything quite like what Jones did on maximum security before or since.

Demara's methods were controversial in another respect: he also discreetly made use of tranquillizers and phenobarbiturates for 'some real bad customers'.

Demara seemed finally to have found his *métier*. His work had value; he was appreciated; he was swiftly progressing up the promotional hierarchy; he was happy and fulfilled. Yet again, it was all about to be snatched away. Inevitably, one day one of the inmates was lying on his bunk reading a back issue of *Time* when he happened to spot a picture of a man who bore an uncanny resemblance to the assistant warden of maximum security. Could their own Ben Jones be the great impostor, Ferdinand Waldo Demara? Demara quietly left before they had time to sack him. 'How many times I have died and how many times I've been orphaned,' he reflected.

Yet another period was spent in a drunken haze. Cashing a cheque in the name of B. W. Jones brought the police and a list of charges which combined could have put him in jail for nearly fifty years. However, the state of Texas was not interested in persecuting Demara: it just wanted him gone. As Governor Ellis put it: 'I didn't want to hurt him. And I didn't want to see him.' Demara's mother covered the bad cheques and the other charges were dropped. Once again, the authorities' unwillingness to wash their dirty linen in public saved Demara's skin.

On his release he went home to Lawrence to find that his father had died. A period of deep depression and introspection followed. He left again, and a couple of legitimate jobs later was bored and unfulfilled. Hearing about a vacancy at North Haven School on an island off Maine, he was again motivated to enter the fray, and as Martin Godgart became an asset to the small community. As well as proving an excellent teacher, he set up and ran the Sea Scouts (every child on the island joined), taught at the Sunday school and played Santa Claus at Christmas. This pillar of the community was eventually arrested, and yet again the charges were dropped. Few people, it seems, ever sought revenge on Demara.

Other escapades followed, and even while Crichton was writing his book new headlines appeared: Genius without Portfolio Unmasked Again; Gentle Masquerader at It Again; The Great Impostor Wanted. Demara was being looked for by another school in Massachusetts – not for fraud, but for back-pay he was owed; the school superintendent explained that Mr Jefferson Baird Thorne, who had disappeared mysteriously, was, quite simply, a genius.

Crichton's book appeared in 1959 when Demara was thirty-eight, and the rest of his story has to be pieced together from disparate snippets of news. The book itself sold well, and the following year was made into a film starring Tony Curtis (also called *The Great Impostor*). Demara himself later appeared in a film (*The Hypnotic Eye*), legitimately this time playing a doctor. He continued to adopt further aliases, but fame had made his lives a little more difficult. He 'faded from sight' in the mid-1960s, but in 1970 turned up as the Revd Dr Fred Demara, taking the pulpit at the San Juan Baptist church, Friday Harbor, Washington, and in 1978 was working as a religious counsellor to the sick and dying at the Good Samaritan Hospital in Anaheim, California. Aware of his notorious past one of his colleagues admitted: 'At first I was very skeptical,' adding, 'but he sort of grows on you.' In 1980 Demara was fêted as a 'life saver' at a reunion of the crew of the *Cayuga*.

It would be agreeable to leave Demara there, among those who knew he was 'six kinds of liar', but who nevertheless counted him as their friend. Many stories, however, last too long to have a happy ending. In the same year as the *Cayuga* tribute, Demara was forced to stop working due to ill health. His lawyer, Martin Belli, said that he became despondent towards the end of his life: 'The strings all ran out on him. There was no way to channel or exploit his tremendous talents.' His doctor, Dr John J. Zane, observed of Demara's declining years: 'He was about the most miserable, unhappy man I have known.' During the last weeks of his life, 'all he said was he wished he could die and go to heaven.' Zane perhaps did not detect a trace of characteristic optimism in this remark; also on an upbeat note, Belli added: 'But I never heard him say he had any regrets about anything.'

Ferdinand Waldo Demara, 'the great impostor', died of heart failure in 1982 at the age of sixty: a man of exceptional gifts on whom, perhaps, a mere one life would have been wasted.

5. 'I Know Who I Am'

Impostors have been seen attempting to steal kingdoms, illustrious names, and large fortunes. They have been in some cases so bold and so fortunate as to be received by parents as their children, and by incredulous wives as their husbands. The audacity of such undertakings is in itself a means of success, because such an imposture is so apparently impossible and so perilous, that suspicions are deadened and doubt slow to arise.

– Moreau de Fourneau

The impostor employs two kinds of strategies in order to deceive us: practical and psychological. His most obvious practical props are physical 'evidence': faked documents of identity, ownership or qualification, and sometimes, if impersonating a real person, objects – authentic or faked – known to have belonged to that person. These concrete items carry an awesome authority which is unlikely to be questioned, but which can rarely do the job on their own. The psychological strategies employed by the impostor serve to cement our intellectual knowledge of someone by operating on our emotions, and our 'common sense'. In many cases both these aspects are operating at the same time.

On the level of practical evidence, how does the impostor go about assembling the paperwork required in order to make his claims stick? Firstly, regardless of content, the thing has got to look authentic. In the age of the personal computer, in which a competent child is able to produce a vast range of convincing and official-looking letter-headings, this is a comparatively easy matter, whereas previously it was necessary somehow to come by the real thing. One of Demara's maxims was 'never be at a loss for a letterhead.' Throughout his careers he systematically filched stationery whenever the opportunity presented itself – even if he had no immediate need for it. From bishops' green writing paper to cardinals' red, from blank birth certificates to death certificates, Demara collected stationery like other people save wrapping paper and rubber bands – on the basis that they 'might come in handy'. When it came to certificates of qualification, it was usually necessary to adapt the real thing, substituting pertinent details. In order to hide the tell-tale signs of scissors and gum Demara would photostat the doctored documents, and using a child's printing kit, rubber-stamp them with the message: 'Certified copy. Original records must be held.' Thus the photocopy was not only explained but its original's authenticity effectively reinscribed.

Having furnished himself with references and qualifications, the impostor professional now faces the problem of how to deal with correspondence between the target institution and the imagined, or innocent, referee. Demara once more has all the answers. In many of the religious institutions he was associated with he made it his business to collect and distribute the mail – a task his colleagues were only too happy to delegate. He was therefore able to 'vet' and veto all incoming and outgoing correspondence, disposing of that which might bring his sins to light, and making substitutes when it suited him. When working nights at an eye hospital, he had access to all the medical staff's pigeon-holes and was able to conduct correspondence on behalf of doctors who remained entirely ignorant that letters were being sent out in their names. On other occasions he simply used the more common expedient of having arrangements at various addresses for collecting mail in various names. For the determined impostor, virtually every practical problem is surmountable. There is always the risk with faked documents that a routine check with the issuing institution will reveal the impostor; however, such checks are rarely made if the documents appear to be 'in order'. The safest way of avoiding this risk is not to alter the documents at all but to 'become' the person the originals describe.

This strategy was employed by Arthur Osborne Phillips, who happened to share the same surname as Dr James H. Phillips, under whom he had served as a medical orderly during the First World War. After the war, Arthur Phillips took the doctor's identity and documents in the secure knowledge that the real Dr Phillips was himself now a patient in a mental institution. He carried off the imposture for thirty years before being caught and convicted.

It is also possible to adopt the identity of someone without ever meeting them. Demara told *Life* magazine how he picked Cecil Hamann, a biologist with a doctorate, from a university prospectus (another kind of item he assiduously collected). He managed to obtain all Hamann's documents, but the birth certificate proved particularly problematic. Although he knew Hamann was from New York state, he did not know in which town he was born (and therefore registered). He explained how he got the system to collaborate in his deception:

I wrote a tearful letter, a real sob story, to the vital statistics office at the state capital in Albany. I told them I'd been abandoned by my parents as an infant and I wanted to know where I was born. I gave them my age. That and my name, Cecil Boyce Hamann, was all they had to go by. But back came the information: Hamann was born in Shelby, Orleans County, N.Y. Then I wrote to Shelby and got his birth certificate.

However, this strategy – technically impersonation – carries a further burden: having adopted someone else's name, qualifications, place of birth and employment record, the impostor needs to be prepared to wear convincingly a personal history that is not his own. Here luck and wit play a large part. 'The great impostor' describes his own strategy:

I call it, Demara's law for passing, or the invisible past. Almost all impostors, I have found, cut out a picture of what they think they should look like and then they begin piling up mounds of plausible sounding information behind that silhouette. Say they are supposed to come from Saginaw. What do they do? They learn the name of the high school, of some streets, all sorts of information. When someone mentions Saginaw they leap right in spouting information left and right. This, they feel, proves they *must* be genuine. But I say, once they mention anything definite, they are now on record. I never mention *anything*. Don't be too obvious about not mentioning anything but always leave them with a shadow. If you meet someone who does come from Saginaw you have got to change the conversation or let him do the talking, which, if you lead him the right way, he will do. It really works. Wherever I have left, people are always suddenly amazed to find they don't know one damn thing about me, where I was supposed to have come from and have been, although they all thought they did, that is until the police began asking for specifics. That's Demara's law for seeming to be real and staying as loose and free as a wild goose.

It is easy to see, in this instance, how the realms of fact (documentary evidence) and fantasy (psychological manipulation) become intertwined. The impostor is continually 'managing' other people's knowledge and perception of him. Importantly, he must not appear to be fighting his corner (once someone suspects him, the game is as good as up); he must behave in such a way that it will never occur to anyone that he might be an impostor.

To this end, the impostor often carefully creates an image of himself which puts him above suspicion. Many impostors have found it useful to give an appearance of wealth, for example. Demara found this an essential prop: 'Always try to appear rich. It automatically confers respect and consideration on a person . . . There is a mysterious awe toward money that rubs off on the guy who has it, don't kid yourself.' Appearing moneyed not only excludes one automatically from the list of likely suspects if a crime is committed, but also usefully excuses eccentric behaviour. This is not to say that the impostor will make a great show of riches (and he usually couldn't, anyway), but that he might subtly let it be known that he comes from an 'old' family, or contrive to be seen visiting the bank, apparently withdrawing large amounts (this is an old conman's favourite: a genuine bill wrapped round a wad of green paper is casually pocketed in the street outside the bank – a vulgar but effective device). No one likes to ask direct questions about it, but word soon gets around.

The appearance of wealth does not break down the intended victim's defences; it ensures they are never up in the first place. An example from London at the turn of the last century illustrates this. The representative of a Bond Street jeweller, having been summoned by Lady Campbell to her house in Cadogan Place, duly arrived, bearing a selection of first-water diamonds from which Lady Campbell could select some stones for a piece of jewellery she wished to give to her niece as a wedding present.

The maid explained that Lady Campbell was 'indisposed' and offered to carry the stones in to her bedroom. The young man was understandably reluctant to hand over £4,000 worth of diamonds to a parlour-maid, and refused to do so. Miss Constance Browne, Lady Campbell's secretary, then appeared. As it was Miss Browne who had arranged the appointment, the jeweller was content to let her take charge of the stones for half an hour, allowing the recumbent Lady Campbell to make her choice, while he remained in the drawing room.

He waited. And waited. After an hour he decided to go in search of Miss Browne, but found the door to the room locked. Further investigation revealed that the window had been nailed shut. By the time he had broken the window and called for help, no inhabitant of the house – which it was discovered had been rented for one month only – could be found. Not only had Lady Campbell never existed, but neither had Miss Browne or the maid: all three had been invented by Louisa Miles, a mistress of disguise and deception whose inventive frauds kept Scotland Yard detectives guessing over a career lasting twenty years.

Louisa Miles created an elaborate illusion of an established and substantial household, but the impostor may make good use of the simplest 'prop'. Demara acquired a large second-hand trunk, covered with stickers from classy resorts. Wherever he went (and given his preference for total institutions, he was usually boarding at his workplace) the trunk told its own story, of a wealthy and sophisticated owner. The essential value of the trunk was that Demara never needed to draw attention to it: people automatically inferred certain things from it. It is always better for the impostor not to tell downright lies but to lead people to arrive at their own wrong (but desirable) conclusions: you let them do all the work. Hence, as mentioned earlier, if you meet someone from your purported home town, you let them do all the talking. When Demara was posing as an academic, he would occasionally be asked a direct question to which he did not have a ready answer. His strategy was simply to turn the question around, showing great interest in the other person's opinion, sometimes even taking notes. His adversary went away glowing with pride, while Demara had unobtrusively managed to fill another gap in his own education.

If the impostor seems to prove that it is in fact possible to fool all the people all of the time, it is important to recognize that he often only has to fool one person. For example, if A introduces himself at a party to B as Hugh Percival, a baronet from Hampshire, provided that nothing about A strikes B as phoney, B will then introduce him to C and D as such, who will in turn introduce him to E, F, G and H. In a social situation the impostor's new identity is reaffirmed each time someone other than himself describes it. In the case of institutions, the acceptance of an identity again usually only depends on one person – for example, if someone presents himself at a university as a doctor of philosophy, only one person will be responsible for checking his credentials. Once that person has accepted the impostor, the impostor has little to worry about, provided that he is able to do the job without arousing suspicion.

The importance of passing the first test – of gaining the belief of one person – is illustrated in the case of Brian MacKinnon. MacKinnon, as mentioned earlier, was a Scot in his early thirties when he passed himself off as a Canadian teenager in order to retake his 'A' levels. When his imposture was exposed, his form teacher said, 'We were a right crowd of dopes. He stood out like a sore thumb.' In fact the first time Gwynneth Lightbody saw 'Brandon Lee', she mistook him for a fellow teacher, and other members of staff commented on his mature appearance. However, 'we assumed everything had been done, and he was just a bit of an oddity.' The staff's assumption was reasonable; Mrs Holmes, the deputy rector, had received a fax from one William Lee regarding his son's wish to attend the school, accompanied by a glowing report from one Marsha Hunt, Brandon's former teacher (MacKinnon had of course penned both documents). She had also interviewed 'Brandon Lee', and at the end of the meeting had asked to see a birth certificate. For some reason she changed her mind, saying, 'No, I'll believe you.' The fact that Mrs Holmes waived the formalities suggests that she had no suspicions about the bright young man before her. He had 'passed' Mrs Holmes, and therefore would 'pass' everyone else, even though both staff and fellow pupils thought he seemed much older than his given age. In a thoughtful article on Brandon Lee, Ian Parker notes how, on that first crucial day at school, staff and pupils alike rationalized their own doubts about the new student. Gwynneth Lightbody told Parker that she had reasoned: 'in teaching you see all sorts of strange sights. It could be he had some illness that made him age rapidly – or something:

Pupils were doing the same, trying to make Brandon fit his own story – by reminding themselves, for example, of the wide range of body types. 'I had a boyfriend who was over six foot then,' one pupil said to me; another said: 'I could think of boys with beards and hairy chests. If someone says they're seventeen, you're not going to turn round and say no, no you're not.' By lunch, it seems, MacKinnon had been accepted as an old-looking, odd-looking teenager – an alien from Canada – rather than an adult who looked his age.

The emphasis given by institutions to paperwork – the way that their members prioritize this kind of 'proof' over the evidence of their own eyes – can be seen in this and many other instances as a fatal flaw. Common sense was telling everyone at the school that this boy was a man, but, as Gwynneth Lightbody said, 'when you're presented with facts . . .'

The facts were no facts; the crucial representative of fact in this case – the birth certificate – had not even been requested. Yet even if it had, it could have been faked. Our society's dependence on the authenticity of such pieces of paper is a more recent phenomenon than we might think. History shows that we used to employ other criteria for determining identity, the credibility of which was as zealously maintained as our modern systems.

In an age when most people could not read, people depended on other signals and cues to assess each other's status. There was generally a far greater emphasis on visual signifiers – the outward signs by which something or someone declared what it was, or who they were. The red and white striped pole announcing the availability of a barber-dentist's services was such a symbol for hundreds of years. The picture element of the pub sign remains one of the last links with this visual system, itself replacing an older symbol, the ale-stake (a stake surmounted by a garland, for example). People as well as places proclaimed their identity by visual signifiers: very often a person's occupation could be instantly 'read' in the way they looked. For example, the out-of-work shepherd put on his smock and took his crook to country fairs, where he simply stood, literally advertising himself. Alongside him stood other men whose clothes and tools also rendered them living signs. The potential employer in search of a particular skill or craft could easily and immediately identify his man by his appearance.

The importance of clothes as reliable visual signifiers of social status in particular was paramount, and consequently sumptuary laws were introduced in many parts of medieval Europe which prohibited the lower classes from 'aping' their betters by wearing their clothes. Women were also forbidden to wear men's clothes. Marginal figures, such as Jews and prostitutes, were required to wear veils, hats or aprons of a particular colour. Rendering status highly visible ensured that everyone knew their place – and everyone else's place. One of the reasons that actors were viewed with suspicion, if not open hostility, lay in their practice of dressing as kings one day and vagabonds the next – or worse, as women. The shape-shifting player resisted a straightforward 'reading', but he was read none the less: the logic of outward-appearance-reflecting-inner-identity when applied to the multi-costumed actor interpreted him as an amoral and sexually suspect figure.

The sumptuary codes faded, in time, from the law books, but the assumptions which surrounded them did not. Although no longer required to by law, people continued to wear more broadly defined costumes. Despite the fact that there was no law preventing a servant girl from wearing her mistress's cast-off evening dress, the considerable weight of social disapproval – from her peers as well as her 'betters' – effectively prevented her from doing so. It was the general reliability of visual signifiers that enabled theatre audiences in the sixteenth and seventeenth centuries to accept plot conventions based on mistaken identity more readily than we do today: the mock marriage was entirely feasible; the (impostor) long-lost cousin rooted in the events of real life.

There were important signifiers in social behaviour, as well as dress. In the past the separate classes moved in clearly defined social circles and largely segregated social spaces. They related to each other and spoke to each other in different ways; the lower orders, for example, automatically making gestures of deference with their bodies and in their speech when communicating with the upper classes. (When Quakers, declaring all men equal in the sight of

God, refused to observe the traditional removal of hats when in conversation with their social superiors, a tremor ran through the upper classes which proved to be an early warning of the earthquake of the English Revolution.)

This emphasis on outward appearances as reliable signifiers of status presented the impostor in the past with a different set of problems from those he faces today. By transgressing the unwritten rules of dress, location and behaviour, which defined who people were, the impostor had the advantage of a camouflage which made people assume him to be 'one of them'.

Although we no longer depend on appearances to the extent that we used to, we can still see today surprisingly strong traces of the preliterate emphasis on appearance in our own culture. While the uniforms of police officers or nurses perform an obvious and useful function, rendering them highly visible, other uniforms are relics of the old you-are-what-you-seem culture. The priest, the lawyer and, to a lesser extent, the scholar have all retained, in our own culture, their costumes from a distant past, which remain outward symbols of their professional status. Non-compulsory, or informal uniforms also persist. For example, the street prostitute continues to be easily marked out by wearing an informal uniform; it continues to be convenient to her, and to her customers, that she is recognizable. (The 'look' of the prostitute is so reliable that women are generally careful to avoid inadvertently straying into her sartorial territory, 'Do I look like a tart?' being a regularly voiced anxiety down the ages between women preparing for a night on the town.) Resistance to the blurring of gender boundaries remains evident, particularly among members of the older generation, who can still be heard expressing disapproval when 'unisex' clothes and hairstyles offer confusing masculine/feminine 'readings'.

In our literate age, with our emphasis on qualifications, references, certificates, computerized data, and so on, we may think imposture is much harder to pull off. We assume, for example, that the widely requested birth certificate has an inherent authenticity. It is this assumption which guarantees we will never check with the registry office. It is shockingly easy to open a bank account in any name, and it is not illegal to give a false name to the police (provided that you are not in charge of a vehicle, under arrest or under oath). Most of the time people are not required to prove who they are. If we see a police officer in uniform, we are not going to ask to see their ID (and if we did, would we know what it was supposed to look like?). If we consult a solicitor, do we ask to see his qualifications? His businesslike suit, the context of his office, his demeanour, all tell us that he is who he says he is; so we are still relying on quite primitive signals to assure ourselves of his identity, and it does not occur to us that things so real as clothes, context and behaviour might be merely costume, set and performance.

Having considered the tactics employed by the impostor in order to gain our confidence, and also how easily that confidence is gained, in order fully to understand our capacity to be conned it is worth considering cases where the impostor has claimed to be a real person. Although these impostors themselves are not of great interest here, as their primary aim is almost always financial gain, what their stories reveal about our capacity to deceive ourselves is significant.

It is tempting to believe that in the face of the most convincing mountain of evidence in support of the impersonator, the simple expedient of calling a witness who knew the person they claim to be should easily settle the matter once and for all. Yet here the water becomes unexpectedly murky, for history shows several examples of people – even and especially close relatives – who disagree violently about whether someone is or isn't the person they once knew.

In 1920 a patient in a psychiatric hospital in Dalldorf, Germany, was reading an article about the murder of Tsar Nicholas II and his family in Russia two years earlier. She noticed a strong resemblance between a photograph of one of the Tsar's daughters and a fellow patient who had been admitted some weeks previously with no

ID, no money and no memory. The hospital summoned one of the Tsarina's ladies-in-waiting, now living in Berlin, to confirm the identification. This she duly did: the mysterious patient was indeed the Grand Duchess Anastasia.

The story of Anna Anderson, as she later called herself, has been told numerous times; many were the strange twists of fortune both in her own account of her life prior to her 'rediscovery' as Anastasia and in the subsequent years spent pursuing her claim to her lost title (and fortune). But what are of primary interest here are the competing testimonies of people who knew the real Anastasia. The lady-in-waiting was not alone: at least a dozen Romanov relatives agreed that Anna Anderson was Anastasia. On the other hand, Anastasia's Swiss tutor (whose wife had been her nurse) and her godmother, among others who had known the princess, declared with equal conviction that Anna Anderson was *not* Anastasia.

How could people who had been on intimate terms with the real Anastasia have been so completely divided over the identity of Anna Anderson? As always, in cases of claims concerning money or status, competing interests were at work. Surviving Romanovs may well have embraced too readily, and failed to question too thoroughly, what must have seemed a dream-come-true: that the Tsar's direct line had not been utterly destroyed by the Bolsheviks, but had been miraculously preserved in this young woman, who after all certainly looked like Anastasia and had scars and other physical anomalies in common with the princess. Moreover, she appeared to remember certain details of family life, 'in' jokes and other references which only someone intimate with the royal circle could know. It may have been the case that some of these relatives – some of whom had not seen Anastasia since she was a child – did not instantly recognize Anna as Anastasia, but faced with the corroborative evidence decided that it was better to err on the side of caution. If she did, after all, turn out to be Russian Aristocrat Number One it would be most inconvenient to be remembered by her as a doubting Thomas.

While those who refused to recognize Anna as Anastasia may well have had equally political or personal reasons for resisting her claim, they proved to be on safer ground. The pro-Anderson lobby must have been moved by powerful motives indeed to accept a Russian princess who spoke no Russian. Anderson explained many years later in her 'memoirs' that it was not that she could not speak Russian but, just as she did not like to talk about the events surrounding her escape (because 'I had suffered such awful things that I did not want to be reminded of it'), she likewise 'had also decided always to speak German, because Russian had become disagreeable to me'. However, considering that her knowledge of Anastasia's mother tongue was a factor so crucial in making her claims stick, this seems perverse in the extreme. Significantly, when Anderson did take the opportunity to give a full account of her life as Anastasia, she also wrote her autobiography in German.

Although some of those relations who had initially identified her as Anastasia later retracted, a hard core remained convinced to the end (including the German Crown Princess Cecilie, Prince Frederick of Saxe-Altenburg and Sigismund of Prussia). Was it the physical resemblance or the details of family life with which she was uncannily familiar that persuaded them she was the real thing? Perhaps more convincing was the affecting personality of Anna Anderson herself, a woman who suffered from mental illness on and off throughout her life, and who probably wished herself a princess, and was easily persuaded by unscrupulous individuals that she was one.

The family and acquaintances of Roger Charles Doughty Tichborne were similarly divided over the identity of the man who came forward in 1866 claiming to be Tichborne, who had been believed lost at sea twelve years previously. An impressive one hundred witnesses testified under oath that the claimant to the Tichborne baronetcy and estate was the man they had known. Those convinced included some thirty of Roger's fellow officers and men from his army days, various friends, tenants, servants, plus the family solicitor and an assortment of magistrates. The Tichborne claimant's greatest champion, however, was Lady Tichborne herself, who, despite the unanimous opposition of the rest of the family, was convinced beyond the shadow of a doubt that the claimant was indeed her son.

On the negative side, it is worth quoting the words of Sir John Coleridge, whose cross-examination of the claimant lasted for 22 of the first trial's 102 days.

The first sixteen years of his life he has absolutely forgotten; the few facts he has told the jury were already proved, or would hereafter be shown, to be absolutely false and fabricated. Of his college life he could recollect nothing. About his amusements, his books, his music, his games, he could tell nothing. Not a word of his family, of the people with whom he lived, their habits, their persons, their very names. He had forgotten his mother's maiden name; he was ignorant of all particulars of the family estate; he remembered nothing of Stonyhurst; and in military matters he was equally deficient. Roger, born and educated in France, spoke and wrote French like a native and his favourite reading was French literature; but the Claimant knew nothing of French [. . .] The physical discrepancy, too, was no less remarkable; for, while Roger, who took after his mother, was slight and delicate, with narrow sloping shoulders, a long narrow face and thin straight dark hair, the Claimant was of enormous bulk, scaling over twenty-four stone, big-framed and burly, with a large round face and an abundance of fair and rather wavy hair.

However, even Sir John had to admit that despite all this, the claimant 'undoubtedly possessed a strong likeness to several male members of the Tichborne family'.

Like Anna Anderson, the Tichborne claimant's principal asset was an accident of nature: a strong visual likeness to his model, which was enough to convince the grief-stricken Lady Tichborne, who had always refused to accept her son's death, that he had at last returned to her. As in the previous case, the unshakeable conviction that he was who he claimed to be outweighed for many people the more compelling objective evidence against him. Again, for many, 'gut instinct' triumphed over bald fact. The things he had forgotten, including, like Anastasia, his mother tongue, were again attributed to stress and amnesia. Others were not convinced, and it is again worth considering the factors which may have accounted for such sharp and implacable divisions arising among people who had known the real Tichborne.

Roger Tichborne had lived with his parents in his mother's native country of France until he was sixteen. If Lady Tichborne had had her way, he would have remained there, and she greatly resented her husband's decision to uproot her son and give him an English education. Such was her opposition that James Tichborne had achieved this by stealth, using the excuse of a family funeral to spirit his son away to the Jesuit College at Stonyhurst. A long period of separation followed, during which Lady Tichborne neither wrote nor spoke a word to her son. It seems quite plausible that when she heard of her son's disappearance her grief was tainted by bitter regret that she had let their relationship deteriorate in this way, and that the possibility that he was alive seemed to offer an end to her feelings of guilt and an opportunity to redeem herself. Others may really have believed the claimant to be Roger, although there were allegations of widespread bribery of witnesses; some may simply have wanted to help make an old lady happy. Needless to say, a mother's identification of her son carried a great deal of weight with people who might otherwise have hesitated. On the other side were the relations who the appearance of the claimant threatened to dispossess and disinherit: from the outset they viewed the claimant with open suspicion and hostility.

It is a strong possibility that, as in the case of the would-be Russian princess, the claimant grew to believe that he really was Roger Tichborne. The campaign had become his life. Over a decade after his release from prison the poverty-stricken claimant sold his confession to a newspaper. However, he soon retracted it. The fact that he clung to his assumed identity to the end is seen in the inscription on his coffin, which names its occupant as Sir Roger Charles Doughty Tichborne.

A third, much earlier, case bears strong similarities to both the examples of 'Anastasia' and the Tichborne claimant, but this time there was an unforeseen twist to the tale. Martin and Bertrande Guerre had been married for nearly ten years, living in Artigat, a village in southern France, when Martin disappeared in about 1548. Bertrande and the family had presumed him dead when, four years later, he turned up again. His appearance had altered somewhat, but most of the villagers – including, crucially, Bertrande – accepted him as Martin Guerre. He knew a great deal about the family's past life, after all, and for three years the couple lived happily together. Bertrande bore the returned Martin two children to add to the son she had before Martin had gone away.

As in many of the cases mentioned so far, powerful motives for believing in the impostor blinded his supporters to fundamental inconsistencies in his impersonation. The facts that the returned Martin had lost a scar above his eye, was shorter and stockier, that his feet, the cobbler noticed, had shrunk, were cheerfully ignored by Bertrande and Martin's sisters. However, it was not until the returned Martin began to take a more proactive role in the family business, upsetting his uncle Pierre (who, after Martin's disappearance, had married Bertrande's widowed mother), that it was deemed expedient to question his identity. The village proved to be split over whether this was the same Martin they had known previously. Of 150 people who testified, although more denied than agreed that this was Martin Guerre, both camps were outnumbered by those who were unable to make up their minds. As was to happen in the Tichborne and Anastasia affairs, court case followed court case, and just as the judges in Toulouse seemed about to come to a decision in favour of the returned Martin, something occurred which ensured the story would one day be made into a film: a one-legged stranger entered the courtroom; the real Martin Guerre had at last returned.

The scene may well be imagined. Horace Fuller captures the moment in his commentary on the case:

It was then necessary to examine, seriously and legally, the degree of resemblance which existed between these two men. They placed them side by side. It was easy to make a comparison of the features, particular marks, and general appearance. According to [Jean de] Coras [an eminent lawyer, MP and Chancellor to the Queen of Navarre] this comparison elicited only exclamations of wonder. Two eggs did not resemble each other more than did these two. He who had seen one had seen the other.

Emotions ran high. Martin's four sisters, who had supported the impostor from the start, now knew and embraced their real brother. Bertrande immediately turned on the impostor who, it emerged, was Arnault du Tilh, known as 'Pancette'. Martin looked on his wife and the man who had been living in his place with an understandably 'hard, wild face'.

It seems possible that had Pancette chosen to keep a low profile as far as the family business was concerned, his imposture might have gone unchallenged – if not undetected. Commentators on the events are divided over whether Bertrande was aware of the imposture; the reader may decide whether it is plausible that a woman might accept a stranger as her husband of ten years, after an absence of four. Did Martin's sisters also fail to recognize that Pancette was not their brother or, seeing the abandoned and probably widowed Bertrande's new-found happiness, decide that discretion was in order?

As in the other examples, the division of opinion over Pancette's identity cloaked competing interests. During the early years of Martin's absence, his uncle Pierre had moved into his place as head of the family, taken up residence in the family home and assumed control of the family's business interests. He, more than anyone else, had reason to resent the intruder, and it was he who led the campaign to unmask him. It is also interesting to note that while Martin's sisters supported the impostor, his brothers-in-law lined up on Pierre's side: while the men felt threatened by the cuckoo in the nest, the women took a more philosophical view of the situation, in which emotional considerations were an important factor. On the scales of reason, the family divided along traditional gender lines. The tendency of the villagers summoned to testify before the court to shrug their shoulders and fail either to confirm or deny the identification can also be interpreted as their unwillingness, whatever their private views, to intervene in what was essentially a family matter. On the other hand, the courts did have a vested interest in the affair: their pragmatic preference was to be able to reach a verdict which would keep the marriage together, and ensure the legitimacy of its children. If the real Martin Guerre had not stepped forward it is quite possible that the case may have gone in Pancette's favour; as it turned out, he went to the gallows, and Bertrande and Martin were reconciled. The marriage later produced another son.

What the events were which led up to Pancette's impersonation of Martin Guerre are not entirely clear. What is known is that, in common with the later 'Russian' and English examples, the Frenchman was mistaken for his model before the imposture occurred to him. Everyone has had the experience of seeing someone who bears a striking likeness to someone else they know, and many have been told they have a doppelgänger. But what kind of personality decides to act on, and exploit, such a random and unplanned event? The answer may be: only someone with nothing to lose – someone prepared to throw up the life they have, exchanging it for the uncertainty of a life that only might become theirs. This recalls the case of Harriet Stokes: she too took her cue from the unsuspecting punter; when a prospective employer mistook her for a boy, she immediately saw the advantage in keeping her mouth shut and played along. The impostor's own life must be a non-starter to embark on an imposture which first suggests its own possibility by such an unpredictable turn of events as someone tapping them on the shoulder and saying, 'Aren't you . . . ?' It must hold few attractions if they feel free to turn opportunist at the first sniff of a way out, and they must feel untethered to the world and unbound by its unwritten laws to be willing so readily to surrender their own identity for someone else's. The fact that they are prepared to take on a new family, a new home, a new history, testifies to the sense in which they must feel they are leaving nothing of value behind them. It is, of course, their consequent ability to immerse themselves so completely in their assumed role that makes them so convincing. There comes a point where they are no longer playing the part, because there is nothing hidden behind it: finally, they may convince themselves that they are who they claim to be.

Let us consider the figures in the shadows who were reborn as Princess Anastasia, Roger Tichborne and Martin Guerre. In 1927 a private detective produced a Berlin landlady who identified Anna as Franziska Schankowska, a peasant girl who had disappeared from her lodgings at the time that Anna was fished out of a Berlin canal and taken to hospital suffering from depression. (It was from here that she was transferred to the Dalldorf psychiatric hospital, where a patient noticed her likeness to the Tsar's daughter.) A member of the Schankowski family also declared Anna was her sister, although this was never proven to the satisfaction of a court of law.

Pancette du Tilh may even have known Martin Guerre. Pancette was a soldier for Henry II and was fighting in Picardy at the same time as Martin, who had been drafted into the army of Philip II of Spain. The fact that Pancette was, on more than one occasion, mistaken for Martin prior to his imposture indicates that they were at least moving in overlapping social or professional circles. Whether or not Anna Anderson was Franziska, the social upheaval in Europe caused by the Great War and the Russian Revolution may well have thrown her into the company of displaced members of the Romanov household, from whom she may have learned odd details which she later saw an opportunity to put to good use. In both her case and that of Pancette, they must have somehow gleaned sufficient personal information to make their claims initially plausible; in both cases they were almost certainly later assisted by others. Even if Anna Anderson had operated entirely on her own, the constant succession of Romanovs and their lackeys who visited her must have furnished her with a growing store of information, in their questioning alone. Although some of these meetings were supervised, no one was aware of what everybody else had said to Anna Anderson, and of course those who believed she was Anastasia must have spoken to her quite freely about the family's history. Bertrande Guerre must also have coached Pancette extensively in the intimate details of her life with Martin for him to answer detailed questions in court correctly.

The impersonators' possession of apparently 'inside' knowledge is designed to be impressive and, intelligently deployed, the smallest detail can become extremely powerful. On one occasion, when an army captain was reminiscing about some wartime hospital visits during which he had accompanied Anastasia, Anna exclaimed, 'The man with the pockets!', a reference to a patient who had stood uncivilly with his hands in his pockets while talking to the princess. On another occasion Anna embarrassed Anastasia's uncle, Grand Duke Ernest, by reminding him of the time he had gone as a German ambassador to St Petersburg to broker a peace deal during the war. The mission was supposed to be a secret. These examples are often quoted in commentaries on the story and were indeed well chosen: the pockets, a detail barely worth remembering but part of the canon of small amusing incidents which form the common ground of reminiscences between old acquaintances; the peace mission, a suitably 'big' secret, impressive in a quite different way. Such piquant snippets of information spoke in favour of Anna's authenticity, even in the face of her ignorance of more ordinary details of everyday life with the Romanovs. Similar to the 'pockets' incident, it is often quoted that Pancette du Tilh, posing as Martin

Guerre, made early and public reference to a pair of white stockings his wife stored in a chest at the family home. The choice of such an intimate domestic detail – and its apparent insignificance – was cleverly thought out. Surely the real Martin would never have occasion to mention the stockings, or where they were kept, to anyone else: therefore this was Martin.

Like his counterparts above, the Tichborne claimant, despite his apparently poor court performance, also had ample opportunity to bone up on his subject. The claimant, known as Castro, was working as a butcher in New South Wales when he came forward (via a lawyer) as Roger Tichborne. (Lady Tichborne had been advertising extensively, requesting information regarding her missing son, and it is not clear whether the initial impetus to identify himself as Roger Tichborne came from Castro or the lawyer.) An old family retainer, Ben Bogle, who had known Roger well was at this time living in Sydney – Lady Tichborne instructed him to go and meet the claimant. It seems likely that at this point Bogle was recruited into the plot, although even if he truly believed Castro to be his long-lost master Castro had ample opportunity to pick his brains on the sea journey to Europe. Either way, when Lady Tichborne first met Castro in Paris, Bogle had enthusiastically confirmed the identification. Lady Tichborne, elderly, short-sighted and an obsessive believer that her only son could not be dead, immediately threw her arms (as one journalist added, 'as far as they would go') around the portly Castro and accepted him as Roger. He then had free access to all Roger's diaries and correspondence, as well as his mother's happy memories of him on which to draw.

After coming to England in order to pursue his claim, it was also later discovered that a number of inquiries had been made on Castro's behalf in order to build up a picture of the man he said he was. Solicitors in his employ had obtained, for example, records of all leaves of absence granted to Tichborne in the Horse Guards, and a list of all the teaching staff at Tichborne's school. It was also noted that the claimant's house in Croydon was 'greatly overstocked with male servants', all of whom had served in Tichborne's regiment.

Logically, as a piece in the *Daily News* argued after the claimant was finally proved to be guilty of perjury and sentenced: 'In a case of disputed identity it is not by a man's knowledge of what he might have learned, but by his ignorance of what he must have known if he were the true man, that he is to be judged.' But in cases of identity people do not always proceed logically; far from it. As the *Daily News* article concluded:

The Claimant's 'feats of memory' give the key to the extraordinary amount of support which he obtained. There are, indeed, plenty of witnesses who affirmed that they remember the face, the walk, the upper part of the face, and what not; but in every case it is evident enough that what had really impressed them was that the Claimant was able to remember something which they remembered.

Castro, it seems, was not even his real name; attempts were later made in court to prove that he was actually Arthur Orton, the son of a butcher from Wapping; a brother was produced who testified to the truth of this. It is worth observing that the people behind these pretenders are all shadowy insubstantial figures: although Anna Anderson failed to convince the courts that she was Anastasia, and Castro failed to prove he was Tichborne, their opponents were unable to prove conclusively who they *really* were. Similarly, very little is known about Pancette du Tilh. Their real lives remain sketchy and uncertain.

These examples serve to demonstrate that although in theory we tend to think that one person could not be mistaken for another by people who have known them well, they most certainly can. Whatever level of physical proof we, as organized groups, rationally demand to ascertain identity, as individuals we are vulnerable to less material suggestion, and for unscientific reasons are able to convince ourselves, in the face of powerful opposing evidence, that A is in fact B. It is also significant that just as the ordinary impostor usually has to convince only one person of his assumed identity, impersonators depend on winning the support of one significant person. No testimony carries so much weight as that of the wife who will confirm that this is her husband, or the mother who is certain that this is her son.

It was widely believed at the conclusion of the Martin Guerre affair that Bertrande, his wife, had actually mistaken Pancette du Tilh for her husband. Yet common sense told people that this was really impossible – they after all had husbands and wives themselves and instinctively felt that such a misapprehension was not credible. Their explanation was simple: Pancette had bewitched Bertrande. While a twenty-first-century reader is unlikely to sympathize with this view, there *is* a sense in which the impostor bewitches his victims, although it is more in the spirit of the fairground fortune-teller, or the mountebank astrologer or spiritualist, than that he is dabbling in the black arts. He observes, listens, guesses when necessary, identifies our weaknesses, calculates his moves and the effects they will have, and when he has processed the information, projects it all back to us as though it originated from him, effecting the astonishing illusion.

Having considered the ways in which the impostor manipulates his victims, and the ways in which we are psychologically and emotionally susceptible to him, it is appropriate to look at the mind of the impostor himself. As some of the examples cited have shown, it is often very difficult to gain a detailed picture of the person behind the mask, and although his motives are sometimes obvious – particularly in the cases where money is at stake – the impostor requires more than a strong motive: his personality must be in some fundamental sense adapted to – or attracted by – disguise.

During the 1950s psychologists began to apply themselves to the phenomenon of imposture. In 1955 Helene Deutsch wrote an influential paper in which, by looking at a selection of cases, she offered a broad psychological profile of our subject. In it she suggests that children from privileged and indulgent homes may feel that nothing bad can happen to them, with the result that when something bad does happen, they are ill-equipped to deal with it, and instead retreat from its reality. This may be coupled with disappointment in a parent. As Deutsch explains it, a child's sense of his self-worth is largely derived through his parent's opinion of him. However, the parent's opinion of the child is validated by the child's own esteem for his parent. Therefore, when a child lionizes a parent, who in turn lionizes the child, if the parent then falls from his pedestal – for example, through illness or business failure – the child's concept of his *own* value suffers a heavy blow. Self-love is sustained in such children by the feeling that they are unique; 'Daddy's special boy' is far less special when Daddy turns out to be as frail and impotent as the next guy. This child is characteristically handicapped by an inability to tolerate authority and lacks a capacity for sustained effort; however, he *is* intelligent. In lay terms, this child is 'spoilt' and faces a crisis when the spoiling stops, making him feel that his identity as a 'special' person is threatened. He feels he has a *right* to be special, and he will prove both to himself and to others that he *is* special.

Where other children might respond by a single-minded pursuit of academic or athletic excellence, for example, or collapse under the weight of their own inertia and feelings of worthlessness, the child who will become an impostor has no patience with working his way up the conventional ladder of effort, achievement, reward. He feels entitled to go straight in at the top and claim the status and success he feels he deserves. Deutsch further observes that this desire to be recognized as special often cloaks an inner perception of his own inferiority: the affirmation of a false identity is actually the denial of his own identity. Thus the impostor is pulled in two directions at once: while he may regard himself as a genius, he will perversely 'court situations in which he would be exposed as the counterpart of a genius – a liar, an impostor'.

When Deutsch's model is applied to what we know about 'the great impostor', Ferdinand Waldo Demara, her theory seems in

1. Truth is stranger than fiction.
Louis de Rougement demonstrates his turtle-riding skills
at the London Hippodrome in 1906

2. The Grand Duchess Anastasia

3. Anna Anderson in a psychiatric hospital in Dalldorf, 1920

5. Chief Buffalo Child Long Lance at the Calgary Stampede, 1923

4. Sylvester Long (left) and his brother

6. Brandon Lee/Brian MacKinnon with fellow pupils (fifteen years his junior) at Bearsden Academy

7. The slightly built Roger Charles Doughty Tichborne was lost at sea in 1854

8. The Tichborne claimant was a 24-stone butcher from Wapping

9. The Dauphin, son and heir of Louis XVI and Marie-Antoinette. The suspicious circumstances of his reported death gave rise to rumours that he had escaped

THE DUKE OF NORMANDY.
SON OF LOUIS XVI.
From an Original Portrait.

10. Karl Naundorff, one of the forty claimants to the title of lost Dauphin

11. Portrait of James Barry
as a young man

12. Dr Barry in later life,
with manservant 'Black John' and Psyche,
one of a succession of white poodles
of the same name

13. James Gray, alias Hannah Snell

14. The Billy Tipton Trio (Tipton is the middle figure)

15. The irrepressible Ferdinand Waldo Demara: The Great Impostor

16. Princess Caraboo of Javasu, alias Mary Baker of Devon

many respects to be borne out. As a child, Demara, true to Deutsch's type, lived in a big house on the finest street in Lawrence, Massachusetts. His father was a flamboyant French-Canadian, his mother Massachusetts-Irish stock. Demara Senior had done well for himself, beginning by opening a cinema and soon building a small empire of picture houses. His parents sent Demara to the local state (public) school, although they could easily have afforded to do otherwise. Crichton notes that right from the start Demara felt he didn't fit in: he was larger than all the other children his age, and his family was the only one not working in some capacity for the mills that formed the town's industry – this on top of his parents' wealth set him apart from the others.

In fifth grade Demara Junior produced a duelling pistol when bullied by a gang of classmates. The police came, and he was, for a short time, a hero among his peers: 'I remember it felt good to be one of the guys. I had never felt like I belonged anywhere.' The boy enjoyed the role of bad guy, and his behaviour deteriorated until the school suggested his parents move him elsewhere. Demara himself later considered that this may have been a key point: 'Maybe that was the beginning of the pattern. Just when I belonged, I didn't.' He was enrolled at St Augustine's, a Roman Catholic parochial school. As a gesture of defiance he resolved not to speak, at home or at school. The silent kindness and understanding of the mother superior, however, impressed and touched him, and made him resolve on a new beginning: 'I decided right then I had some special sacred mission and I made up my mind to become a very devout boy.'

Demara might have regained his balance at this point, but his world was about to be turned upside-down, exactly in accordance with the pattern Deutsch identifies: at the age of eleven his father's business collapsed, and the family home was repossessed, along with many of their belongings. The adult Demara recalled his father telling him, 'None of this belongs to us any more. Someone is going to come and take it away.' The boy Demara wanted to be told the situation was temporary, and that they would return some day; he told his sister it was 'just like a vacation'. She was having none of it: 'We're poor people now. We don't belong here any more.' Demara was warned that whatever he didn't pack from his room would be left behind. He took nothing. To add insult to injury, his father took a job as a projectionist in one of his old cinemas at $28 per week.

Demara tried to assert his status by saving his money and buying expensive chocolates for his whole class – this incident and two early experiments in arson indicate a boy who wanted to make an impact in the manner Deutsch describes. And then his sister died. Home must have been an extremely unhappy place by the time Demara, aged fourteen, set off for school one morning never to arrive. Having sold his bicycle in town for $8 he bought a train ticket and headed for the Trappist monastery at Valley Falls, Rhode Island.

An interesting pattern was emerging, which does not form part of Deutsch's analysis. When writing about the circumstances under which, two years later, Demara left this first monastery, his biographer observes: 'If there is one good thing about having no possessions in a monastery, it is that leaving poses no problem.' Yet travelling light was something Demara had done from an early age: all but evicted from the family home, he had chosen not to take one toy, one book, one object of sentimental value with him. When he had run away to the monastery he had taken only his bicycle, which he immediately sold. At the age of sixteen Demara was already in the habit of travelling with no 'baggage', nothing to remind him of who he was and who he had been. Perhaps he rejected possessions because they had proven, in the past, unreliable. Or perhaps he was rejecting the comfort derived from associations – with the past, with people. He who travels light is always travelling. Demara also appears to have taken little account of other people's possessions, given that whenever he needed a car he simply took the nearest available vehicle. The only baggage he seems to have accumulated over the years was his store of faked documents and letter-headings, and the only possession mentioned in his biography is his highly prized green trunk, which was more of a stage prop than a personal effect: 'almost as good as a second set of credentials'. This possession itself was an impostor: the travels its stickers described were not Demara's own, its impressive exterior bore no relation to the catalogue of lies which lay within.

Returning to Deutsch's psychological profile of the impostor, it is easy to identify the same patterns present in Brian MacKinnon's imposture as Brandon Lee. Delusions of grandeur, which she also describes as characteristic, are evident in MacKinnon making Lee's parents a Regius professor of zoology and an opera singer: his own father had been a fireman, while his mother was a nurse and later a warden in a sheltered housing scheme. The fall in the father's status is also there: MacKinnon's father had to quit the fire service after an injury at work and became a lollipop man. It was immediately following his father's death from cancer that MacKinnon put his plan into action. Perhaps the most audacious aspect of the Brandon Lee imposture also resonates with Deutsch's view that the impostor often seems perversely to court exposure: when he decided the only route back into medical college lay via returning to school under another name, he chose the same school which he had left thirteen years earlier.

In Ian Parker's incisive account of MacKinnon's imposture, he also draws some conclusions about the kind of person MacKinnon was, or is, observing that his 'mission required . . . a fairly empty social landscape'. In other words, no friends to recognize him. The impostor's inability to sustain personal relationships – seen in Demara's fleeing the loyal Catherine – is also borne out by MacKinnon's rejection of a close girlfriend whom he was in love with but whom he felt distracted him from his purpose. Again, the rejection, or absence, of close relationships peculiarly fits the impostor for his role. Parker also suggests that the popular Brandon Lee was a vehicle in some ways for the isolated Brian MacKinnon to make a relationship with the world: 'Brandon was born of Brian's obsession [to become a doctor], but he was also something of a relief from it. Brandon got Brian out of the house, like an agoraphobic's chaperone.'

This concept of the faked identity forming a kind of *alter ego* may be useful in understanding the impostor. It may be that the impostor is attempting a kind of self-healing. There do seem to be two elements at war within impostors such as Demara and MacKinnon: the self that believes in his own talent, intelligence, creativity and destiny – his 'drive' – and the self that perceives himself as society is labelling him, as a failure. Because it is continually being rein-scribed by people and authorities outside the impostor, the 'failure' side threatens to win this struggle. The impostor's survival strategy is therefore to divide himself into two people: only then can he fully engage with his successful, ambitious aspect; only then can he suppress his inferior, inadequate side. The divided self enables the impostor at last to move forward and embrace his destiny, and leave his lacklustre twin behind.

Aspects of Deutsch's model impostor-in-waiting can be recog-nized in many instances. The interesting case of David Hampton (who impersonated Sidney Poitier's non-existent son) received widespread publicity, in which some details of Hampton's character emerged. A family friend remembered Hampton, who was born in Buffalo in 1964, as 'a very clever kid, very articulate', although his school records were patchy and troubled. According to Hampton, his one desire was to get out of Buffalo: 'There was no one who was glamorous or fabulous or outrageously talented there. I mean, here I was, this fabulous child of fifteen, speaking three languages, and they didn't know how to deal with that.' Both Hampton's undoubted intelligence and his own high opinion of himself were classic signs of what was to come. In addition, it emerged that his relationship with his father had broken down, Hampton Senior having refused to support the career in the arts his son wished to pursue.

There is usually very little, if any, available material on the childhood of impostors (most accounts focus on the imposture itself, and the adult perpetrating it), so it is impossible to make a remotely scientific case for what factors may 'breed' imposture. However, where such background information does exist it is surprising how often aspects of the patterns described here can be detected. In his frank biography of his father, *The Duke of Deception*, Geoffrey Wolff had the advantage of being able to consult relatives about his subject's childhood, as well as extensively researching school records and letters. The picture that emerges echoes many of the 'classic' circumstances already described. As an impostor, Arthur Wolff does not properly belong in this book, as his interest was always financial (he was, as Wolff Jr candidly explains, 'a bullshit artist' and 'a confidence man'), however, his background is pertinent to the subject.

Arthur Wolff appeared to be made of 'the right stuff': educated at Groton and Yale, he had been a fighter pilot in England during the war, transferred to the OSS, fought with the partisans in Yugoslavia, and with the Resistance in France. 'A pretty history for an American club man,' his son comments. 'Its fault is that it is not true.' There had been no Groton, no Yale, no military service of any kind.

Arthur Wolff's parents (like Demara's) were both from immigrant families. His mother was forty and his father, a doctor, fifty-two when he was born in 1907. The fact that he was a 'late' baby, combined with the fact that thirteen years earlier the Wolffs had had a baby girl who died in infancy, possibly contributed to the intensity of their feelings about Arthur. 'My father's health was studied and maintained, he was petted and adored,' Geoffrey writes; but while Arthur's mother 'doted on her little boy, dressed him like a doll and praised him ceaselessly', his cousins recall Arthur's father's 'insane tantrums around his son: they remember him chasing the boy, trying to hit him with a chair, threatening to kill him with it, but they don't remember why':

My father was thought by his friends to be generous, talented, bright and charming. His charm disarmed them and his mother, but never his father. To please The Doctor required attainments his son was too young to possess, so my father must very early have become a student of evasion, plotting ways around the judgment and daunting standards of someone sixty-five when he was thirteen.

The Wolffs had a huge house, and their staff included cook, maid and chauffeur. As a boy, Arthur was, according to a cousin, 'beyond imagination spoiled. I remember going to his room, filled with every single thing made for a child, and the room looked like a hurricane had come through it; you couldn't walk across it without breaking a toy because there was no room on the floor for them all. It was grotesque, and cruel.' Geoffrey observes that 'The Doctor begrudged his son time, and instead of time preferred to give him things,' with the result that Arthur as an adult 'thought of possessions as the fundamental, material manifestations of love'.

Arthur's father was an excellent doctor, and also an inventor, designing, among other things, an improved pneumatic tyre. But while other Hartford doctors became millionaires, Dr Wolff 'grew poorer as he lived richer'. He was also believed to have been short-changed by the hospital where he worked, due to the staff's reputed anti-Semitism. In 1922 the big house was sold and replaced by a far more modest residence.

Young Arthur could not brook denial and threw outrageous tantrums when crossed. He grew into 'a wild boy' who broke windows, charged items to his mother's shop accounts without permission and 'borrowed' money from his classmates. By the time he was thirteen his father could no longer control him; a succession of boarding schools followed. Although his early grades show that he was an extremely bright and capable child, 'once his intelligence was beyond dispute, he began to backslide.' He ran up huge bills in local stores, which were always left to his parents to pick up, before graduating to bouncing cheques – now, with a grandiose air, signing himself Arthur S. Wolff III.

A long career of imposture, fraud and deception followed, with the inevitable result that when the author wished to visit his aged father, he was obliged to travel to a California prison. Several hallmarks of the classic impostor-childhood are evident in this tale: the spoilt and lionized child, the intense parenting, the transformation of the father's fortunes, graduating to a boy who spent money he didn't have in the belief that he was somehow entitled to a certain lifestyle. The desire, too, of being seen as a person of significance is also reflected in his later invention of a materially successful and personally heroic past (Groton, Yale, a valiant military career). Perceived as a failure by his unrealistically demanding father, Arthur Wolff proceeded to take what he believed he could never earn. He too divided himself into two: the side that was doomed to disappoint was rejected, along, incidentally, with his inconvenient Jewish heritage; the other side enthusiastically embraced the known, solid values of the security and approval he identified with material wealth and social status.

The extent to which the impostor believes his own tale also indicates how successfully the impostor self is able to repress the self it seeks to discard. Demara freely admitted that there were several occasions when his identity was justifiably questioned and he experienced what felt like genuine emotions of affront. When Navy HQ ordered the captain of the *Cayuga* to suspend the ship's doctor, Demara seems really to have believed Plomer's questions 'ridiculous' and 'an outrage'. Similarly, when the prison authorities confronted him with the *Life* article at Huntsville, Demara was hurt and angry: 'For the time at least I think I forgot I was guilty.' Even more interesting was his reaction when suspicion was cast over his documents at the New Subiaco abbey. In recollecting the incident years later Demara retained a sense of indignance: 'I don't think a doctor of philosophy had ever driven through the place before I got there. And one probably hasn't since. Disgraceful performance!' The fact that he *wasn't* a doctor of philosophy is entirely eclipsed by his galling sense of injustice. This sense of grievance, of feeling unjustly persecuted by small-minded people, is typical both of Demara and MacKinnon, and of many other impostors.

In his biography of Demara, Crichton attempts to get a handle on what is actually going on in Demara's case: although he does seem to have the textbook background in common with impostors studied by contemporary psychologists – 'At an early age he lost his social status and everything that went with it and many feel he has been going through life in another guise trying to find it again' – Crichton suspects that there was a great degree of personal enjoyment to be derived from Demara's many lives:

. . . the simplest truth about the man is that life suddenly and almost miraculously becomes exciting and challenging the moment he drops his own cloak and puts on the protective plumage of another. It is a game and, at times, a great game. It is tense, it is serious and funny, it is dangerous. It is self-expanding at the same time and it is self-destructive. It is also a heady opiate that, once tasted, makes everything else seem flat and stale and, even unreal.

It becomes, he even suggests, an addiction, the next hit always holding the promise of being the best yet. Demara admitted to *Life* magazine that 'being an impostor is a tough habit to break', and both Marvin Hewitt and Brian MacKinnon acknowledged the obsessive nature of their drive to pursue their chosen course.

Not all impostors easily fit Deutsch's model. When Marvin Hewitt (the highschool drop-out who posed as a physics professor) was interviewed by the press, he had a very straightforward explanation for his actions. Hewitt had been an exceptionally bright child, quickly outstripping not only his peers but his teachers. He had completed all the highschool mathematics courses by the time he was eleven. The fact that he was different caused him to become alienated from other children. While his teachers were 'nonpercep-tive and couldn't understand what I was talking about', the boy Marvin 'could not go around and talk relativity to other kids of eleven'. Even as he excelled academically, he became isolated within the education system, describing his superior understanding as 'insulation'. He realized he had reached the limit of what school could offer him and continued to educate himself in the public libraries. His interest in science was wide-ranging, and he read extensively in calculus, engineering and psychology. 'Perhaps because of association, I became interested in works on child psychology as I recognized myself as a brilliant child.'

In other impostors this claim would be read as a typical *delusion de grandeur*, but Marvin Hewitt really was brilliant. The tragedy that was looming was that his father, a labourer, and later a police officer, flatly opposed any talk of further education. Sergeant Samuel Hewitt, *The New York Times* mentioned, was killed in Marvin's home town of Philadelphia, chasing a car thief in 1947, when his son was twenty-five. The connection it neglects to make is that Marvin Hewitt began impersonating qualified academics in the same year. Hewitt himself gave no clues as to whether this was significant, telling a journalist that, apart from his genius, 'there were some other elements in his psychological complex, but they were of a personal nature, and he did not wish to discuss them.'

Robert Crichton found Ferdinand Waldo Demara evasive in a different way when he looked to 'the great impostor' himself for an explanation for his career. Demara tried to laugh the question off, before saying, 'I have thought it out and I believe it's truth. It's rascality, pure rascality!' Yet this upbeat response may mask real psychological damage, both leading up to the imposture and inflicted by the demands of the imposture itself. An arresting officer once suggested to Demara, 'Every time you take on a new identity the whole world opens up for you, doesn't it? I mean, it's all fresh and wide open like the day you left home.' Demara replied with deadly seriousness, 'Now I'm telling you the truth and then I don't want any more of this bull. Every time I take a new identity some part of the real me dies, whatever the real me is.' Yet Demara shows more self-knowledge in this admission than many others. When MacKinnon was put on the spot, he burst out, 'To fuck with identity. It's just a name. I know who I am.'

6. Dr James Barry:
'A Gentleman Every Inch'

Who shall decide when doctors disagree?

– Alexander Pope, *Moral Essays*

The history of imposture in the field of medicine has recorded no example more extraordinary and impressive than that of James Barry. In August 1816 he arrived at the Cape of Good Hope on the first of many postings overseas. By his own reckoning he was seventeen years old, yet he held an MD from Edinburgh University and had three years' experience as a hospital assistant (the most junior commissioned officer in the medical department of the army). Barry's origins were obscure, and he did nothing to clarify them. He was believed by some to have been the illegitimate child of a nobleman, others asserted he was of noble, if not royal birth. The one known fact was that the young doctor's sponsors included the influential Beaufort family. Lord Charles Somerset, second son of the Duke of Beaufort, was at this time the governor of the Cape, so Barry found himself among friends in Cape Town.

Once installed, Barry quickly earned a reputation for his prodigious talents. It was not long before he was appointed physician to the governor and counted many members of the Cape's fashionable and affluent set among his patients. One correspondent wrote to the neighbouring Governor of St Helena:

I have . . . here quite a prodigy as a physician, a Doctor Barry, whose skill has attested wonders since he has been here. Indeed it would be well worthwhile for an invalid to come here solely for the purpose of obtaining his advice.

St Helena's most famous inhabitant at that time was the exiled Napoleon Bonaparte, and when the son of his private secretary, the Count de las Cases, fell ill, the highly recommended Dr Barry was sent for. The count recorded in his journal the fact that Barry had been described to him as 'an absolute phenomenon', and that he had performed 'extraordinary cures' at the Cape, one of which had 'saved the life of one of the governor's daughters after she had been given up'. However, when the doctor arrived, escorted by a sea captain from St Helena, the Count de las Cases was taken aback by Barry's youthful looks: 'I mistook the Captain's medical friend for his son or nephew. The grave doctor who was presented to me was a boy of eighteen.' Dr Barry prescribed fresh air, exercise and regular baths, duly effecting a complete recovery in his patient, and his fame in the colony increased.

The count was not the only person to find Dr Barry's appearance remarkable. One account put it most delicately, stating that he 'was a gentleman every inch of him: though this is not literally saying very much for him, seeing he was but a little man'. Estimates of his stature ranged between five feet to five feet six inches. His hair was variously described as 'reddish', 'sandy', 'light' and 'dyed red'.

Some saw him as well proportioned, although small, others as ill proportioned. We are also told he had a long nose, prominent cheekbones, and 'a rather lugubrious expression of countenance'. According to a Dr Bradford, 'He sought every opportunity of making himself conspicuous, and wore the longest sword and spurs he could obtain.' Several commented on the fact that Barry's appearance and manners were 'most singular' and that there was 'something extraordinary' about him.

The lack of consensus over Barry's appearance is perhaps telling. Accounts of his temperament seem to reveal a similar combination of apparently contradictory qualities. Widely agreed to be quarrelsome, while some saw him as irritable, vain, 'rather bombastic in speech and repellent in manner', others traced more attractive qualities: he was clever and agreeable, generous, kind, well informed, a superior conversationalist. Some found both positive and negative qualities reconciled in the doctor: it was acknowledged that 'selfish, odd, and cranky as he was, he had kindness for the poor, and was charitable without ostentation'; and that 'however eccentric', Barry was of 'a class of men second to none in nobility of purpose, practical sympathy and largeness of ideas'. Surgeon-General McKinnon was to hear plenty of bad press concerning Barry, but personally maintained that he was 'a pleasant and agreeable man. He neither cursed nor swore, but behaved himself like a gentleman. I have heard many reports about him, and most of them were false, the people making them being obviously interested parties.'

All these qualities are perhaps reconcilable when one considers what Barry was trying to do, and the nature of the beast he was up against. His insistence on rigorous hygiene, for example, was well ahead of his time, and he pioneered the idea of preventive medicine, considering overcrowding and poor sanitation prime causes of illness. Barry quickly discovered, however, that in the army it was one thing to identify a problem and quite another to rectify it. The 'interested parties' to whom McKinnon referred constituted those who bore the brunt of Barry's frequent outbursts of disgust at the deplorable conditions he found being endured in military hospitals. His regular and scathing reports on his findings were met by his superiors (unused to such savage criticism of the system, especially from within it) with a combination of outrage and petulant hurt feelings. The medical department groaned under its own ungainly weight; everybody knew that. And nothing could be done, everybody knew that too. Then along came a mere boy, squawking shrill complaints at unwashed floors, dirty linen and overflowing chamber-pots. Inevitably, mischievously, Barry's complaints and requests for supplies and staff always found their way back to the local officials who were implicitly to blame for the inefficiency and neglect he reported. He was not popular in such circles, a situation his lack of tact and patience did nothing to improve.

As far as the authorities were concerned, the brilliant young doctor was a mixed blessing. On the one hand he seemed to be in constant collision with his colleagues, both inferior and superior, while on the other his skill and decisiveness – especially in difficult operations – were widely acknowledged. On occasion, frustrated by the inefficiency and indolence of the decision-making machine (which failed even to supply him with the stationery he required to fulfil the medical department's endless administrative demands), Barry would take matters into his own hands.

Fed up and angered at the red tape which seemed designedly impenetrable, Barry's lack of patience quickly became as famous as his undoubted skill. Nevertheless, the medical department had been sufficiently impressed by Dr Barry to offer him the post of colonial medical inspector when the incumbent resigned in 1822. Barry was then twenty-three, and the post was an important one; until recently the duties of the inspector had been carried out by a board of several doctors, but an economy drive led to the board's authority being invested in one man, whose remit included the vetting of all drug imports to the colony, the licensing of all doctors and apothecaries, and the supervision of all medical practice. In short, Barry was now a force to be reckoned with in the Cape. Again, his reports to his superiors failed to win him friends:

Apothecaries are practising medicine, physicians are keeping shop and shopkeepers are selling drugs. To my certain knowledge many persons have been poisoned by patent medicines given improperly.

Barry also concerned himself with areas of medical practice in the Cape which his predecessors had ignored. Visiting the leper colony at Swellendam he was appalled to find its inmates starving, filthy and maltreated, and reported:

Nothing could excel the misery of the 120 lepers squalid and wretched beyond description. I found the Medical Department neglected. The doctor seemed not to take the slightest interest in the poor people entrusted to his care.

Barry prescribed an improved and more varied diet, advised the benefits of frequent sea-bathing, insisted that the lepers' sores were frequently cleaned and dressed, and appealed to the governor for cooks and nurses to be provided. He agreed. Barry now turned his attention to the lunatics in the Somerset hospital, concerning which he wrote:

The whole establishment [is] void of cleanliness, order or professional care. The wards are as dirty as the patients. Nothing but a general reform could improve the place, which does not deserve to be dignified with the title of Hospital.

Barry was making enemies as fast as he was making improvements. His interest in the welfare of the poor blacks – whether lepers or mentally ill – was resented by the wealthy whites who were used to running things without interference. To the importers of patent medicines, the pharmacists and the local doctors, Barry assumed the role of a professional pain in the arse. His influence with the governor, to whom many complaints were made about Barry, also frustrated them. Another strategy would have to be found to deal with Dr Barry. One Sunday, the story goes, Barry went to church, and finding the governor's pew empty, walked out again. A rhyme soon travelled the drawing rooms of Cape Town:

> With courteous devotion inspired
> Barry came to the temple of prayer
> But quickly turned round and retired
> When he found that *his* Lord was not there!

Soon afterwards an obscene placard was erected near Dr Barry's house, alleging that an improper relationship was being conducted by Dr Barry and the governor. Although its exact wording has not survived, it contained a reference to the governor as 'Dr Barry's little wife'. Could it be that Lord Charles Somerset and Dr James Barry were lovers? The evidence seemed to suggest otherwise; the young doctor was said to have 'a winning way with women', and was known as a flirt – at least – and a lady-killer – at most. The doctor was certainly extremely popular with his female patients, and one adjutant was moved to request Barry 'to discontinue visiting his wife just at the hour he had to be on parade or in the orderly room'. Yet it was observed that none of the unattached young women were able to pin Barry down, and he remained a lifelong bachelor.

Whether true or not, the slur on his reputation did considerable damage. Although the authorities were able to rescue the governor's name, the mud stuck to Dr Barry. However, it was not in Barry's nature to keep a low profile. Inspecting the 'Tronk' (the town prison) with Judge Kekewich, Barry reported that prisoners were to be found in conditions of unparalleled filth and squalor, naked and without bedding. Broken bones were left untreated, and the prisoners' meagre soup-ration was served in communal tubs without the provision of spoons, obliging them to slurp 'like pigs' from a trough. 'I do here, my Lord, declare,' Barry reported, 'that I never witnessed any scene more truly appalling than this. Mr Kekewich went out in disgust.'

Once again, the officials responsible took offence. But they were soon to have an opportunity to get their own back on the little doctor. Aaron Smith, a sailor, had got drunk one night and broken into the house of Mr Denyssen, the Dutch Fiscal (a powerful man in the colony). Once Smith was behind bars, the prison doctor declared him 'deranged in his mind' and the Fiscal applied to Barry to have him transferred to the lunatic asylum. Before authorizing the transfer, Barry examined Smith himself, finding him 'perfectly sane in mind and by no means a subject for the Somerset Hospital'. This decision might have gone unchallenged had Barry refrained from remarking:

Probably H.M. Fiscal's application for Aaron Smith's admission into that establishment has been in the spirit of 'pure charity' for the benevolent purposes of having the wounds inflicted upon this poor man by the Dienaars (on the day of his admission to the Tronk) professionally attended to.

Aaron Smith was not released, and Barry was summoned to appear before the local court of justice in the hope that he would withdraw his remarks. Barry tore up the summons. On the second summons he appeared in court but refused to speak. The Fiscal sentenced him to one month's imprisonment. Barry appealed to his friend the governor, who suspended the sentence, but reproved Barry for his conduct in the affair. Still Barry was not satisfied and agitated for the sentence (albeit suspended) to be revoked. The governor, who at this time was under pressure to return to England to face charges of incompetent government of the colony, could do without the added nuisance of the Barry affair, which also, inevitably, revived the scandal advertised by the placard a few months earlier. He easily succumbed to pressure to abolish Barry's post and replace it once more with a committee, on which Barry would be offered a junior position. Stripped of his powers as colonial medical inspector, Barry could neither bark nor bite. He was understandably aggrieved:

Thus, in the midst of public and important duties, scarcely yet completed, I was disgracefully virtually dismissed from my Office. And I must here repeat, to the utter ruin of my professional character and prospects in Life. As to the temporary inconvenience of pecuniary matters, I have not, I do not give them a thought. I had, indeed, flattered myself that I was bartering my time, my health and my talents (such as they are) to the Public Benefit, for honest fame, not sacrificing them to infamy.

In his dual role as physician to the governor and the great and the good of Cape society and colonial medical inspector, Dr Barry had scrupulously applied the same standards of medical care to rich and poor, black and white, sane and insane, convicted felon and law-abiding civilian. He had worked tirelessly to establish the humane treatment of society's misfits, pioneered the vital role of simple hygiene in the care of the sick, and even supervised the replacement of the city's open sewers with iron pipework. For his pains, he lost both posts, and in 1826 was reduced to assistant staff surgeon, on a wage of 7s. 6d. per day.

While Barry the reformer had fallen from grace, Barry the brilliant surgeon came to the rescue. One day he was called out to a woman, one Mrs Munnik, who had been enduring a difficult labour for several hours. Barry quickly realized that the only option was to perform an emergency Caesarean section. The problem was that Barry had never seen the operation performed, and had only read about it. He also knew that in Britain no mother had survived the operation. He moved the patient to the kitchen table, ensured everything was scrupulously clean and set to work, speed being of the essence. Both mother and baby were saved. The grateful parents named the child James Barry Munnik. The Cape was not going to be allowed to forget the little doctor.

Promoted to staff surgeon in 1826, and following a brief spell of service on Mauritius, Barry finally returned to England. His exploits were well known to the army medical department, and the fact that he had technically come home without leave to do so seemed typical, but not excusable. Summoned before Sir James McGrigor to explain himself, Barry appeared not to understand what all the fuss was about, and said simply, 'I have come home to have my hair cut.'

Barry later wrote that he came home to tend Lord Charles Somerset, who had left the Cape before Barry and was seriously ill. Although he recovered, he was to die two years later (in 1831). Also in that year Barry was posted by the army medical department to Jamaica, where he served apparently uneventfully for four years. Then he was sent to St Helena to take charge of the regimental hospital. He was soon in trouble again. The hospital had a military and a civilian wing – Barry was responsible for both. Although satisfied with the accommodation for soldiers, Barry found the overcrowded, mixed-sex civilian wards 'confused and disgusting'.

The solution he suggested was to turn an empty building adjacent to the hospital into an entirely separate civilian hospital, where women, men and the insane could be separately quartered. In the mean time, however, Barry was having great difficulties in procuring even essentials for the existing hospital. In St Helena it was the commissariat, working under the control of the treasury, who organized supplies for the army. A row developed between Barry and the commissariat, the latter denying it had any responsibility to provide for civilian patients, while Barry maintained that it was responsible for supplying all hospitals *administered* by the military, regardless of whether the patients were troops or civilians. The commissariat was immovable. In frustration, Barry went over its head, and wrote direct to the Secretary at War. News of the letter got out and Barry found himself under house arrest, awaiting a court martial for 'conduct unbecoming to an officer and a gentleman'. As Barry saw it, 'It was probably the first instance of an officer being brought to trial for the performance of his duty.'

The court accepted that Barry was justified in writing the letter, and the treasury ordered the commissariat to provide supplies for the civilian wing of the hospital. Despite being officially exonerated, Barry had again made powerful enemies. Although he had achieved a great deal for the hospital, he was to pay a heavy price. When the next opportunity presented itself – and given the fact that tact and Barry were strangers, it did not take long before the governor found a pretext to get rid of him – Barry was sent home under arrest. The disgrace nearly broke him. A journalist witnessed his departure from the island, accompanied by his servant and his dog:

On one of those still sultry mornings peculiar to the tropics, the measured step of the doctor's pony woke up the echoes of the valley. There came the P.M.O., looking faded and crestfallen. He was in plain clothes. He had shrunk away wonderfully. His blue jacket hung loosely about him, his white trousers were a world too wide, the veil garnishing his broad straw hat covered his face, and he carried the inevitable umbrella over his head so that it screened him from the general gaze. The street was deserted, but other eyes besides the writer's looked on the group through the Venetian blinds. No sentry presented arms at the gates, and the familiar quartet proceeded unnoticed along the lines to the ship's boat in waiting.

One phrase had damned Barry, he later learned. A report was issued by the board established to examine Barry's case:

The Board is willing to hope for the sake of truth and candour that Dr James Barry might possibly only have intended an allusion to the defective state of the accommodation and not a reflection on the administration of the duties of the hospital and the Board feels happily relieved from all necessity for further comment by the impossibility of its being believed that H.E. Major-General Middlemore or Lt. Col. Anderson [. . .] could have tolerated a 'confused and disgusting' administration to have existed for a day.

Barry was now in his forties. Whether he had been broken by the system, or whether maturity and experience had taught him to avoid confrontations with the authorities, his subsequent postings were relatively uneventful. Staff surgeon once more, Barry worked for the medical department in the Windward and Leeward islands, and later in Malta. In 1851 he was sent to Corfu, having been promoted to deputy inspector-general. Two years later, on the outbreak of war with Russia, Barry volunteered for a posting at the front but was refused. Within eighteen months nearly a quarter of British troops were dying in the Crimea; not only through the war itself, but due to cholera, dysentery and starvation. At Barry's suggestion, many of the wounded were brought to Corfu.

The men arrived in rags infested with vermin, suffering from cholera, fever and frost-bite, as well as war wounds. Of the 462 cases brought to Barry's hospital on one ship, he lost only 17 men – less than a single day's death toll in Scutari. Although Barry protested at the usual inefficiencies and abuses (no clothes were provided for the men, and the army insisted on drilling convalescent troops), he had learned not to upset the authorities. Undeterred by failing to secure a post at the front, he decided to spend his leave in the Crimea. Here he was to meet another great reformer who was beginning to make headway establishing the basic principles of order and cleanliness in military hospitals. Florence Nightingale and James Barry should have had a lot in common. Both had experience of grappling with an obstructive and inefficient army medical department: both had to deal with officials 'whose only object', as Nightingale observed, was 'to keep themselves out of blame'. Both were dedicated to the task of alleviating the unnecessary sufferings endured by the ordinary soldier. Both believed in the simple expedients of hygiene, good diet, fresh air and exercise. Their meeting was a disaster.

Nightingale described the encounter in scalding terms:

I never had such a blackguard rating in my life – I who have had more than any woman – than from Barry sitting on his horse while I was crossing the hospital square with only my cap on in the sun. He kept me standing in the midst of a crowd of soldiers, commissariats, servants, camp followers, etc., everyone of whom behaved like a gentleman during the scolding I received while he behaved like a brute.

Barry, she declared, 'was the most hardened creature I ever met throughout the army'.

Barry had evidently lost none of his charm. Next he was

dispatched to Canada, where his practical streak was again in evidence. He deplored the troops' unvarying diet of boiled beef and the uncivilized practice of billeting army wives in barrack rooms with other soldiers; he requested feather, rather than straw mattresses for the hospitals, and books for the troops. Following a severe bout of influenza and bronchitis in 1859, Barry came home. Aged sixty, and weakened by illness, he was retired against his wishes. Despite having upset and infuriated many people during his career, he had a surprising number of friends, and he spent much of his time as an itinerant guest at their various homes. In 1865, however, having settled in lodgings in Marylebone, Barry succumbed to an epidemic of diarrhoea.

The death-bed scene of the notorious yet brilliant doctor, attended by his faithful African servant, was given a nice ring of Victorian sentimental melodrama in the account of it which appeared in Charles Dickens's magazine, *All the Year Round*:

To his valet's consternation, he refused to see a doctor. 'Black John' could do nothing but sit by his master's bed, and wait. James lay dozing and powerless. It was after midnight when he rallied. He sat up and spoke to John, wandering at times, and expressed concern at his long attendance through so many hours; he would have John take some slight stimulant, which the faithful soul declined. Suddenly James fainted on his pillow. The valet used restoratives, which revived him.

'John . . .' gasped the invalid, 'this must be death.' But John did not think so.

'You are only weak, sir,' he said. 'Let me give you some champagne and water, or the least drop of brandy in a wine-glass of water.' For James would take such stimulants in great extremity, and he was now in great extremity.

He sipped a little from the glass, and said, more gently than usual: 'Have some yourself, John; you need it, and you will not mind drinking after me.' They were his last distinct words.

'When I was a boy,' Barry once said, 'I was told that when I began a story, to begin at the beginning and continue to the end.' But in Barry's case, what should have been the end proved yet another beginning. For when the old man's body was prepared for burial, Dr James Barry was found to be a woman. More astonishingly, by unmistakable marks on the body, it was deduced that Dr Barry had at some point borne a child.

It is quite possible that Barry's true sex might never have come to light. Her final illness came suddenly, but on other occasions when she had been seriously ill she had issued strict instructions that she was to be left in the clothes she died in, and her body sewn up in a sheet. But come to light it had, sending a seismic wave through the army medical department. As the scandalous rumour spread, the Registrar General, George Graham, was moved to request from Dr McKinnon, who had issued the death certificate which designated Dr Barry *male*, a statement of the doctor's true sex, 'not for publication, but for my own information'.

McKinnon explained that, having been 'intimately acquainted' with Dr Barry for many years and having attended him during his last illness, it quite reasonably never occurred to him, when issuing the death certificate, to check the sex of a man he had known so well. It was not until after he had issued the death certificate that the woman who had laid the body out came to see him:

She wished to obtain some perquisites of her employment which the Lady who kept the lodging-house in which Dr Barry died had refused to give her. Amongst other things she said that Dr Barry was a female and that I was a pretty Doctor not to know this, and that she would not like to be attended by me.

I informed her that it was none of my business whether Dr Barry was a male or a female – and that I thought it as likely he might be neither, viz. an imperfectly developed man. She then said that she had examined the body and that it was a perfect female and farther that there were marks of her having had a child when very young. I then enquired how have you formed this conclusion? The woman pointing to the lower part of her stomach, said, 'From marks here, I am a married woman, and the mother of nine children. I ought to know.'

The woman seemed to think that she had become acquainted with a great secret and wished to be paid for keeping it. I informed her that all Dr Barry's relatives were dead and it was no secret of mine, and that my own impression was that Dr Barry was a hermaphrodite.

But whether Dr Barry was male, female or hermaphrodite I do not know, nor had I any purpose in making the discovery, as I could positively swear to the identity of the body as being that of a person whom I had been acquainted with as Inspector-General of Hospitals for a period of 8 or 9 years.

The behaviour of the layer-out requires some explanation. The 'perquisites' – or 'perks' – referred to were effects belonging to the deceased which were traditionally offered to the layer-out, constituting an informal part of her payment. These had been denied to the layer-out in this case, leaving her feeling justifiably aggrieved. It seems extremely likely that she would otherwise have kept Dr Barry's secret to herself but now saw an opportunity to put pressure on the army to recompense her. McKinnon's dismissive tone in describing the interview, and especially the suggestion that the layer-out aimed to blackmail someone, is unbecoming: he had simply been caught out. His version of events raises other questions. If he had believed that Barry was a 'hermaphrodite', would he really not have taken the opportunity of Barry's death to examine the body? The possibility of seeing such a physical anomaly must occur possibly once in a lifetime: is it credible that he would pass up such a chance? It seems that this was a matter of professional – and masculine – pride. Either he *had*, in fact, examined a body he suspected was sexually unusual, discovered that Barry was a woman and decided that discretion was in order, or it had never occurred to him that Barry was anything other than a man, and he consequently had not bothered to examine the body at all, other than to establish that Barry was dead. The 'hermaphrodite' theory, in this analysis, was hastily thought of after it had been demonstrated that McKinnon had known a man well for over a decade without realizing that he was a she.

The extraordinary story of Barry's lifelong deception was duly published in the national press and reprinted in the *Medical Times and Gazette* with some additional reflections, suggesting that the discerning had never been taken in at all. The journalist, who had never met the doctor, did not hesitate to apprise his readers of the 'facts' of the case:

The deceased was very well known, and many were the stories and surmises circulated during his (?) lifetime. The physique, the absence of hair, the voice all pointed one way, and the petulance of temper, the unreasoning impulsiveness, the fondness for pets, were in the same direction.

That a woman could have got so far in a man's world was explained simply: 'In 1813, when the deceased entered the army, the Professional qualifications required for the services were not of the highest order.' The editorial also cast doubt on reports of Barry's decisiveness and skill as a surgeon.

The medical department was quick to respond to the press reports that Barry was a woman, with a statement by Edward Bradford, Deputy Inspector-General of Hospitals, who had met Barry. While he acknowledged Barry's 'singular appearance' Bradford was emphatic that Barry was *not* a woman:

He was quite destitute of all the characters of manhood. His voice was that of an aged woman. [. . .] When suddenly called on for a duty which he disliked, he went to bed and wept like a child till the danger had passed.[. . .]The stories which have been circulated about him since his death are too absurd to be gravely refuted. There can be no doubt among those who knew him that his real physical condition was that of a male in whom sexual development had been arrested about the sixth month of foetal life. It is greatly to be regretted that the opportunity of his death was allowed to pass without exact observation of his real condition by a skilled person.

The establishment had spoken. No further correspondence on the subject appeared in the medical press for thirty years. Then, in 1895, an inquiry addressed to the *Lancet* prompted a steady stream of correspondence from people who had met or heard of Barry. Lt Col E. Rogers, who wrote a novel based on Barry's life, had known his subject briefly:

In 1857 I travelled with this remarkable character on board the inter-colonial steamer plying between St. Thomas and Barbados, when I occupied the same cabin, I in the top and she in the lower berth – of course, without any suspicion of her sex on my part. I well remember how, in harsh and peevish voice, she ordered me out of the cabin – blow high, blow low – while she dressed in the morning. 'Now then, youngster, clear out of my cabin while I dress,' she would say.

Another correspondent had been a good friend of Dr Jobson, who had studied medicine with Barry at Edinburgh University, and had also joined the army with 'him':

One of [Jobson's] fellow students was remarkable by the persistency with which he avoided his fellow students, and he was also laughed at because, in contradistinction to the shooting-coats which all the other students wore, he invariably appeared in a long surtout. However, although he kept the other students at a distance, he soon became friendly with Dr Jobson and invited him to his lodgings where he introduced him to his mother, with whom he lived.
Both Dr Jobson and Dr Barry resolved to go into the army, and were together at a depot where Dr Jobson was astonished to find that Dr Barry was afraid to go home by himself through a rather rough part of the

town, but asked Dr Jobson to go with him. Dr Jobson, who, although a little man, was devoted to athletics, was much disappointed that he could not teach Dr Barry to box. He never would strike out, but kept his arms over his chest to protect it from blows.

Dr Jobson and Dr Barry were appointed to different regiments, and they never met again, although Dr Jobson heard of him occasionally as performing all the duties of an army surgeon, and also of his performing serious operations in the hospital at Malta. When she died and it was discovered that she was a woman and had been a mother Dr Jobson was as much astonished as anybody; for, although he remembered the above-mentioned womanly traits, they had never caused him to have the slightest suspicion of her sex.

Thirty years on from her death, that Barry *was* a woman seemed universally accepted; at this distance of time, however, opinions differed on how successful her imposture had been during her lifetime. One claimed that it had been widely believed that Barry was a 'hermaphrodite', while another held that 'it was a matter of common repute that she belonged to a different sex than the one indicated by her clothes.' A third noted that 'neither the landlady of her lodging nor the black servant who had lived with her for years had the slightest suspicion of her sex.' Although it is possible that some people may have guessed the truth, another piece of information that emerged from the correspondence in the *Lancet* was that at least two people claimed to have certainly known Barry's secret. Someone signing himself 'Colonel' volunteered the following anecdote:

I was quartered as a subaltern in Trinidad while Dr Barry was serving there in the capacity of principal medical officer. One day a friend of mine, an assistant surgeon, asked me to walk with him into Port-au-Prince. 'The P.M.O.,' said he, 'is down with fever at the house of a lady friend but has given strict injunctions to us not to visit him. Nevertheless, I feel bound to call and see how he is. Will you come with me?' On arrival my friend entered Barry's bedroom, while I remained on the verandah. In a few minutes he called me excitedly into the room, exclaiming, as he flung back the bedclothes, 'See, Barry is a woman!' At that moment the P.M.O. awoke to consciousness and gazed at us bewilderingly. But she quickly recovered presence of mind and asked us in low tones to swear solemnly not to disclose her secret so long as she lived.

If this account was authentic, the two men had faithfully kept Barry's secret until long after her death. Was their gentlemanly silence, we may wonder, a testament to their honourable behaviour towards a vulnerable woman, or their loyalty to a brother officer?

So how convincing was Barry's imposture? It is interesting to note that those closest to Barry, her immediate colleagues, her servants, her landlady, the one close friend of her student days, did not suspect the truth, while those on the fringes of her circle (and those who never met her) were quick to assert that her true sex was an open secret. There are compelling reasons for believing that no one guessed. The most powerful of these is that, as we have seen, Barry had made a lot of enemies; there were plenty of people looking for a reason to get rid of the little doctor, who seemed to cause trouble wherever 'he' went. If there was such a strong suspicion that Barry was a woman, why did no one use it as the looked-for opportunity to discredit and dismiss him/her?

It seems very likely that attitudes to women in the culture of the time simply precluded the possibility of Barry being a woman from entering most people's minds, however odd the voice or appearance may have been. We are dealing with a period when it was widely believed that women were simply incapable of mastering the skills required by the medical and other professions. To begin to suspect that Barry was a woman would have required an imaginative leap comparable to that which would permit a person today seriously to begin to wonder whether their dentist actually hailed from Mars. In the light of the prevailing attitudes to women, very few men must have been willing to admit they had been 'taken in' by Barry.

The process of mythologizing Dr Barry now began in earnest. The doctor was characterized, for example, as shrewish and governed by her (often violent) emotions. One account has Barry so enraging one governor, that His Excellency seized 'the little fellow' by the collar and dangled him out of the window. In another version it is the governor who is 'seized by the doctor and flung out of the window'. If these instances, which seem too incredible even for Barry's extraordinary life, satisfied a largely male audience who preferred to believe that Barry was, deep down, a mere creature of emotional instability, like other women, then the stories of her as a fearless duellist may have had an almost erotic appeal, rather like that which accounted for the popularity of the swashbuckling cross-dressing heroines on the contemporary stage. She was variously reported to have fought one, or two duels; to have killed her opponent, to have shot him 'through the lungs', or to have herself sustained a wound in the leg. One version had her duelling with a dragoon, after which 'Hands were shaken,' and the combatants became 'good friends for life'. But if correspondents were competing to produce the best Barry story, Sir Josias Cleote had one to top the lot. He wrote to the *Lancet*:

I am the only officer in the British army who has ever fought a duel with a woman. When I was aide-de-camp to Lord Charles Somerset at the Cape a buxom lady called to see him on business of a private nature, and of course they were closeted for some time. Dr Barry made some disparaging remark about this. 'Oh, I say, Cleote,' he sneered, 'that's a nice Dutch filly the governor has got hold of.' 'Retract your vile expression, you infernal little cad,' said I, advancing and pulling his long ugly nose. Barry immediately challenged me and we fought with pistols, fortunately without effect.

Given Barry's aversion to doctors, and flat refusal, however ill, to be physically examined, it seems extremely unlikely that she would have put herself in a position where she might be wounded.

The duels, like the defenestrations, are part of the myth-making machinery Barry's own deception had set in motion, and it is possible that she even encouraged similar rumours during her life – they certainly aided, rather than harmed, her screening of her true sex.

Although Barry's true sex was revealed after her death, no one knew *who* she was. In the absence of any other known name, her tombstone marks its occupant as Dr James Barry. Nor was it known why she had embarked on a career as a man. While facts were absent, stories were plentiful. The American traveller and writer Mark Twain had been told that 'she was a daughter of a great English house . . . She had disgraced herself with her people; so she chose to change her name and her sex and make a new start in the world.' The Earl of Albemarle had heard she was 'the legitimate grand-daughter of a Scotch Earl . . . the *soi-disant* James Barry adopted the medical profession from attachment to an army-surgeon . . .' A journalist added to this rumour further dramatic speculation: 'Was it,' he asked, 'an early folly that led her to find too late that men betray, and did she embrace the army as a means to soothe her melancholy, or with the hope of meeting and shooting her betrayer?' A more specific rumour suggested that Barry was the illegitimate child of one of the Beauforts/Somersets. Following the placard scandal in Cape Town, a libel had been repeated in the House of Commons accusing Lord Charles of committing 'an unspeakable atrocity with his reputed *son*, the household physician'. We may have to conclude with one of the *Lancet*'s correspondents that 'What romance or tragedy led Dr Barry to act as she did will not, I fancy, ever be known . . .'

It is significant that of all the 'reasons' posited for her imposture, the notion that she may simply have wanted to become a doctor was by no one admitted as a motive. That there was perhaps no 'romance', and only the 'tragedy' of being a woman, was not in the reckoning. The way in which imposture is reported and interpreted is in many respects as socially significant as the imposture itself. The response of a jealously patriarchal establishment which, it must be remembered, rationalized its exclusion of women, was inevitably resistant to the meaning of Barry's imposture. The significance of the affair was consequently talked down, from a range of standpoints: denial that any imposture had taken place (i.e., Barry was not a woman); denial that the imposture had been successful (i.e., Barry was a woman, but had never been a convincing man); acceptance of the imposture but minimalization of its impact or meaning (i.e., Barry had only got away with it because any fool could gain medical degrees in her youth); determined reinscription of Barry's essentially feminine frailty (i.e., she had done it all because of some man). The whole story had to be 'spun' and stripped of any subversive potential.

There is a possibility that Barry's imposture *was* a deliberately subversive act, but that she might have been its instrument rather than its instigator. June Rose, author of Barry's most recent, comprehensive biography, cites compelling evidence in favour of Barry's mother being sister to the artist James Barry. Yet this is less helpful than it seems; her Christian name is still unknown, as is the identity of her father. There are several contenders for the latter title: the patronage of the Beauforts suggests that she may have been the illegitimate offspring of one of their number (possibly even of Lord Charles Somerset himself, Governor of the Cape of Good Hope at the time of Barry's posting there – this would account for their apparently suspiciously close relationship, and also the rumour that Barry was Somerset's bastard 'son'). The Latin American exile General Francisco Miranda and David Steuart Erskine, Earl of Buchan, also both exerted influence on the young Barry. She dedicated her MD thesis to both these men, and they were also acknowledged in her name, which she signed in her schoolbooks James Miranda Steuart Barry. It is impossible to know whether either of these connections was forged because of a friendship with her uncle, or a more intimate relationship with her mother. Buchan's connection with Barry is significant in another respect: he was an early feminist, and had published on the subject, describing the education girls received as a kind of 'cerebral foot-binding'. Is it possible, therefore, that Dr James Barry was the result of some kind of experiment? Could Barry the artist and General Miranda have collaborated in a plan dreamed up by Buchan to 'prove' that a girl, given the same opportunities as a boy, could put them to as good use? Perhaps the germ of the idea *did* come from the young Barry herself, and her indulgent patrons went along with it. Unless new evidence comes to light, these questions can never be answered. It cannot help but be observed, however, that Barry appears to have shared an 'in' joke with the patrons she acknowledged in her dedication to her MD thesis. She prefaced the thesis with a quotation from Menander, which she rendered in the original Greek: 'Do not consider my youth, but whether I share a man's wisdom.'

What, with the benefit of hindsight, do we now make of that extraordinary meeting with Florence Nightingale? Why did the mere sight of Nightingale appear to enrage Barry – to the extent that Nightingale, with her vast experience of the very worst of the British army's medical department, considered Barry the 'most hardened creature' she had ever encountered in the establishment?

Perhaps Barry recognized in Nightingale the woman she had never been allowed to be, a woman who exercised her considerable talents within a man's world, but as a woman. Or perhaps Barry had so successfully sublimated her own sense of her gender that when faced with a woman who insisted on being taken as seriously as a man, she felt threatened. She may even have reacted through fear that Nightingale would somehow 'see through' her imposture. Nightingale too might not have taken Barry's outburst of spleen to heart had she known the truth. Nightingale had, after all, thought of telling her mother when she controversially set off for her medical training: 'You must now consider me . . . a son.'

Nightingale is a uniquely useful figure against which to consider what Barry's life, had she led it as a woman, could have been – at best. In fact, the girl Barry could never have achieved what

Nightingale did. Nightingale was from a 'good' family and had her own funds behind her, whereas Barry, it seems, was a bastard whose family had fallen on hard times and was dependent on the goodwill of her uncle's friends. Moreover, Nightingale did not seek to encroach on the territory of the (male) surgeon; nursing was an extension of a domestic occupation that had been traditionally carried out by women. Nightingale's aims were to clean up the nursing profession which, as Barry would probably have put it, did not at that time deserve to be dignified with the title of 'profession', being largely carried out by untrained, 'unrespectable' women, notorious for drunkenness and incompetence. Nightingale sought, and achieved, all kinds of reforms which would improve the lot of the common soldier, whom she witnessed being killed by the neglect of their own army in greater numbers than they were falling in battle. She had a mountain to climb, and met resistance and resentment every step of the way. Her sex was usually no more than an additional burden to her, its only advantage lying, as she once observed, in the fact that 'A woman obtains that from military courtesy . . . which a man . . . partly from temper, partly from policy is effectually banned.' Barry – crucially – failed to show Nightingale that famous military courtesy towards women – inadvertently paying her an honour she understood herself – of treating her like a man. When we question how convincing Barry's imposture really was, it is worth remembering that as the diminutive, smooth-faced, high-voiced doctor was shrieking at Florence Nightingale, it never occurred to the Lady with the Lamp that she was looking at a member of her own sex.

If Barry had ever read Nightingale's *Cassandra* she might have felt ashamed at her treatment of a fellow-traveller. 'Why have women passion, intellect, moral activity – these three – and a place in society where no one of the three can be exercised?' she asked, observing that 'women often long to enter some man's profession where they would find direction, competition (or rather opportunity of measuring the intellect with others)':

A woman cannot live in the light of intellect. Society forbids it. Those conventional frivolities, which are called her 'duties', forbid it. Her 'domestic duties', high-sounding words, which, for the most part, are but bad habits (which she has not the courage to enfranchise herself from, the strength to break through) forbid it.

What are these duties (or bad habits)? – Answering a multitude of letters which lead to nothing, from her so-called friends – keeping herself up to the level of the world that she may furnish her quota of amusement at the breakfast table; driving out her company in the carriage. And all these things are exacted from her by her family which, if she is good and affectionate, will have more influence with her than the world.

It was what she saw as the enslavement of women of her class to the daily round of trivial pastimes, which were deemed the only occupation suitable for them, and designed to keep them busy but ineffectual, that caused Nightingale to conclude: 'Nothing can well be imagined more painful than the present position of woman.'

And what do we now make of Barry's popularity with her female patients? Was she gentler and more understanding of women and their bodies than the run-of-the-mill army physician? Perhaps, and it is an attractive though admittedly unscientific thought, her skill in the critical Caesarean operation was influenced by a more intimate and instinctive understanding of female anatomy than anyone could ever have guessed at the time. As for her reputation as a lady's man, there are at least three admissible explanations. Firstly, it was a blind: just as a man who may fear he will be recognized as gay may go out of his way to prove his masculinity, so Barry played up her chosen gender. Secondly, she may genuinely have sought and enjoyed the company of women whenever possible, living and working as she did in almost exclusively male society. Thirdly, and we will meet this theme again in connection with male impersonators, she may have been a lesbian.

This seems doubtful. The scandal of the Cape surrounding Barry and the governor, Somerset, may well have cloaked a real affair. It is feasible that if, as June Rose surmises, the Beaufort/Somersets were 'in' on Barry's secret, a sexual relationship developed between the young Barry and the widowed Somerset. But if Barry was an illegitimate blood relation of Somerset's, as also seems possible, the picture becomes more complicated. That there was indeed a pregnancy is also not certain. Stretch marks can be caused by rapid weight-gain and loss caused by illness. Yet, as Ruth Richardson, who has also investigated the Barry story, has noted, the layer-out, who was the only person to inspect Barry's corpse, would have had considerable experience of bodies both living and dead, doubling, as she traditionally would have, as a midwife, and it was she who noted and interpreted the stretch marks. Barry did have periods of leave which remain gaps in what is known of her life, when she could indeed have concealed the later stages of pregnancy and a birth. The fact that she hid her own sex so successfully for so long suggests that she would have been capable not only of concealing the existence of a child – who, at this point in history, could easily be 'farmed out' to a wet-nurse, and thence to an adoptive family – but of sublimating her own emotional and psychological reaction to such an event. However, such speculation remains just that: Barry was experienced at hiding her self.

What happened to the child borne by the woman known as James Barry is not known. Yet the name of James Barry, which history could so easily have erased, was destined to live on down the generations by other means. The baby saved by the doctor, when she performed one of the first successful Caesarean sections in the world, was named James Barry Munnik. *His* son was also named after Barry, as was his godson, James Barry Munnik Hertzog, later General Hertzog, Prime Minister of South Africa. The custom of naming the firstborn Munnik sons after James Barry has continued to this day. The current James Barry is, agreeably, a doctor.

7. Other Singular Gentlemen

What am I that their [other women's] life is not good enough
for me? Oh God what am I? . . . why, oh my God, cannot
I be satisfied with the life that satisfies so many people?

– Florence Nightingale, note to herself, 1851

James Barry and Harry/Harriet Stokes, whom we met earlier, were
not alone in preferring the freedoms and privileges afforded by life
as a man; neither were they alone in carrying the imposture through
until they died.

During the California gold-rush, the life of the stagecoach driver
was as arduous and hazardous as that of the miners themselves, and
frequently more so. The reinsmen, as the stage-drivers who 'held
the ribbons' were called, ran the regular risk of being stopped at
gunpoint as they carried their precious cargoes out of the gold-fields,
and many were killed. Passengers' lives also depended on the
skilfulness of the reinsman as he negotiated terrain which was
fraught with natural hazards as well as the ever-present threat of a
hold-up. A good reinsman was therefore worth his weight in gold,
and Charlie Parkhurst was one such driver.

As is often the case in tales of the Old West it is difficult to
establish where reality ends and myth begins, but we can at least
be satisfied that Parkhurst was a legend in his own lifetime. The
received wisdom was that 'in more than twenty years no highway-
man had dared to hold up a stagecoach with Charlie Parkhurst on
the box, for the first two who tried it had been shot dead in their
tracks.' He was also famed for his ability to drive at breakneck

speed, which minimized the danger of attack, and it was claimed that he saved several lives when 'he whipped a team across a tottering bridge just before it went down.'

We do have a reliable witness in the shape of J. Ross Browne, an authentic chronicler of nineteenth-century California, who was offered the opportunity of travelling 'on the box beside old Charlie' in the 1860s. Although less comfortable than travelling inside the coach, such an offer was a great and rare honour and not to be refused. Browne left us this vivid picture of 'Old Charlie':

I was proud and happy to sit by the side of Charlie – especially as the road . . . over which we passed after dark, branches off over hills, and along the sides of hills, and into deep canyons, and up hills again; dark, dismal places in the midst of great forests of pine, where the horses seem to be eternally plunging over precipices and the stage following them with a crashing noise, horribly suggestive of cracked skulls and broken bones. But I had implicit confidence in Old Charlie. The way he handled the reins and peered through the clouds of dust and volumes of darkness, and saw trees and stumps and boulders of rock, and horses' ears, when I could scarcely see my own hand before me, was a miracle of stage driving. 'Git aeoup!' was the warning cry of this old stager. 'Git alang, my beauties!'

'Do many people get killed on this route?' said I to Charlie, as we made a sudden lurch in the dark and bowled along the edge of a fearful precipice.

'Nary a kill that I know of. Some of the drivers smashes 'em once in a while, but that's whisky or bad drivin'. Last summer a few stages went over the grade, but nobody was hurt bad – only a few legs 'n arms broken. Them was opposition stages [i.e., a rival company's coaches]. Pioneer stages, as a genr'l thing, travels on the road. Git aeoup!'[. . .]

'How in the world can you see your way?'

'Smell it. Fact is, I've travelled over these mountains so often I can tell where the road is by the sound of the wheels. When they rattle I'm on hard ground; when they don't rattle I genr'ly look over the side to see where she's agoing.'

'Have you any other signs?'

'Backer's another sign; when I'm a little skeer'd I chew more'n ordinary. Then I know the road's bad.'

'Don't you get tired driving over the same road so often?'

'Well, I do – kalklate to quit the business next trip. I'm gettin' well on in years, you see, and don't like it so well as I used to afore I was busted in.' [This was a reference to the only time he took a tumble, breaking several ribs.]

'How long have you been driving stage?'

'Nigh onto thirty years, an' I'm no better off now than when I commenced. Pay's small; work heavy; gettin' old; rheumatism in the bones; nobody to look out for used-up stage drivers; kick the bucket one of these days, and that's the last of Old Charlie.'

'Why, you must have made plenty of friends during so long a career of staging.'

'Oh yes, plenty of 'em; see 'em today, gone tomorrow! Git alang!'

Not long after this interview Charlie indeed retired from driving and successfully ran his own stage station and saloon before moving into the cattle business. Forced to give up ranching due to sciatic rheumatism (which disabled many of the early stage-drivers) he eventually retired completely, and died alone at home in late December 1879.

As in the case of James Barry, Charlie Parkhurst's true sex emerged only when the body was being prepared for burial. Unlike in Barry's case, where the absence of a medical examination by a qualified doctor had enabled doubt to be cast on the testimony of a mere woman, Parkhurst's neighbours, who discovered her body and its secret, summoned a doctor, who confirmed the astonishing fact that Parkhurst was a woman, and also definitely established that she had at some point been a mother.

In respect of her early life, Charlie Parkhurst had more in common with the master chimney-builder Harry/Harriet Stokes than with James Barry. Just as Stokes had run away from home as a child, Parkhurst had run away from a New Hampshire poorhouse at a very early age; like Stokes she had gained employment as a boy – in her case she became a stable-lad, and her employer coached her in reinsmanship. Her career as a stage-driver eventually took her to California where, apart from her renowned skills as a driver, she seems to have appeared unexceptional, playing dice and cards with her colleagues, drinking and smoking. It was noted only that she didn't talk about personal matters, and never swore. It evidently did not occur to those who met her that Parkhurst was not a man, and J. Ross Browne's account nowhere suggests he noticed anything peculiar in that direction about the stoical old driver. Yet like Barry, someone somewhere knew the truth – for even if these women had succeeded in bringing their babies into the world alone, they had certainly had some assistance in breeding them. The private lives of such women remain their most successfully kept secrets, of which even the grave did not rob them.

The lifelong gender impostures perpetrated by Stokes, Barry and Parkhurst enabled them to lead full and active lives in the world in fields in which a woman would never have been given a chance to prove her skills. Moreover, there was doubtless an economic imperative behind their disguise: there were few opportunities for single young women to earn their keep, however enterprising, and the workhouse or the whorehouse – or even the madhouse – would have been their most likely destinations had they attempted to 'make it alone' as women. This was, after all, the nineteenth century, and the necessity for such deception was to recede as in the next century women gained property rights, the vote, and eventually at least theoretical rights of equality in the workplace. Prejudice and sexism of course persisted but not, it may be believed, to the extent that women would have to disguise their sex in order to succeed in certain professions.

So when Billy Tipton, jazz pianist and saxophonist, died in 1989, his adopted sons were as amazed as his fans to learn that 'he' was really a 'she'. Born in 1914, Tipton had been a popular and successful musician whose career had extended from the big-band scene of the 1930s and 1940s to the well-regarded Billy Tipton Trio of the 1950s, and beyond. Off-stage, Billy was a scoutmaster, husband and stepfather to three boys.

Fascinatingly, Tipton had four 'wives', the final union lasting eighteen years, and appears to have been an active and skilled lover. Tipton had devised a general purpose excuse for 'his' unusual style of lovemaking: he had been injured in a car accident. This had left him with a genital disfigurement (which was why he liked the lights off) and unhealed ribs (explaining the bandages around his chest). The accident had also left him sterile, and he made use of a prosthesis. His last wife, Kitty Kelly, who had been traumatized by a rape when a young girl, claimed they never had sex, although he certainly had a sexual relationship with his other wives.

Billy had been born Dorothy Lucille Tipton and as a small child had displayed exceptional musical talent. At the age of nineteen, after failing to penetrate the male domain of the jazz world as a young woman, she 'suited up' and landed her first job. And so it went on. The fact that her work involved a lot of travelling was in her favour: only the folks back home knew the truth (indeed when she made her disguise permanent, her father resolved never to see her again). Dick O'Neil, who played drums with the Tipton Trio for a decade, interviewed after the revelation of her true sex, recalled that Tipton had sometimes been teased for having a baby-face and high singing voice. 'But I would almost fight anybody who said that. I never suspected a thing.'

Fortunately for posterity, Tipton spoke to at least one of those 'in' on the secret, a trusted cousin, to whom she said: 'Some people might think I'm a freak or a hermaphrodite. I'm not. I'm a normal person. This has been my choice.' But if her imposture gave her a life she would never otherwise have been able to enjoy, it was also responsible for prematurely ending it: Tipton was too afraid of exposure to go to a doctor, although she knew she was gravely ill.

Tipton's wives unanimously claim not to have known their

husband's true sex. This general possibility is strongly resisted in one of the accounts of the life of Harry Stokes, the Salford chimney-builder. It is known that Stokes's first wife knew there was something decidedly lacking in her husband, having declared him 'not a man' after their wedding night, but the woman with whom he lived until his death (some reports say they married), Frances Collins, steadfastly denied having discovered his secret:

She declares with solemn earnestness that she did not know, until informed the other day, that the person with whom she had been living for 25 years, sleeping together night after night in the same bed, was a woman, and her own children looked upon Stokes as their step father. She asserts that she took Stokes into the house in the first instance out of pity, to shield him from the persecution to which he was subjected. It may be that out of a sense of shame the old woman thus attempts to conceal her knowledge of Stokes' sex, [when] she did in reality know from the first that the person was a woman . . .

Collins was fifteen or twenty years older than Stokes, and this fact plus her claim that she sheltered Stokes because she felt sorry for him (his first wife having sounded it about that he was sexually inadequate), make it possible that their relationship was not a sexual one, which might make her case more plausible. Although it is naturally difficult to believe that a woman would not know that she was living under the same roof with a person of the same sex, the possibility must be admitted. For example, surely if Tipton's last wife had known 'he' was a 'she' there would have been little risk in Tipton revealing this fact to a doctor during her final and fatal illness. Also, while women of Frances Collins's generation might well feel that public denial of private knowledge was necessary to protect their reputation, Tipton's wives lived in an age where (a) people were beginning to talk more openly about such matters and (b) any of the four would have made money by selling the story of their strange marriage. It nevertheless remains a significant fact that even those wives who have been prepared to talk exceedingly frankly about the sexual aspect of their marriage to Tipton continue to maintain their innocence of her true sex.

As Marjorie Garber has queried, when it is said that 'he' was *really* a 'she', what is the force of that reality? If most people who knew a person, and even those who knew them intimately, knew them as a man; if that person looked like a man, behaved like a man, and even thought like a man; were they not more *really* a man than a woman? It is significant, for example, that after Billy Tipton's adopted sons were told of (and accepted) their father's true sex, they continued to talk to the press of Tipton unaffectedly as 'he' and 'him'. Although the physical proof was incontrovertible, the Tipton they had known was more *real*. 'I'm just lost,' one of them told a reporter, suffering understandable confusion as a result of the discovery; yet at the same time he affirmed the identification which was concrete to him: 'He'll always be Dad,' he said.

The examples cited so far have been women whose true sex did not emerge – at least publicly – until death robbed them of control of their secret bodies, yet there are many examples of women who passed as men but were 'found out' during their lives. Most of the documented cases were soldiers, in an environment where the cut and thrust of daily life must have rendered their physical secrets much more difficult to keep to themselves.

When women were discovered in the ranks of European and American armies they had often already earned such a degree of respect from their comrades-in-arms that they were allowed to remain there. Such women were characteristically outstanding soldiers, and a significant though small number of such exceptions were made; Napoleon, for example, knew of several cases of female soldiers illegally serving in his own ranks, but acknowledging their proven courage and martial skill, authorized their continued service. In some senses these women encountered more problems than those whose true sex was never discovered; although their comrades might be aware that they were women, whenever they encountered a stranger, a man was seen. Sometimes these dual-gender soldiers were able to turn their true sex to their advantage, at other times it could be a distinct disadvantage. Although women soldiers can only strictly be termed 'impostors' when none, or few, are aware of their true sex, useful insights into gender disguise, and reactions to it, can be gleaned from their stories.

The life of Thérèse Figueur is one such case in point. Her mother died as she gave birth to Thérèse in 1774 in Burgundy, and her father's second wife proved to be a violent alcoholic. When she was nine Thérèse's father also died, and she was saved from the orphanage only by the intervention of an uncle, who arranged a foster home for her at Rueil, where she made firm friends with a boy called Clément Sutter.

Clément, at the great age of eleven, was a drummer at the local barracks, and presumably it was through him that Thérèse gained her early impressions of military life. However, another uncle soon whisked her away to Avignon, where her training at a cloth-merchant's proved less attractive than the company of her uncle, who was embroiled in a Royalist anti-revolutionary uprising at the time, and commanded a company of gunners. It was at this point that her uncle – possibly feeling that she would be safer if Convention forces captured Avignon – allowed Thérèse to wear a uniform.

The liberty this afforded the nineteen-year-old Thérèse was a revelation: 'I could go about with him anywhere and everywhere,' she wrote, 'even on campaign.' And she did. On an early sortie, when their column dispersed in disorder at the approach of hostile scouts, it was Thérèse who held her ground, having the presence of mind to pick up a still-burning fuse from the ground where it had been dropped, and fire the cannon. On being captured by the enemy she learned she had put eight men out of action. After two weeks of waiting to be either shot or guillotined she prevailed on her jailer to gain her an audience with the Citoyen Général, to whom she revealed her true sex. The general, both impressed and amused, offered to reprieve her and her uncle if they transferred their allegiance to the Republic, an offer they accepted. The general also dubbed Thérèse 'Sans-Gêne' (a play on the words 'sexless'/'shameless').

From this point on 'Sans-Gêne' deserved her name, flitting back and forth between genders according to which was most useful in the prevailing circumstances. Masculine attire was her preferred choice, and on occasions when she made use of women's dress to extricate herself from sticky situations, she clearly saw it as 'disguise' – apparently unaware of the irony.

In an incident which is strongly reminiscent of Barry's stand-off with Florence Nightingale, when Figueur, in military mode, was confronted at a dinner party with a comparable figure of female power, she reacted with similar hostility. The terrifying 'la belle Lyonnaise' was a patriot of sinister reputation justly feared by Figueur's more worldly companions. None the less, overcome with feelings of 'horror and disgust' Figueur publicly berated the lady for her ill manners (she was combing her hair at the table). On the other hand, when she saw defenceless women victimized by men she seems to have felt an obligation to defend them. When travelling in a coach she cautioned a policeman who was embarrassing a servant girl with his lewdness to watch his tongue – a confrontation which almost came to blows. And when a cook for the Republican army who was breast-feeding her baby was taunted by a passer-by, Figueur 'told him what I thought of him, in language of a strength and pungency which he richly deserved'. Other women, such as the Empress Joséphine (whose husband, early in his career, had been called a coward and challenged to a duel by Figueur), regarded her as an entertaining curiosity, although Figueur couldn't bear being treated – by women at least – 'like some strange kind of animal'.

There was another aspect of their cross-dressing which made women soldiers perhaps more sensitive to the good opinion of others. Women who dressed in men's clothes risked being tainted by an old popular association between transvestism and prostitution.

Indeed, many of the European directives to evacuate the battlefield of women were designed to shake off the female camp followers servicing the soldiers' sexual needs, who sometimes constituted a small army themselves and occasionally dressed as men in order to avoid being apprehended. This emphasized the proverbial link which labelled the cross-dressed woman a loose woman; as the serving woman whom Figueur had defended ungratefully remarked to a fellow passenger when she learned the she-soldier's secret: 'Well, I wasn't going on talking to her – not likely! A woman who dresses up in men's clothes like that can't be any better than she should be.'

Thérèse's story also offers confusing signals as to her sexual orientation. On the one hand, as a dashing dragoon, she was involved in such an intense relationship with a sixteen-year-old girl in Castres that when the girl fell pregnant Thérèse was obliged to give ocular proof to both the girl and her mother that she could not possibly be the father. Yet when a Republican Adjutant-General was sufficiently attached to Sans-Gêne to offer her marriage, with the guarantee that she could 'remain a man and retain her rank', she agreed. She was, however, plagued by doubts as the wedding day drew near. She dreaded:

. . . the boredom of etiquette. I should be always having to mind my p's and q's, always pulling a grave face. My husband would, likely enough, have a jealous fit and start playing the tyrant. Then there would be rows and squabbles without end. I began to feel thoroughly scared.

When she arrived at the town hall at the appointed hour, she felt 'Our witnesses and the numerous friends about me seemed horribly like the members of a procession about to conduct the victim to the slaughter.' The bride and groom took up their positions before the official presiding over the ceremony: seeing before him two almost identical coated, waistcoated and breeched figures, he pointedly demanded which was the bride? Everyone laughed –

including, to the bride's wrath – the groom. Figueur later recalled, 'I felt very much like giving the offensive gentleman one in the face.' She announced the wedding was off and marched out.

A further problem experienced by women who lived as men but whose sex was an open secret was that they could not always be sure by which standard they were being judged. When anyone dealt with Harry Stokes, James Barry, Charlie Parkhurst or Billy Tipton, these women – ironically – knew they were 'on the level', 'man to man'. By contrast, the women soldiers could never be certain that they were playing the same game or by the same rules as the men who were privy to their secret. For example, Thérèse Figueur was understandably crushed when she mistook sexual attraction for professional respect. When she fell into the company of General Bernadotte (who was later to become the King of Sweden) she took pride in the fact that he put in a special request to his colonel to have her seconded to his staff. Summoned to his presence, her heart sank as the general began to talk of the sleep he was losing over her, and how from the first moment he saw her . . . but surely she had felt there was something special between them? 'I hung my head,' recalled Thérèse, 'and said nothing.' Undaunted, Bernadotte pressed on, explaining that due to his wife's ill health, 'when I'm on campaign I must have the society of a woman, a friend.' He promised that Thérèse would be well rewarded for keeping him company. Her account of her reaction aches with disappointment: she evaded his attempt to kiss her:

. . . without violence or anger, but I felt stunned, hurt, and filled with a profound sense of sorrow. The man's countenance, so handsome, so dignified; his uniform covered with gold lace, the great diamond star and the broad red ribbon on his breast . . . and then that he should hold me thus cheaply, I, who, like him, had fought on the field of battle, sword in hand. A blush of shame mounted to my brow. I tried to speak, but could only utter a few incoherent words, and even they were interrupted by a sort of convulsive movement of my whole frame.

'A married man . . . And I was so proud of all you had done for me . . . So then it was not as a brave soldier that you thought of me . . . You treat me like the most worthless of creatures.' The humiliation, the mortification of the thing choked me. I could not go on.

The next day Figueur returned to France.

Figueur wanted to be admired for her qualities, rather than her sex, yet she did not deny – rather she celebrated – her feminine side, and felt that she combined both male and female instincts. Although she wrote that 'Nature, in jesting mood, had caused me to be born a girl,' she was clearly proud of what she saw as her feminine sensibilities: as she worked tirelessly in Burgos to relieve the suffering of its war-weary civilians, 'I became conscious within me of those charitable instincts which nature has implanted in every feminine heart.' As it happened, the acts of kindness for which she became well known in this period were later to save her life when, as a soldier about to face an enemy firing squad, she was recognized as the 'soldier-maid' who was 'so kind to the poor'.

She also identified her care for her appearance – which she maintained in the face of great difficulties – as a legacy of her essentially female self. When imprisoned in Lisbon in deplorable and sordid conditions she gives the following account:

Amongst our number were some Spanish civil servants and employees who had seen service in the Government of King Joseph. Many of them had their wives with them, and the unhappy women were terribly dismal and forlorn. I did my utmost to encourage them and keep up their spirits. The rats were a great trial. They ate and befouled our rice. In prison men are careless of their persons, but women never forgo the desire to adorn themselves. That is one of the things in which they like to display their superiority over the other sex. My uniform coat was in holes; I mended it with some cloth I got from two of the tails. My under-jacket was in excellent order. I told myself that a belt of fur all round it would make it look like a hussar's pelisse. I saved and saved for weeks on the half-ration of rice until I got together about twelve French sous, with which I purchased a fur cap from an English soldier. Cut with strict regard to economy, it enabled me to give the desired finish to my pelisse. I had got three shirts, one of which I sacrificed to repair the other two and to make myself half-a-dozen collars. By similar means, I made myself a blue cloth cap with a broad band of lace round it. I washed my linen in a bucket, and ironed it by sitting on it. Anyhow, I managed somehow or other always to look decent.

Perhaps it was only in the heat of battle that Thérèse Figueur really became Sans-Gêne – or sans everything. Due to that widely attested phenomenon whereby all thoughts of individual interest are swept aside in an adrenalin rush, she on one occasion volunteered to resupply an isolated battery, holding a crucial position. She had galloped across a stretch of land swept by enemy fire, delivered her precious cargo of ammunition, returned, and jumped up and down with satisfaction before realizing she had a bullet in her shoulder. This kind of bravery was typical of her; on another occasion she single-handedly saved two soldiers who had fallen into a fast-flowing river from drowning. And perhaps this is the key to the gender-bending female soldiers: their ability completely to forget themselves – their sex was just one irrelevance among many.

After a period of imprisonment in England, Figueur returned to France in time to hear of the surrender of Paris. Her soldiering days over, at the age of forty she opened a café. It was not long before her path crossed, once again, that of Clément Sutter. Her childhood friend the drummer boy had come home a war hero and prevailed upon Thérèse to marry him. This time she was ready to make the commitment and formally quit her life of adventure. Typically, her recollection of her feelings has about it the flavour of someone resigning themselves to a demanding and arduous campaign:

Once I had signed the register, I said good-bye to all ideas of independence. My sole thought was to make my husband happy. I made up my mind, as any soldier should, that there was no going back, and that it was my duty to give strict obedience to the orders of the leader I had chosen. The orders were never harsh. I had for a husband, the man I loved best, a brave, loyal, sober, steady man, with an even, gentle disposition, a man who adored me, and, what was not to be despised, a fine specimen of manhood, the handsomest member of the force. He had an open, good-looking countenance, he stood five foot two, with a fine broad chest glittering with the cross of the Legion of Honour and the medal of the Civic Guard, which he had won on the 15th August. Add to that, a calf so big that my waistband would only just go round it. And then, in addition to all that, a sergeant's epaulettes and General d'Espinoy's promise to exchange them soon for the epaulettes of a commissioned officer.

But there was to be no happy ending for Thérèse: the expected promotion never came, and Clément died, leaving her in great poverty. The female dragoon died in an almshouse in 1861, aged eighty-seven.

One year before the birth of Thérèse Figueur, in 1773, Félicité de Fernig was born near Valenciennes, her sister Théophile three years later. Their father and brother were already soldiers when, at the ages of sixteen and thirteen, the girls disguised themselves as boys and joined the local Garde Nationale. Although fellow members of the troop were in on the deception their commandant was not. The girls succeeded in keeping a low profile until one day a visiting general drew the commandant's attention to the furtive behaviour of the two young volunteers, who appeared to take great pains to avoid eye-contact. The commandant had good reason to have rumbled the girls' true identities before this: they were, after all, his daughters. The ensuing scene, described by writer and politician Alphonse Marie de Lamartine, would have provided perfect material for a patriotic artist to create a monument to the spirit of the Republic:

Théophile and Félicité realising that their secret was out, fell on their knees, blushed and burst into tears, acknowledging their misdeeds, and, flinging their arms about their father's knees, implored him to forgive the deceit they had practised upon him. M. de Fernig, himself in tears, embraced his daughters and presented them to Beurnonville, who described the whole scene in a dispatch which he sent to the convention.

The Mlles de Fernig – needless to say – acquitted themselves magnificently at every opportunity and were held up as models of patriotism (after the style of Jeanne d'Arc) to which their male comrades should aspire. The sisters' biographers, however, are always pleased to draw attention to the fact that they never lost sight of their feminine instincts. While in the heat of battle they charged, holding the horses' reins between their teeth, leaving their hands free to fire and reload their guns, dispatching enemy grenadiers right and left, after their victories they visited the battlefield and:

. . . laying all their soldiers' bravery aside, fell a-weeping, like the two kind-hearted girls they were, as they surveyed the scene of desolation, on every hand corpses ripped open, and wounded men in the throes of death.

The de Fernig sisters, however, blotted their copybook with the Republic by supporting the dissident Dumouriez and were banished from France, returning only when the government changed. As O. P. Gilbert noted, 'From the time they put off their uniforms and put on petticoats, there is nothing of very striking interest to record in the lives of the two sisters.' They married, Félicité taking as her husband a man whose life she had saved some time before, and who had been searching for her ever since. In concluding their story Gilbert observes with some satisfaction:

. . . how easily the two soldiers who for so many months had borne themselves with such manly heroism resumed the gentler characteristics of their sex. Indeed, they threw themselves into the part with zest, displayed no small talent for coquetry, took great interest in the upbringing of their children, as well as in the making of preserves.

So far our male impersonators have tended to be heroic figures. Catalina de Eranso, however, represents the darker side of the type. She was born in 1592 in Spain. Having enjoyed a comparatively unrestricted childhood, during which she was able to indulge in the same games and adventures as her brothers, she was, like many girls of her class, at an early age entered into a convent. The life evidently did not agree with her (she may have been sexually abused), and in 1607, when she was fifteen, she absconded, fitted herself out with men's clothes and embarked on a life of crime and violence.

Although, in the course of her various careers, she encountered her brother and her father, and happened to enlist as cabin boy on a ship captained by her uncle, none of these relations recognized her. Yet when, in an act of bravado, she visited her old convent in the flamboyant trappings of a wealthy lord, she was thrown into confusion when her former sisters addressed her by name. Her travels took her through Spain and much of South America, and her occupations included those of valet, page, train-bearer, shop manager and clerk, as well as sailor and – more gloriously – soldier. Her irregular careers of robber, thief and general bad lot also saw her in and out of a string of religious establishments, where she sheltered from the consequences of her crimes.

Whatever qualities made her the exceptionally courageous and effective soldier she undoubtedly was were unfortunately entirely undisciplined in other areas of her life. Brutality and violence seem to have come to her as easily as breathing. She stabbed and slashed the face of a man and killed his companion – all this arising from the unpardonable crime of blocking her view in the theatre. More tragically, in responding to a challenge to answer for the deaths of two men she had killed in a fight over a game of cards, she unwittingly killed her own brother. 'I remained dumbfounded,' she economically commented in her memoirs.

As well as sustaining numerous injuries in her martial activities (official and otherwise), a lifestyle which meant she spent considerable periods on the run often found her enduring great physical hardships. On a perilous crossing over the Andes with two other deserting soldiers, starving and lacking water, she and her companions were reduced to eating their horses. Obliged to continue on foot, her companions later died of cold and exhaustion, while Catalina survived, only to continue a life which had become a sequence of heinous crimes and narrow escapes from retribution.

Unlike Thérèse Figueur, Catalina de Eranso seems to have felt no obligation to sisterly behaviour towards her own sex and twice found it expedient (for financial and other equally self-serving reasons) to become engaged to be married – on both occasions, equipped with whatever she needed at the time, disappearing on the eve of the wedding. When employed by a wealthy lady in La Plata, Dona Catarina de Chaves, she accepted with some relish that lady's instruction to disfigure the face of a rival.

Only towards the end of her career, when she was so badly wounded that the surgeon insisted she make her confession before he would operate, did she reveal the secret of her true sex. The surgeon saved her life and held his tongue. She was by this time infamous throughout South America, a wanted man. But she could not remain one step ahead of the law for ever, and one night, finding herself completely surrounded in the town of Guamanga, put a gun to her head. The local bishop somehow broke the self-destructive spell and prevailed on her to hand over her weapon and go with him. She recounted, for the first time, her whole story and, agreeing to return permanently to female dress, entered a convent:

The news of this event ran like wildfire up and down the land and caused throughout the 'Indies' a wave of universal astonishment, not only among those who had known me before, but among those who had subsequently become acquainted with my adventures.

She was eventually permitted to return to Spain on the understanding that she would continue to forswear male dress. She agreed; however:

. . . when the ship was only one day out to sea, [she] thrashed three officers with whom she was playing cards, and slashed the Captain's face with a pocket-knife, with the result that she was promptly dumped ashore on the coast of Peru.

She found another ship; this time the captain took the wise precaution of locking her in her cabin for the duration of the voyage. However earnestly she had made her promises, she disembarked at Cadiz dressed as a gallant cavalier. More adventures followed and Catalina's right to wear male dress was eventually authorized by Pope Urban VIII. It does not seem likely that in her later years Catalina developed the de Fernig sisters' interest in the making of preserves. However, it is not known how or when Catalina, who had set such a low price on the lives of others, met her death, although it seems likely to have been on the battlefield, back in South America.

It is worth considering why these women should have been such exceptionally courageous and dedicated soldiers. It would be wise to acknowledge that perhaps merely the fact of their being women had drawn attention to the daring nature of the exploits which in men might have been less remarked upon. Yet it also seems likely that in order for women to be prepared so thoroughly to transgress the prevailing cultural values, to risk everything, disregarding the shame and stigma associated with women who wore men's clothes – let alone being prepared to give their lives, unasked – that such women were necessarily going to be highly motivated and extremely brave.

It is also important not to romanticize the powers-that-were who recognized and approved their achievements. These female soldiers were not perceived as in some sense the best of their sex, and proof of what women could do, but as *exceptions* to their sex, salutary but atypical examples. Both the emphasis on the fact that these women were often easily able to return to their 'natural' roles when the fighting was over, insisted on by biographers, and the nickname 'Sans-Gêne' are telling. In a culture which depends on the sexual status quo, the ideal story of the woman-as-man impostor – if a soldier – ends not in battle, blood and guts, but in marriage, children and jam.

In fact, much more insight into the personal experience of women practising gender imposture can be gained by looking at the lives of more ordinary she-soldiers, including the ones who did not pause to light the abandoned cannon but fled with the rest of the men; those who were motivated to begin a career of imposture not by patriotism, but by self-preservation, or even, by accident.

The freedoms that life as a man offered crucially included the ability to earn a man's wage, and this was the primary motivation for many women who joined the army, and was certainly the case with Deborah Sampson, the best known of the American military women. An adventurous and energetic young woman, at the age of twenty she enlisted in the 4th Massachusetts regiment in the borrowed clothes of a friend's son. It is refreshing to learn, in this catalogue of exceptional female heroism, that the young Sampson's first act was to take her bounty to the nearest tavern where she 'called for spiritous liquors, got excited and behaved herself in a noisy and indecent manner'.

This early promise of aptitude for military life was borne out as 'Robert Shurtleff' went on to fight for two years in the Continental Army during the War of Independence. Close physical intimacy with her comrades never presented a problem for Sampson; even on occasions when she had to sleep with other soldiers, she stated that 'They as little suspected my sex as I suspected them of a disposition to violate its chastity, had I been willing to expose myself to them, and to act the wanton.'

Like many women-as-men Sampson was prepared to risk her health rather than make herself vulnerable to discovery. When her regiment was vaccinated against smallpox in 1782, Sampson absented herself rather than face the possibility of detection. In fact she had only succeeded in delaying discovery, as the following year she succumbed to the disease during an epidemic and the doctor treating her quickly discovered the truth. Impressed, he promised to keep her secret. Sampson's fear of exposure was such that when in the same year she was wounded in the leg and shoulder, although the injuries were not mortal, she later recalled, 'I considered this as a death-wound, or as being equivalent to it as it must, I thought, lead to discovery.' Her principal concern was the possible reaction of her comrades, whether the friendships she had made with them would withstand the revelation, and whether she could bear what she interestingly described as 'the shame that would overwhelm me'.

Sampson was not to die on the battlefield, nor, like Thérèse Figueur, in penury. After the war she married and had children but never let go of her years as a soldier, publishing her memoirs in 1797 and embarking on a highly successful lecture tour in 1802 in which she thrilled audiences both with her story and by going through her military exercises with her musket. Sampson was now forty, a mother of two, and seemed anxious to play down the sense in which she might seem to have wished to challenge traditional female roles. Her lecture was therefore framed as an apology for her 'uncouth' actions, her 'good intentions' offered up as mitigation for 'a bad deed', one of 'error and presumption'; and in case any of her audience still had doubts, she ended her performance with an encomium on the virtues of female domesticity. Yet it is difficult to square this repentant attitude with other things she told her audiences, such as this more militant description of her transgressive act: 'I burst the tyrant bonds which held my sex in awe and, clandestinely or by stealth, grasped an opportunity which custom and the world seemed to deny, as a natural privilege.' Just as she had been forced to disguise her sex in order to take part in the war, Sampson was obliged to 'dress up' her feelings about what she had done for her audiences. The problematic nature of her position is revealed in the description of her war service which was given to the House of Representatives in the course of her long battle for backpay:

Deborah Sampson exhibited an extraordinary instance of female heroism by discharging the duties of a faithful, gallant soldier and at the same time preserving the virtue and chastity of her sex unsuspected and unblemished and was discharged from the service with a fair and honourable character.

The recurring problem was how to convey the idea that it was possible for Sampson to have been a 'good' man without having been a 'bad' woman. She did eventually succeed in receiving both her pay and a pension, but the difficulties began again after her death in 1831 when a special act of Congress was required in order to facilitate payment to her surviving relatives. This Congress did, satisfying itself that it was setting no dangerous precedent, 'as there cannot be a parallel case in all time to come'.

England, as a maritime nation, had its share of sailors who were eventually revealed (or revealed themselves) to be women; two of the most famous were Mary Anne Talbot and Hannah Snell. Both women ended up at sea not because of any lust for glory or adventure, and not for patriotic reasons, but as the result of ill-treatment by men charged with their protection. Mary Anne Talbot was born in 1778 with the dubious honour of being one of sixteen illegitimate children sired by Lord William Talbot, Baron of Hensol; her mother died giving birth to her. The semi-orphan passed from wet-nurse to miserable boarding school, and from the hands of one unscrupulous guardian, a Mr Sucker (who had charge of a fortune left to her by her sister until she should come of age), to the hands of another, one Captain Essex Bowen, who made her his mistress and subsequently enlisted her under the name John Taylor as his footboy when he set sail for San Domingo.

Captain Bowen was the only person who knew her true sex, a fact which he used to control her; Talbot, for her part, demonstrated extraordinary courage in 'keeping up appearances'. As a drummer-boy at the battle for Valenciennes in 1793, the fifteen-year-old concealed the fact that she had been wounded, and later dealt with the injuries herself. Valenciennes was to mark a turning-point for Talbot, for the battle did her the service of claiming the life of her persecutor and abductor, Captain Bowen. Talbot now learned from letters in Bowen's possession that Mr Sucker, her original guardian (who had no more deserved that title than had Captain Bowen), had swindled her out of her fortune. Talbot privately vowed revenge, although she was not able to accomplish this for several years; in the mean time she had little option but to continue to work as a sailor.

During a subsequent hair-raising encounter with the French fleet, Talbot 'felt not the least intimidated' and although wounded in the leg by grapeshot continued to stagger about the deck until, as a result of her exertions, 'part of the bone projected through the skin in such a manner as to wholly prevent my standing.' The surgeon ('after making me suffer the most excruciating pain') was unable to extract the grapeshot, and Talbot never recovered full use of the leg. She was later captured by the French and imprisoned at Dunkirk for eighteen months, during three of which she was kept in complete darkness, fed only bread and water and deprived of human company, except for the keeper, who once came in to ask whether she was dead yet.

She eventually returned to London in 1796. Having managed to keep her sex a secret all this time, she was obliged to reveal it when seized by a press-gang the following year. She subsequently experienced great difficulty extracting the money due to her from the Navy Pay Office at Somerset House, and was repeatedly fobbed off and sent hither and yon, until, in utter frustration, 'I made use of language which gave offence to some of the gentlemen, and was immediately conveyed to Bow Street.' The magistrate, far from fining her, looked into her case, and she finally got her money. Her war wounds reopened and became infected. More pieces of shattered bone were surgically removed but the tissue did not heal; the regular mention she makes of this leg in her story thereafter (the weeping wounds continued to issue fragments of bone, and eventually even the offending grapeshot itself) indicate that it blighted her life thereafter. All this time, despite pressure to revert exclusively to female dress Talbot had continued to find her masculine appearance more comfortable. In any case, she had some unfinished business to attend to before she was prepared to relinquish male dress. It was time to pay Mr Sucker a visit.

Mr Sucker was doubtless surprised and intrigued when a young man visited him at home one day, inquiring after his ward, Miss Talbot. Sucker explained that, regretfully, Miss Talbot had died on a sea voyage in 1793. Thereupon the stranger drew his sword and announced that he – or rather she – was in fact Mary Anne Talbot, come to claim her inheritance. The terrified Mr Sucker admitted that the fortune was spent and Talbot was obliged to leave empty-handed. Although she had not laid a finger on him, she was to learn, three days later, that the shock of this dramatic confrontation had killed Mr Sucker.

There is little doubt that the effect Talbot produced on Sucker had much to do with her appearance; how seriously, in contrast, he would have taken the return of a friendless young woman can only be guessed. However, Sucker's death did nothing to improve Talbot's financial situation. She took a succession of menial jobs, and spent some time on the stage, playing roles of both sexes, before the debtors' prison at Newgate beckoned. As one of her more recent biographers, Julie Wheelwright, notes, 'Her life was beset by chronic illness and the poverty that plagued most single, working-class women of late eighteenth-century London.' In many senses, then, Talbot's gender transformation had only postponed her inevitable fate. After serving her term in prison, she found work as a servant at the home of Robert S. Kirby, a publisher who encouraged Talbot to write her story, which he published in his *Wonderful Museum* magazine accompanied by an appeal for financial assistance. Although she was never by any means well off, she attracted sufficient sympathy to become, in her turn, a victim of imposture, when a woman in a Light Horseman's uniform, claiming to be John Taylor (Talbot's alias) was arrested for soliciting wealthy Londoners for money. Mary Anne Talbot died at the age of thirty, largely as a result of wounds she had been dealt as a soldier.

Talbot was less apologetic than Deborah Sampson had been for appropriating male clothing and, having been used to it from a much earlier age, found it and the privileges it afforded far more difficult to put aside after she had quit the Navy. She had, after all, never worn women's clothes in her adult life and reasoned that 'having been used to a male dress in defence of my country, I thought I was sufficiently entitled to wear the same whenever I thought proper.'

But it was not merely a matter of clothes. It had been observed of Deborah Sampson that as a forty-year-old respectably married woman, 'she conversed with such ease on the subject of theology, on political subjects and military tactics that her manner would seem masculine.' Mary Anne Talbot not only disturbed her landlady by frequently wearing her seaman's clothes, but by the fact that she was 'more inclined to masculine propensities, such as smoking, drinking grog, etc., than what became a female'. When Talbot died, Kirby reprinted her story, adding some reassuring notes of his own for those readers who might be concerned that 'long habits of association had blighted the delicacy and modesty which are such ornaments to a female'. While he acknowledged that Talbot had contracted 'all that blunt generosity of spirit and good nature peculiar to British seamen', he insisted that she had retained 'much of the sensibility of her sex, and to a friend or acquaintance she was ever willing when able to render either pecuniary assistance or personal service'. Once again, in this period a woman's achievements in a male role could only be acknowledged and admired if the audience of her tale was assured that the masculine part of her never eclipsed her essentially feminine self. The notion of a woman who not only *seemed* like a man, but *was* like a man, was not a concept deemed either worthy of celebration or entirely healthy.

It was not until sailor 'James Gray' and shipmates were convivially ensconced in a corner of a London pub, back pay safely pocketed, that the young marine stood before the assembled company and announced, 'Gentlemen, Jemmy Gray, you will find, will, before we part, cast his skin like a snake and become a new creature.' Gray then turned to a man who had been a regular bedfellow and declared, 'Had you have known, Master Moody, who you had between a pair of sheets with you, you would have come to closer quarters. In a word, gentlemen, I am as much a woman as my mother ever was, and my real name is Hannah Snell.'

Her shipmates were understandably astonished to hear her revelation, and then full of praise and admiration. Master Moody, however:

. . . carried the testimonies of his respects to a much higher pitch than any of his comrades, for he protested solemnly and seriously that he was become all of a sudden so enamoured with her, on account of her numerous and praiseworthy qualifications, that, if Mrs. Hannah had as favourable opinion of him as he had of her, he was very ready and willing to commit matrimony with her that very hour as an incontestable demonstration of the sincerity of his love and affection.

Hannah 'modestly refused the generous offer', knowing all about all-of-a-sudden enamourments, having committed matrimony once, and once too often, and having determined 'never to submit to the marriage yoke any more'. Like Talbot, it was because of a man that Snell became a man. She had married, at the age of twenty, a Dutch sailor, who 'turned out the worst and most unnatural of husbands . . . who not only kept criminal company with other women of the basest characters, but also made away with her things in order to support his luxury and the daily expenses of his whores'. When Hannah was seven months pregnant her husband abandoned her. Her baby was born and died seven months later, after which Hannah resolved to pursue her husband. To this end, in 1745, in the name and clothes of her brother-in-law, James Gray, she joined the company of a British warship. She served, as soldier and sailor, for the following four and a half years without her true sex being guessed.

Due to her dexterity, commitment, 'natural intrepidity and peculiar sprightliness' she was quickly appreciated as an asset on board; or, as her first biographer put it, as 'a little tar of note'. After some time on the high seas she learned from a shipmate that her husband had been executed for murder, whereupon 'she was determined, if possible, to acquire some honour in the expedition, and so distinguish herself by her intrepid behaviour.' As a child, Hannah already showed signs that the 'seeds of heroism' were becoming implanted in her nature, and by the age of nine she had formed her playmates into a company of troops which she marched about her home town of Worcester. At the siege of Pondicherry, India, in 1748, she faced the gruelling reality of this childhood game:

James Gray was one of the party that was ordered . . . to fetch up some stores from the waterside that had been landed out of the fleet, in doing which they had several skirmishes, and one of the common men was shot dead close on her right side, upon which she fired and killed the very man that shot her comrade, and was very near Lieutenant Campbell when he dropped.

She was also in the first party of the English foot that forded the river to get over to Pondicherry, which took her up to her breast, it being so deep, and was likewise very dangerous, as the French kept continually firing on them from a battery of twelve guns.

On the 11th of August she was put on the piquet guard, and continued on that guard seven nights successively, and was one of a party that lay two days and two nights without any covering in going through the barrier, and she was likewise put on duty in the trenches some part of the siege; she was obliged to sit or stand all the while near middle-deep in water.

At the throwing-up of the trenches she worked very hard for about fourteen days . . .

During the engagement she took eleven shots in her legs, and one, more dangerous, in her groin. As she lay in the hospital a new battle of competing agonies commenced between her mind and body:

The wound being so extremely painful [the bullet was still lodged in her groin], it almost drove her to the precipice of despair; she often thought of discovering herself, that by that means she might be freed from the unspeakable pain she endured by having the ball taken out by one of the surgeons; but that resolution was soon banished, and she resolved to run all risks, even at the hazard of her life, rather than her sex should be known.

She allowed the doctors to treat the injuries to her legs but continued to conceal the other wound. She eventually extracted the ball herself in a 'full hardy and desperate manner' by digging her finger and thumb into the deep narrow wound and pulling it out.

Although Snell was able to evade detection at this crucial point, there was always the day-to-day business of living as a man to contend with. Her girlish looks were noted, yet ignored; as mentioned earlier, the nature of her imposture was simply beyond the imagination of most people with whom she came into contact. She was teased for her lack of facial hair but so were many young recruits; more blatant proof was in evidence when she was stripped to the waist and whipped on board ship (for a misdemeanour of which she was innocent):

. . . the boatswain of the ship, taking notice of her breasts, seemed surprised, and said they were the most like a woman's he ever saw; but as no person on board ever had the least suspicion of her sex, the whole dropped without any further notice being taken.

As in many other cases of imposture, witnesses were so confident of the (in this case sexual) identity of the person that they dismissed what their own eyes were seeing.

Following her return to England and her revelation of her true sex to her shipmates, like both Sampson and Talbot, Snell took to the stage for a while, in 1750, singing songs and performing military exercises in her uniform. She continued to capitalize on her novelty value by opening a public house, 'The Widow in Masquerade', in Wapping. Her portrait was painted several times, and her biography was published in the same year. Her first biographer noted that Snell had done far better for herself as a result of her imposture than she could possibly have in her own identity. During her stage career, he noted, she was contracted for a season on a weekly salary, 'which is such a stipend that not one woman in ten thousand of her low extraction and want of literature could by any act of industry (how laborious soever) with any possibility procure'. Despite her vow never to remarry, Hannah Snell did take two further husbands before her death in 1789 in Bethlehem hospital, to which she had been committed three days earlier, having gone suddenly and inexplicably insane.

Other than this sour end, Snell had enjoyed financial security and public recognition since quitting the service. Like Sampson and Talbot, she was a curiosity rather than a source of pride in the potential abilities of the fairer sex, and admiration of these three women focused less on their heroism than on the fact that they had succeeded in preserving their 'virtue' while living almost exclusively in the company of the opposite sex.

This contemporary obsession with female chastity – which in these cases was doubly commended in the face of such a degree of perceived temptation and opportunity – had the effect of obscuring the fact, clearly spelt out in all three women's own words, that they each had important and meaningful relationships with members of their *own* sex. Hannah Snell, as James Gray, found 'a kind of a sweetheart' in a Miss Catherine in Portsmouth, who wanted to marry Gray; Deborah Sampson, as Robert Shurtleff, felt an 'irresistible attraction' to a Miss P. of Baltimore, feelings which were equally warmly reciprocated; and Mary Anne Talbot, as John Taylor, if not attracted to other women, was certainly attractive to them and suffered the unwanted attentions of a determined young woman in Rhode Island. (Talbot later lived under her true identity with a close female friend.) These significant transgressive relationships attract no adverse comment from contemporary biographers and commentators, whose preoccupation with the threat men posed to women's virtue excluded other possibilities from their field of vision.

Although it initially seems a possibility, it is in fact difficult to argue that any of these women were necessarily lesbians, who actively sought a masculine lifestyle. The facts that Talbot was put to sea against her will and that Snell set out initially in pursuit of her errant husband, seem not to fit with this proposition. Also the fact that both Sampson and Snell later chose to marry may suggest (but of course does not prove) that they were not lifelong lesbians. What seems more likely is that the activity of imposture itself created sexual tensions between the women-as-men and other women. These women were not part-time soldiers and sailors; they were 'being' men twenty-four hours a day, seven days a week, and had often been living this life from an early age. They learned not only to live in the world as men, but to *see* the world as men, and that included seeing women as 'other'.

This is not to say that their same-sex passions were not 'real' or authentic; they were merely vastly complicated. Of course these women preserved their chastity despite living surrounded by men, but this was because they had ceased to have emotional needs or sexual feelings; their imposture had transformed them both inside and out.

None of the soldier women discussed here had intended a lifelong gender deception, and following their reversion to female dress also reverted (with the exception of Talbot, whose early death prevents any conclusion being drawn on the subject in her case) to hetero-sexual relationships. By contrast, Stokes and Tipton, who remained men to their dying days, were undoubtedly lesbians: had they not been attracted to women, both could easily have avoided marriage and its attendant risks of discovery. Living as men therefore provided for them not only the economic advantages and social privileges of masculinity, but also enabled them openly to conduct sexual and emotional relationships with women. Is it significant that Barry and Parkhurst (who are both exceptions in having borne children while living their entire adult lives as men) both appear to have been loners?

All of this points to the conclusion that there is no typical gender impostor, no classic pattern of circumstances leading up to the imposture and no single model to the imposture itself. The only common and crucial feature these characters shared was that the lives they led as men would have been utterly inaccessible to them as women. Their situation was heavy with irony: while the strain of keeping their secrets must sometimes have been almost intoler-able, and their loneliness at times unimaginable, they also experi-enced a freedom of speech, movement, action and ambition flatly denied their conventional sisters.

The near-impossibility of women (*as* women) being able to secure a fraction of the freedoms and achievements detailed here was neatly illustrated by Virginia Woolf. She did this by providing an answer to a sample charge: that a woman would never have been able to write the plays of Shakespeare. Woolf accepted the charge, but her explanation had nothing to do with the inferiority of women's intellectual or creative abilities, but the inferiority of their education and opportunity. In order to illuminate her point she invented the improbable figure of Shakespeare's sister.

For a start, Judith Shakespeare, of course, is not sent to the grammar school in Stratford-upon-Avon. However, Woolf generously gives her the benefit of access to her brother's books, although her reading – and especially her writing – attracts only disapproval. She is soon under pressure to marry, which will put to an end, once and for all, any idea she has of being mistress of her own destiny. Woolf again reprieves her, allowing her to run away to London. Here she is turned away from theatres, where women are not allowed to act, let alone presume to write, as a result of which, single and destitute, she is rescued by a man by whom she becomes pregnant and, in the face of her lover's reaction, commits suicide. In the test case of Judith Shakespeare, Woolf found patriarchal society guilty of the death of female creativity. Even, on the rare occasions when women did slip through the net, against all odds managing to make their mark on the world, history as written by men largely failed to acknowledge their contribution. So it was, also, with those women who lived as men.

When Lamartine wrote of the exploits of the courageous de Fernig sisters he was moved to demand of his readers:

Where are their names on the marble tablets and our triumphal arches? Where are their portraits at Versailles? Where are their statues on our frontiers which they watered with their blood?

These rhetorical questions pretty well sum up the fact that history has largely failed to recognize the achievements of these undoubtedly peculiar but – in various ways – brilliant women. James Barry, for example, has yet to receive the recognition that is her due as the first female doctor. In the history of women in jazz, Billy Tipton's name is never mentioned. And so on. This is, perhaps, not merely proof of the feminist argument that history as written by men renders the history of women as 'invisible' but a direct result of the fact that these women used imposture in order to achieve what they did. However impressive their record, their strategy of subterfuge somehow excludes them from taking their place in either traditional (largely male-produced) history, or the history of women. They remain neither fish nor fowl, neither heroines nor heroes, but shadowy and marginal figures, individuals as unlikely as Shakespeare's sister.

8. Chief Buffalo Child Long Lance: 'One Hundred Per Cent American'

Oh, look down upon Long Lance,
Thou knowest Long Lance,
The Sun, the Moon, the Day, the Night;
Tell me if it is real,
This life I have lived,
This death I am dying.
Ah, the clouds are leaving my door,
The Outward Trail is no longer dark,
I see – I understand:
There is no life, there is no death;
I shall walk on a trail of stars.

– 'The Death Song of Long Lance'

Chief Buffalo Child Long Lance was one of the most famous native Americans of his time. In the late 1920s Red Indians, as they were sometimes called, fell into two categories in the minds of many Americans. There was the romantic figure of the Plains Indian, a feathered noble savage with an ancient and mysterious culture, and there was the lazy and resentful Indian, the menial urban 'half-blood'. Chief Buffalo Child Long Lance defied both these stereotypes: charming, handsome and urbane, the snappily dressed young journalist's achievements were widely reported. The *New York Herald Tribune* proclaimed in January 1930:

He is, to use a much abused phrase correctly, a 100 per cent American. Buffalo Child Long Lance, full blooded American Indian, chief of the

Blood band of the Northern Blackfeet, athlete, soldier, author, explorer and scholar.

The Toronto *Star Weekly* emphasized the young Indian's gallantry, noting that in 1915, although he had been appointed to West Point by President Wilson himself, because there was a war on in Europe, Long Lance 'did a very fine thing': he resigned from West Point, went to Canada, enlisted in the Canadian army as a private, and in a few weeks was overseas. He was wounded eight times and came out of the army a captain, decorated by three governments for gallantry in action.

It should perhaps be explained that for an Indian to gain admittance to the prestigious US Military Academy at West Point was no mean feat: only three non-whites had graduated from the college in over a century. To then leave in order to fight in a real war was typical of the phenomenon that was Long Lance.

There seemed no end to his achievements. He had also published a book and starred in a movie – both to critical acclaim. In addition to all this, he was believed to be 'the youngest chief west of the great lakes and one by blood inheritance'. Long Lance was, everyone agreed, a phenomenon.

He had certainly come a long way from the childhood he described with compelling detail in his autobiography:

The first thing in my life that I can remember was the exciting aftermath of an Indian fight in northern Montana. My mother was crying and running about with me in my moss bag-carrier on her back. I remember the scene as though it were yesterday, yet I was barely a year old . . . I do not remember anything more until I was four. And then I came to life again one day in mid-air. I was in the act of falling off a horse. I do not remember sitting on the horse's back, but I remember falling through the air, hitting the ground and lying there on my back, looking up in bewilderment at the spotted belly of the black-and-white pinto as it stood over me . . . From this incident on, I remember things distinctly.

I remember moving about over prairies from camp to camp . . . Mystery pervaded everything . . . And our fathers themselves were facing a big mystery which they could not fathom: the mystery of the future in relation to the coming of the White Man.

Later, the young Indian became fascinated by these pale strangers:

They interested me, these white-skinned people. They knew so many things. I saw in them what the white man calls *romance*. And that feeling has never left me. Even today I see romance only in the swirling turbines of factories and steamships, in the railroad, in the subway, in the radio and in the marvellous discoveries of science and medicine. These people so impressed me that I decided 'I am going to be like that.'

And so Long Lance began his long journey, attending the famous Indian School at Carlisle dedicated to giving the Indian 'a white man's chance' and going on to college and military training. He proved his patriotism by fighting in France in the Great War, returned a hero and began a career as a journalist in 1919 at the Calgary *Herald*. The 'Chief', as he was known at the paper, was popular with his colleagues and cut his teeth on the sports pages. In 1921 he began to cover a story much closer to his heart, when he wrote about life on the Indian reservations of Western Canada. His articles were extremely popular, and he went on to write for the Vancouver *Sun* and Regina *Leader*, as he travelled the country on the Indian trail. Long Lance's early articles showed the extent to which he had absorbed popular attitudes to Indians. He approvingly reported that the government had provided houses and 'proper' clothing for the Indians. The more uncivilized rituals had been abolished, and the Indian children were receiving an English/ Canadian Protestant education. However, he soon began to realize the price the Indians paid for 'civilization'. On one reservation the local doctor informed him that three out of four Indians died before the age of twenty. Among the novelties the Europeans had brought the Indians was tuberculosis.

At the Sarcee reserve Long Lance found a tribe that was literally dying, and lost no time in communicating this impending disaster to his readership:

The majority of the babies born on the Sarcee reserve die before they have reached the age of five, and a great proportion of the remaining one hundred and fifty Indians are past the age of 50 or 60 years . . . Seven deaths have occurred so far this year, with no births.

He also drew attention to the fact that while the Indians were permitted to sell their land, they did not control the money this raised:

Before the Blackfoots give up any of their treaty land for money that will be added to their tribal funds at Ottawa, they want the assurance that, instead of being used to pile up abstract interest on paper, these funds will be available for tribal improvement, and particularly towards establishing better medical and educational facilities.

He now began openly to criticize the authorities, questioning the outlawing of certain Indian ceremonies. 'Why is the Indian compelled to throw aside every native custom that formerly gave him self-respect?' he wrote. 'Why cannot he be allowed to remain a decent Indian instead of being forced into a ragged nondescript?' When the Allied Tribes made their representations to government, Long Lance spelt out their demands for his paper's white readership:

They are asking for the right to use the water on their reserves for irrigation purposes; for the right to fish for salmon for their own use; for the right to hew down timber on their own reserves.

Long Lance discovered the lives of the Indians of Saskatchewan to be more heavily regulated even than those of blacks in America's Deep South. An individual could not leave the reserve without permission from the government agent; he needed a permit before he could sell any of his farm's produce and had to seek permission from the agent to hold a traditional dance. Long Lance had seen enough. Now widely travelled and well acquainted with the facts, he began to make use of the many connections he had made in other parts of the country to secure aid, advice and support for the Indians of British Columbia from their more emancipated cousins. Although it was difficult for Indians to organize politically, and the Bureau of Indian Affairs could expel any journalist or 'political agitator' from a reservation, without giving a reason, the authorities, far from seeing Long Lance as a troublemaker, perceived him as an 'ideal' Indian, having fully assimilated the dominant culture. They had little idea of what he was up to in his travels and always gave him full cooperation and access to the reserves. At one time Long Lance would have appreciated what the Bureau of Indian Affairs was trying to do; it believed that the only way to help the Indian was by making him throw off his superstitions, stopping his children speaking 'mumbo-jumbo' and instead teaching them English, dressing and housing him like his conventional neighbours. It was their benevolent intention to make his descendants indistinguishable from the rest of society. Long Lance now saw the government's 'good intentions' depended on the annihilation of a whole way of life. He wrote that the Indian did not fear change, but worried that his son will 'be made into a white man, and that he might be lost to his home and people'. Perhaps this fear echoed Long Lance's own anxieties about his cultural identity.

Long Lance moved on to the Winnipeg *Tribune*, where he began to write about the Manitoba Indians. Although he was now a respected journalist, Long Lance still encountered racial prejudice where he was not known and was on at least one occasion refused entry to a hotel. On other occasions the Chief turned his racial difference to his social advantage; on the one hand he was among the first bright young things in Winnipeg in the roaring twenties to perfect the Black Bottom, and on the other, he could always draw on his exotic heritage to startle party-goers with a war whoop (which, it was said, could be heard several blocks away) or astonish and enchant the ladies with an authentic Indian war dance. He was a party animal, and to the forward-looking and hedonistic post-war generation, the perfect party guest.

However, Long Lance would have remained a local hero, and probably a temporary one, had not his stories begun to appear in national Canadian and American newspapers, which they did early in 1923. His articles ranged from vivid eye-witness accounts of ancient Indian rituals, such as the Blackfoot Sun Dance, to pieces based on interviews with elderly Indians, which exposed several of the convenient 'paleface' myths about Indian history. Possibly due to resentment from some quarters of the Native American community that he was using his Indian connections for self-publicity, his political activities came to an end, and in the summers of 1924 and 1925 Long Lance took a post as press representative for the Canadian Pacific Railroad, based at the fashionable and exclusive Banff Springs Hotel in the heart of the Canadian Rockies. Long Lance fulfilled his role – to advise and entertain wealthy tourists – to perfection. What better host to the rich at play than the well-groomed, well-spoken young Indian, at once subservient and noble, uniting both the wistfulness and the appeal of a beautiful wild animal tamed? Long Lance was now a Professional Indian.

In March 1927, after moving to New York City, Long Lance was commissioned by Randolph Hearst's Cosmopolitan Book Corporation to write his autobiography, which was published the following August to extravagant praise, catapulting him to fame. The foreword was by the humorous writer Irvin S. Cobb, then the most widely read and highest paid short-story writer in America. Although given to 'darkie' jokes, Cobb was an Indian enthusiast and collector of native artefacts and had befriended Long Lance, who became a frequent and welcome guest at Cobb's home on Long Island. This racial distinction made by most whites between 'Negroes' and 'Indians' was one of which Long Lance was only too aware, as he was admired and fêted at a time when many New York hotels, restaurants, theatres and even churches refused admission to blacks.

By autumn 1929 Long Lance was a celebrity in his own right, fulfilling many speaking engagements, being paid $100 a time (then a handsome fee) and endorsing a running shoe for the B. F. Goodrich Company. Long Lance appeared to have reached the peak of his fame. Then he became a film star. The makers of *The Silent Enemy* intended to make a film which showed Indian tribal life as it really was, eschewing the inaccurate cliché of the warlike Redskins of contemporary Westerns. Authenticity was the key, both in the photography of the wildlife on whom the Indians depended (the 'silent enemy' of the title meaning hunger) and in the portrayal of the Indians themselves. To this end hundreds of real Indians were employed on the film, many of whom did not speak English. The old chief in the film was to be played by the Sioux, Chauncey Yellow Robe, a great-nephew of Sitting Bull. He also advised on many details of the production. Long Lance provided both the necessary integrity and 'star quality' as the energetic hero Baluk.

The film was shot in the icy backwoods of northern Canada, and the film-makers' insistence on authenticity made it something of an ordeal for all concerned. Long Lance was at one point mauled by bear cubs, and his final stunt, in which he was required to spear a bull moose, was so dangerous that he made out a will on the eve of the shoot.

In May 1930 *The Silent Enemy* was released and became an instant hit with the critics, one of whom named it 'the only significant film to be produced in this country for a long time'. On his return to New York Long Lance's exotic good looks, as well as his glamorous achievements, put him on the 'A' list for society events. He socialized with the rich and famous, performing his war dance on request and dating starlets and showgirls. A couple of months earlier, he had met Anita Baldwin, one of the richest women in America, twice divorced and now in her mid-fifties. Baldwin, an insecure and unhappy woman, became strongly attached to the still youthful and charismatic Indian, encouraging him in his new-found interest: flying.

However, Long Lance's star was waning. He seemed unhappy and had begun to drink heavily. Anita Baldwin offered him a job, first as her secretary and then as her bodyguard on a trip to Europe. An anxious woman, Baldwin confided in Long Lance, telling him of her money worries, her fears for her life, the constant importunities of people asking her for money. A miserable child-hood and two unhappy marriages had made her paranoid and disillusioned. However, she did charitable works and contributed to various good causes – perhaps by this stage she saw Long Lance as one such cause. He behaved so badly on the European trip, however, drinking and being subject to extreme mood swings, that on their return to the US Baldwin left him in New York, as he had become 'too much of a responsibility'.

Having had few significant relationships prior to his involvement with Anita Baldwin, Long Lance pitched straight into another, probably more meaningful relationship. He fell in love with Elisabeth Randolph Clapp (known as Bessie), an eighteen-year-old dancer from a wealthy and socially prominent family, and seemed for a time to be happy. Bessie was certainly madly in love with him, and even after her marriage to another man, wrote to a close friend, 'I love him to this day'; 'the sweetest memories of all my life are the hours we spent together! I can never, never forget him'; and, despite a dutiful afterthought, described him as 'the one real love of my life (besides my husband)'. Yet when this devoted and beautiful young woman wanted to marry him, Long Lance claimed he was already engaged. As Bessie said: 'being an Indian, he wouldn't break his word to her.'

In late December 1931 Long Lance, many of whose old friends

had drifted away, returned to Anita Baldwin, who promised him further flying lessons and to help him get his own plane if he gave up his fast friends, other women and drinking. The plane did not materialize and by this time visitors to Baldwin's home noted that Long Lance was often drunk and abusive to her guards. He continued his playboy lifestyle, and Baldwin distrusted him sufficiently to have him followed. On 18 March 1932 Bessie Clapp telephoned Long Lance to tell him that she had got married and would like him to meet her new husband before the couple flew out to Japan. Long Lance politely declined the offer, regretting that he was about to return to Canada. The following night Long Lance shot himself at Anita Baldwin's home. *The New York Times* reported:

Chief Buffalo Child Long Lance, 36-year-old Indian author, was found shot to death yesterday in the home of Anita Baldwin, wealthy daughter of the late Lucky Baldwin, mining magnate. The authorities said it was suicide. Frank A. Nance, County Coroner, said there would be no inquest. Officials said they were unable to learn why Long Lance ended his life. The body, bearing a bullet wound in the head, was found by a Baldwin servant, and a revolver identified as belonging to the Indian was found near by. Servants told the authorities he had been drinking heavily . . .

None of Long Lance's friends believed he had committed suicide. Why should he? He had been drinking heavily, it was true. Had the news of Bessie Clapp's marriage tipped him over the edge? If he was in love with her, why had he turned her down, claiming he was already engaged? Was it simply the pressure of fame? Or was Long Lance's depression caused by having travelled so far from his roots that, rejected by Indian culture as a 'white boy', yet always an alien (albeit a glamorous one) in the dominant society, he now belonged nowhere? This last explanation is nearest the truth.

Since the appearance of his autobiography discreet inquiries into Long Lance's background had been making him uncomfortable.

Chief Buffalo Child Long Lance had not attended West Point nor had he been decorated once, let alone three times, in the Great War. He had never been promoted above acting sergeant. He was not thirty-five when he died, but forty-one. He was not a chief. He was not a Blackfoot. He was not, even, a Red Indian. The private detective employed by Anita Baldwin to look into his history reported that Long Lance's father was a 'full-blooded Negro'.

Chief Buffalo Child Long Lance was born Sylvester Clark Long on 1 December 1890, hundreds of miles from the Great Plains, in Winston-Salem, North Carolina. The question of his parents' racial identity is probably impossible to settle. Canadian historian Donald Smith, who first fully researched Long Lance's story, has pieced together the following picture. The family believed that Sylvester's great-grandmother had been an Indian slave. She had a daughter by Robert Carson, a white slave-trader and plantation owner. This daughter, Adeline, also had a daughter, Sallie, by a white man, senator Andrew Cowles, a regular visitor to Carson's plantation. Sallie, who would have been one-quarter Indian and three-quarters white, was Sylvester's mother. His father Joe was a slave in the family of the Revd Miles Long. Joe believed his father was white and his mother was a Cherokee slave. These accounts, combined with Sallie's, made Sylvester slightly more white than Indian. Turning to the physical evidence, photographs of Sylvester's family are less than helpful. They do not seem distinctively black, white or Indian, although the viewer might accept any of these labels. Joe Long wearing a suit, having a formal portrait taken in a photographer's studio, could be a European; Joe Long in dungarees, posing with a broom outside the school where he worked as janitor, seems to be an African-American. While Sylvester's brothers, snapped in a nonchalant attitude seem to have African features, Sylvester styled as a Plains Indian appears, at least to non-Indians, utterly convincing. Context and costume – as ever – heavily influence our 'reading' of such images.

With no hope of ever being able to prove their ancestry Sallie and Joe Long had good reason to cling to the stories they had been told about their forebears. In Winston, North Carolina, one was either white or coloured and that was that. It seems likely that Sylvester's background was a mixture of black, white and Indian. South and North Carolina abound in groups who are, in the words of one writer, 'neither fish nor fowl', as marriages between Indians and white settlers occurred at least as early as the late sixteenth century. Later, the fact that white men routinely 'took' Indian and black slave women, with or without their permission, ensured that the purity of both the black and the Indian races became diluted with each succeeding generation. If Joe and Sallie Long were, as seems likely, a mixture of African, European and Native American blood, they were by no means unique in this. However, as far as the authorities were concerned, anyone not entirely white was entirely black. The segregation laws in the South meant that Sylvester faced a future of separate and inferior schooling and could not hope for much more than the most menial occupation. He would never stand beside a white man on equal terms at a work-bench, would never eat at the same table, never drink from the same water fountain, never attend the same church nor even use the same urinal as a white man.

It was not only the laws which established and maintained segregation which restricted the lives of black people in the South; a whole culture of segregation ensured that the colour bar was scrupulously maintained. It could be as dangerous to breach this racist etiquette as it was to break the segregation laws. Stetson Kennedy's *Jim Crow Guide to the USA* demonstrates the informal rules of behaviour which helped to keep non-whites firmly in their place, and which still applied in the late 1950s:

Interracial etiquette prescribes that nonwhites always be introduced *to* whites, never vice versa . . . Under no circumstances does interracial etiquette permit you to shake hands with a person of the other race anywhere in segregated territory [. . .] If you are white, *never* say 'Mr',

'Mrs', 'sir', or 'ma'am' to nonwhites, but always call them by their first names. If you are nonwhite, *always* say 'Mr', 'Mrs', 'sir', or 'ma'am' to whites, and never call them by their first names [. . .]

Regardless of your age, class, distinction, or education, you are apt to frequently be called 'boy' or 'girl'. However, if your hair is actually grey you are more likely to be called 'uncle' or 'auntie' [. . .]

When in segregated territory it is decidedly dangerous to enter a white person's front door if you are nonwhite. On the other hand, if you are white you will find that a white face is the equivalent of a search-warrant anywhere in the South, enabling you to enter the front door of any nonwhite's dwelling . . . It is regarded as improper for a nonwhite to sit down in the parlour of a white home . . . If you are white, the etiquette says you may feel free to sit anywhere in a nonwhite home, without waiting for an invitation [. . .]

If you are a nonwhite man in segregated territory you are required to remove your hat while talking with white persons [. . .] in fact, you may be arrested for wearing your hat while talking to a white person [. . .]

Whether walking on the pavement, or even driving in a car, the black was without exception required to give way to the white. When boarding buses and trams, blacks were expected to wait until all whites had entered. Segregated seating on the bus of course ensured that blacks had to stand rather than sit in an empty seat designated 'whites only'. Blacks were often denied entry to shops or made to wait until all white customers had been served. They were often not permitted to try clothes on, or, if buying a hat, made to suffer the indignity of being required to wear a cloth skull-cap. Here personal recollection is as vivid as empirical fact in conveying the atmosphere of the time. The black American blues musician Johnny Mars (who was brought up in the South under the colour bar) recalls waiting for his sister in a shop while she bought something. He noticed that the white shopgirl, having inadvertently touched his sister's hand when she was paying, automatically pulled out a handkerchief and carefully and ostentatiously wiped her hands afterwards.

Both the formal legislation and the informal codes of behaviour were rationalized and informed by academic reasoning which went largely unquestioned. The impossibility for a coloured boy like Sylvester Long of ever having the opportunity to prove his abilities is amply illustrated by the sort of attitudes which were seen as respectable and reasonable at the time he was growing up:

The mind of the Negro can best be understood by likening it to that of a child. For instance, the Negro lives in the present, his interests are objective, and his actions are governed by his emotions.

So far as the Negro problem affects the United States, it arises from the presence within the country of approximately ten million persons, Negroes of an alien, inferior and unassimilable race.

The Negro has no invention, but he can be trained to do good mechanical work.

In consequence of his emotional dominance the Negro has feeble inhibiting power. Whatever feeling, desire, or passion seizes him for the moment, tends to express itself in immediate action. Lack of inhibition in the Negro explains his sexual incontinence and his disposition to quarrel, fight and steal.

The mental development of the Negro race is sufficient to allow us to infer that they are considerably less gifted than the White race; that in power of reasoning, as well as in energy and in ethical standards, they are bound to be different from and inferior to the Whites.

The Negro cannot think for himself and is lacking in reflective faculties; he cannot do anything except by imitation; he imitates the Whites in everything but the right thing; like the monkey, his sensual nature is the limit of his ideals. He learns to read and write very readily, but beyond that his mind is dull and vacant. We have records of full-blooded Negroes being educated but they are prodigies.

By defining blacks as essentially lesser mortals, white culture justified their inferior status as citizens. Such attitudes were as good as invisible chains, which continued to bind the Long family and millions of others well after the abolition of slavery in a position of abject subservience. That blacks were destined to live on a horizonless desert is reflected in the map of Sylvester's early life. Living at 4½ Street, he attended the equally dour sounding Depot Street School for Negroes. Sylvester, anticipating the so-called life Winston-Salem had to offer a coloured boy, decided something had to change. In the true spirit of a romantic hero he ran away and joined the circus.

The circus opened Sylvester's eyes to a whole new world. While the details are somewhat hazy, it seems that at some point the young Sylvester came into contact with a Wild West show – possibly Buffalo Bill's famous outfit – and he saw, for the first time, non-white men taking centre stage, being admired and applauded by white audiences. His experience with horses in the circus seems to have enabled him to get a job on the Wild West show. When his potential employer took him for an Indian, he knew better than to contradict him. (This 'mis-take', of course, resonates strongly with turning-points in the lives of other impostors.) He lived and worked with 'real' Indians, picking up a smattering of Cherokee spoken and sign language and absorbing details of the culture and Indian stories and legends.

Adopting Native American identity explained away Sylvester's non-white appearance but also had other distinct advantages. Although Indians were regarded by many white people as, like blacks, biologically inferior to whites, there were important differences in perception. Firstly, the Indians comprised a nation, with which white men had been at war. (The subjugation of all tribes had been achieved by 1890, the year Sylvester Long was born, and a year which saw the last episode of white violence against Indians, when 300 unarmed men, women and children were massacred at Wounded Knee.) Many whites therefore had an – albeit grudging

– respect for the Indian, and others felt some shame at the way they had been treated. In the South 'respect' towards a Negro or 'shame' at how they had been treated were simply not in the white vocabulary. Thomas F. Gossett, in his study of race, describes the background to the differences in white North Americans' perception towards 'Negroes' and 'Indians':

One can find in nineteenth-century America much more praise of the Indian than of the Negro, though the Negro was allowed to survive as a slave whereas the Indian was either slaughtered or banished to lands where it was impossible for him to thrive. De Tocqueville observed that the Negro and the Indian were fundamentally different in character. 'The servility of the one dooms him to slavery,' he said, and 'the pride of the other to death.'

Other men [. . .] compared the Indian and the Negro, nearly always to the advantage of the Indian. 'The indomitable, courageous, proud Indian,' exclaimed Louis Agassiz, 'in how very different a light he stands by the side of the submissive, obsequious, imitative negro.'

Indians themselves compounded the 'difference' as they too were quite capable of racism against blacks, particularly in parts of the South where there were three layers of segregation, and they intensely resented being confused with 'niggers', whom they excluded from their schools and colleges. Some tribes had also kept black slaves. It was clear to Sylvester, at least, that since he couldn't pass as white, being Indian was infinitely preferable to being black.

By the summer of 1909 Sylvester had decided that his only ticket out of the life Winston-Salem had in store for him was to gain acceptance as a Red Indian. Yet he set his sights considerably higher than the life the circus had to offer. The first step in his campaign was to get himself into the most famous Indian school in the US at Carlisle, Pennsylvania. In order to qualify he knocked a year off his age – this little lie was to be the first of a series of deceptions which on their own were unimportant but which when put together over a period of years created an entirely new persona. The aim of the Carlisle Residential School was to give the Indian 'a white man's chance'; Sylvester graduated top of his class. At college he shifted his place of birth from Winston to Cherokee county, and by the time he left St John's Military Academy – where he enjoyed the status of being the only Indian and was known as 'Chief' – he had Indianized his surname Long into the heroic-sounding Long Lance.

Long Lance's next target was to get himself admitted to the prestigious United States Military Academy at West Point. This would be no mean achievement, only three non-whites having graduated from West Point in over a century. Long Lance appealed to President Woodrow Wilson, describing himself as a member of the Eastern Cherokee Tribe (untrue) and aged twenty (at twenty-four, his true age, he would not qualify). The president's endorsement of Long Lance's candidature received wide press coverage, which emphasized his identity as a 'full-blooded Cherokee'.

Astonishingly, after all this preparation by an extremely able student and athlete, Long Lance flunked the West Point exam. His biographer Donald Smith believes this was a deliberate strategy, reasoning that Long Lance had learned from friends at his old school that the War Department was having some difficulty authenticating his origins and had decided to abandon a course which would almost certainly have revealed his imposture.

Still determined to make a name for himself, he headed north, and in August 1916 he enlisted in the Canadian Army and was soon on a ship to the killing fields of Europe. Reluctant to let go of his dream altogether when he enlisted, under the heading 'previous military experience' he unflinchingly wrote 'West Point'. During his war service Long Lance was promoted to acting sergeant, but promoted himself in letters home to lieutenant. Canadian Indians were one of the more exotic aspects of the Great War, having a well-earned reputation as crack shots; the ebullient and charismatic Long Lance attracted sufficient attention to warrant an article in the US press, which depicted him as an Indian scholar and military hero. He was injured twice and finally moved to a desk job in London.

After the war Long Lance headed for Alberta, Canada, and a new beginning. In Western Canada Long Lance found that although Indians were discriminated against, he encountered nothing like the prejudice endured by non-whites in the Deep South. In the byline to his first article for the Calgary *Herald* he took the opportunity of establishing a few new 'facts' about himself. He moved his birthplace again, to eastern Oklahoma (1,500 miles from North Carolina). He had been educated at West Point (no change there) and had been an intelligence officer in Italy during the war, receiving the Croix de Guerre for bravery, and promotion to captain. Popular at the paper, once again known as 'Chief', Long Lance worked hard, developed a well-groomed and suave appearance and began dating white women (in his home town men could be lynched for even looking at a white woman in the 'wrong' way).

Knowing what we now know it is easier to understand Long Lance's naivety in his early articles on the Indians. Despite his claims, he had never been on a reservation before, his parents had never lived on a reservation. However, the Indians appreciated his attempts to tell their story, and in 1922 the Bloods honoured him by formally adopting him into their tribe and giving him a Blackfoot name. After the old chief, Mountain Horse, had completed the ceremony, naming him Buffalo Child, Long Lance was as much a Blackfoot as Edward, Prince of Wales, whom Mountain Horse had adopted three years earlier during the prince's royal tour of Canada. Long Lance chose to ignore the fact that the title was honorary: his dream had come true; he had been reborn as a Plains Indian.

Having had several photographs taken in his tribal regalia, Long Lance moved on to the Vancouver *Sun*, by which time he had carefully altered all references to himself as a Cherokee in his portfolio of articles, carefully inserting in their place Blood or

Blackfoot. His reasoning was entirely logical: Cherokees were largely integrated, although second-class citizens; in the south it was not unusual for a non-white person to have some Cherokee blood. The Plains Indians of the north-west, however, were seen as 'real' Indians, having remained largely insular societies, living on isolated reserves, and retaining much of the traditional appearance and culture of their forebears. Long Lance knew that people were much more likely to take him – and his writing – seriously if he was a 'full-blood' Blackfoot, rather than a doubtful Cherokee. Perhaps more importantly, unlike in Carolina, no one would suspect an Indian from the North of being part black. Long Lance's Indianization was now complete: the part-black, part-white, part-Indian Sylvester Clark Long from Winston, Carolina was gone; in his place stood the full-blood Blackfoot, Buffalo Child Long Lance.

As he began to write for the Canadian and US national publications, he of course became more widely known. Long Lance must have been supremely confident in his constructed persona to court publicity as energetically as he did. In fact, his lies became increasingly reckless: in one interview he claimed he was a chief, in another, that the Plains Indians all looked upon him as their leader. He also awarded himself two university degrees. Again, knowing what we now know, his sheer nerve seems astonishing. His editor and good friend at the Winnipeg *Tribune*, Vernon Knowles, asked him:

. . . if he ever felt any of the savage urge supposedly underlying the superficial in all his race. 'No,' he replied. And then he added, quite seriously, 'Except once. The first German I knew I killed in the war – I bayoneted him during an attack at close quarters. You know, I had a frightful time restraining the impulse to scalp him. Just why, I never have been able to fathom. It must have been hereditary impulse for I'd never seen anybody scalped nor had I any inclinations that way before.'

When he was commissioned to write his autobiography, Long Lance realized he had a lot of homework to do. He spent a great deal of time with Mike Eagle Speaker, an Indian with whom he had become blood brothers, filling in the gaps in his knowledge of the Indians' way of life. In the autobiography Long Lance dressed up much of Mike Eagle Speaker's childhood as his own. The strongly authentic flavour of the book is a testament to Long Lance's journalistic skills. However, anyone examining the book closely would have noticed important errors, as did Charles Burke, Commissioner of the Bureau of Indian Affairs (US), when he tried to find out more about its author. He discovered that Long Lance had failed the West Point entrance exam, that he was not a Blood Indian and only an honorary Blackfoot. For some reason Burke, who was unusually sympathetic to the Indians' problems, did not challenge the publishers, but in thanking them for the complimentary copy they had sent him, casually termed it 'a publication of fiction'. It was at this moment that Long Lance conveniently disappeared to northern Canada to make *The Silent Enemy*. On the set he was also evidently under some pressure; living and working with 'real' Indians put him in an especially vulnerable situation. Chauncey Yellow Robe in particular had his suspicions about Long Lance but, like Charles Burke, kept them to himself. The much publicized will Long Lance made at this time was designed to consolidate his account of his roots, naming his brother as Michael Eagle Speaker and leaving his estate to the St Paul's Blood Indian School, ensuring that various people on the crew witnessed the will. Back in New York he evidently felt secure and again succumbed to the temptation to enhance his past further. He told a journalist he was wounded eight times in the war and was decorated by three governments. He was very publicly digging his own grave.

Chauncey Yellow Robe, who had proved himself a stickler for authenticity on *The Silent Enemy*, had also discovered Long Lance was not a Blackfoot and alerted William Chanler, legal counsel for *The Silent Enemy*. When confronted by Chanler, Long Lance tried to talk his way out of it, but Chanler was not convinced and had his background investigated. The deeper he dug the more likely it seemed that Long Lance was by Southern racial standards a Negro. During February and March of 1930, the rumour began to leak out. Irvin S. Cobb, who had written in the preface to Long Lance's autobiography:

I know of no man better fitted to write this book about the true American Indian. I claim there is authentic history in these pages and verity and most of all, a power to describe in English words the thoughts, the instincts, the events which originally were framed in a native language. And I claim the white man will owe him a debt for this work of his.

. . . soon changed his tune. He was frankly disgusted that he had been taken in, exclaiming: 'To think that we had him here in the house! We're so ashamed! We entertained a nigger!' Cobb's shame was rooted deep in his racism: he had been deceived into giving himself the opportunity of liking and respecting a black man. Although most of Long Lance's friends refrained from such poisonous outbursts, many of them drifted away.

However, the scandal was still not public, and with the publicity tour for *The Silent Enemy* about to begin, it was not in the filmmakers' interests to discredit their star. As an insurance policy they secured signed affidavits from Winston, Carolina, stating that Long Lance was white and Indian. As long as they could prove he wasn't black, they had ceased to care what tribe he came from. However, Long Lance knew this was not a pardon, merely a stay of execution. It was at this point that the heavy drinking started. By the time he met Bessie Clapp, true love had come too late. Already embroiled with the complex and demanding Anita Baldwin, he was losing the plot, and disentangled himself from Bessie, pretending he was already engaged. Isolated, Long Lance became progressively more dependent on Baldwin, who in turn became increasingly disenchanted with his dark moods, his drinking and womanizing. When

Bessie Clapp, perhaps the only woman Long Lance ever really loved, called to say she'd got married, he must have realized, finally, that he would never be able to allow anyone to get really close to him. And the immediate identity crisis loomed: he couldn't carry on being an Indian any more, and he couldn't face going back to being black. There was literally nowhere to go, no one to be.

After Long Lance's suicide, Vernon Knowles, his friend and colleague, wrote:

Chief Buffalo Child Long Lance, probably the world's best known American Indian, is dead. Child of the teepees, Canadian soldier of the Great War, graduate of Carlisle University, master in the realm of arts and letters, chief of the Blackfeet, magazine writer, author of books, newspaperman extraordinary, rollicking, jovial spirit and genial soul – if there is anything in the belief of his people in the existence of a Happy Hunting Ground in the hereafter, I wish him all the happy hunting that he could have wished himself.

Clearly his friend had not yet heard the rumours about Long Lance's imposture, but perhaps if he had he would have generously concluded, as did many Native Americans, that Long Lance was a Redskin 'in his heart'. There is little to add to this tragic story except to observe that, when Long Lance shot himself, America lost a great journalist, an acclaimed film actor and a champion of the downtrodden. Yet had America had its way, that same man's greatest service to his country would have been sweeping the sidewalk in North Carolina.

9. Other Foreign Bodies and Exotic Aliens

Impostures succeed because, not in spite, of their fictitious-
ness. They take wing with congenial cultural fantasies . . .
– Hillel Schwarz, *The Culture of the Copy*, 1996

The appeal of a Native American identity for Long Lance is comparable in many ways with the attraction of masculine identity for
James Barry: it offered an escape route from a life which had clearly
defined and narrow parameters. Both Long Lance and Barry were
able to develop their natural talents and abilities to an extent which
the bounds of the identities they were born with would never
have permitted. The idea of becoming a 'Red Indian' had other
attractions, however, which appealed to men who were not black.

Grey Owl never claimed, like Long Lance, to be one hundred
per cent Indian. Although photographs of the great man offer an
utterly convincing portrait of an Ojibwa Indian, his blue eyes were
accounted for by his mixed parentage: he explained he was born
in Mexico to a Scottish father and an Apache mother and later
settled with the Ojibwas. Other parallels with Long Lance are
illuminating. Like him, Grey Owl sought to reinscribe his Indian
identity by writing about Native American life, publishing four
bestselling books. In common with many Native Americans (and
Long Lance), Grey Owl served in the First World War where
Indians were renowned for their marksmanship. Whereas Long
Lance had taken up the cause of Native Americans, whose culture
was being systematically eradicated by white colonial and federal
administrators, Grey Owl, returning from the war, was horrified

at the devastation being wrought by the mining and timber industries, and promoted the values of conservation: he became the prototype eco-warrior.

Grey Owl owed much of his enlightenment, as he freely acknowledged, to his wife Anahareo, an Iroquois Indian eighteen years his junior. It was Anahareo who, by adopting two orphaned beaver kittens whose mother had been killed in one of Grey Owl's traps, caused him to reconsider his attitudes and approach to the natural environment, and to reinterpret it as something which should be protected rather than plundered. He gave up trapping and hunting and began his career as a writer and lecturer in order to raise money for the preservation of wild animals. Grey Owl recounted his and Anahareo's adventures in his first book, *Pilgrims of the Wild*, and she appeared in many of the films made by him, with the result that in the public's eyes she became 'just as much a hero' as he.

Like Long Lance, Grey Owl was a talented writer, having 'a genius for describing animal life' and he proved an equally enthralling speaker. Just as people in their thousands bought his books, on his first lecturing tour in Britain over a quarter of a million people flocked to hear him describe the natural world rapidly vanishing in the North American territories. On his second tour he was presented at court, his tales thrilling the young princesses Elizabeth and Margaret. An exhausting American tour in 1928 proved too much; shortly afterwards, weak with fatigue, he caught pneumonia, and died.

Only then did the man behind Grey Owl begin to emerge. A fellow naturalist wrote an obituary for the Toronto *Star* in which he claimed that Grey Owl was actually an Englishman named Archibald Belaney. A debate began: those, for example, who had served in Flanders with Grey Owl spoke of the way he crawled, undetected, across no-man's land; his sharp-shooting and knife-throwing skills; his 'gift of absolute immobility for long periods' – all of which proclaimed him a true Indian. His publisher, Lovat Dickson, and Anahareo, also backed up his story. Yet at the same time investigative journalism turned up fact after fact which cast doubt on Grey Owl's origins. It was Lovat Dickson, the man perhaps least disposed to disbelieve Grey Owl, who, in his attempts to gather evidence to support what he believed to be Grey Owl's authentic account of his birth and background, uncovered the whole truth.

Archibald Belaney was born in 1887 to an English father and a European-American mother. His father was a man of undisciplined appetites, hopeless with money, women and drink, apparently merely the last in a long line of disastrous Belaney males. When the couple separated, Mr Belaney left the country (he was later to die in a drunken brawl) and Mrs Belaney took a younger son, Hugh, with her to London. The four-year-old Archie was sent to live with two maiden aunts in Hastings. It appears that as a boy he became fascinated by the idea of the 'Red Indians' and spent hours reading and fantasizing on the subject. At the age of eighteen he persuaded his aunts to send him to Toronto – ostensibly to study farming, but his private plan was to 'become' an Indian. During the months leading up to his departure, he prepared himself for his new life:

He knew that he would have to be hardy. He trained himself rigorously to go without food or drink of any kind for a day, sometimes two at a stretch. Some nights he would sleep on the hard floor of his room, or creep out into the garden with a blanket, and sleep curled up under a tree until dawn.

Like Long Lance – and many other impostors – Grey Owl found it impossible to sustain close relationships. Lovat Dickson discovered that he had had not one but four wives. Soon after arriving in Canada he settled with an Ojibwa tribe and married Angele, an Ojibwa woman. She was succeeded by his English childhood sweetheart Constance Ivy Holmes, whom he married while convalescing in Hastings in 1917. It seems that the hiatus provided by the First World War marks the point where Grey Owl made the transition from a naturalized to a 'natural' Indian. It was after the war that he met and married Anahareo, his most significant partner, and began the career that made the name Grey Owl famous. The relationship collapsed in 1936 (although this fact was not communicated to Grey Owl's fans), and he later married a young French-Canadian, Yvonne Perrier. He died shortly afterwards at the age of fifty.

Why did Archibald Belaney become Grey Owl? He was certainly not in it for the money. His publisher reports that Belaney went 'white as a sheet' when told how much he was to be paid for the first British lecture tour, and though his books ran through multiple editions and were widely translated, 'he was completely disinterested in money, and never once inquired how we were doing.' Most impostors, as has become apparent, are products of their time and of their background. Belaney's success as Grey Owl, particularly among his large British following, can also be partly explained in the light of the period.

Just as Long Lance's appearance in the US in the 1920s had peculiarly fitted the glamorous and exotic (not to say escapist) appetites of the time, Grey Owl's appearance in England on his 1935 lecture tour caused a sensation: he 'spoke pure romance' to a people living in the shadow of depression and impending disaster. As his publisher described his appeal:

The voice from the forests momentarily released us from some spell. In contrast with Hitler's screaming, ranting voice, and the remorseless clang of modern technology, Grey Owl's words evoked an unforgettable charm, lighting in our minds the vision of a cool, quiet place, where men and animals lived in love and trust together.

This provides a context for Grey Owl's popularity, rather than an explanation for Belaney's imposture. For that, his background seems to offer likely clues.

The damage done to the boy Archie by his parent's abandonment of him is perhaps incalculable. Into the breach stepped the two maiden aunts from Hastings, who seem irresistibly to insist on a stereotypical image from childhood fiction: one physically large and commanding, the other small and hesitant. Although Ada was the younger sister, it was she who dominated: 'Carrie was Ada's shadow, a constant, muffled echo.' Even Lovat Dickson, who interviewed Belaney's aunts while attempting to establish Grey Owl's identity as authentic after his death, noted in Ada's manner a pride in her 'ability to crush people'. Her love for the nephew she adopted was 'fierce and possessive'. As a child:

Ada dominated his life. She became both mother and father to him, and he never knew whether he feared her or loved her. She bathed and dressed him when he was too young to do these things for himself; she taught him his prayers, read him stories, tucked him up and kissed him goodnight. But her wrath was terrible when it was kindled; she was the only one who ever punished him, and so was the only one he ever wanted to please and impress.

Anahareo, who of course imagined someone in Mexico when Grey Owl spoke of his aunt, gained the impression that:

. . . she over-indulged her vanity by attempting to turn her nephew into a super-being. Her approach to that end was much too severe, and as Archie said, 'She only succeeded in making a devil out of me.'

Belaney appears to have had a double dose of the kinds of fathering common in the lives of other impostors. On the one hand there was the absent, rejecting (real) father, and on the other there was the demanding, judgemental and domineering Ada, a father-figure in skirts. He couldn't win. His ambivalent feelings towards Ada were revealed in the fact that while he *wrote* of his aunt in glowing terms, he *spoke* of her in quite a different tone, telling Anahareo 'I hated her guts. She was a good-looking woman, always primped and starched, a snob and a perfectionist to a T. All she lacked was a human heart.'

Long Lance and Grey Owl both became champions for the underdog, whether that was the Indian people or the animals. Perhaps that was because they both conceived themselves to be of that class: Sylvester Long as a black in the Deep South, Archibald Belaney as an unwanted child foisted on an aunt he could never please. Both undoubtedly primarily sought escape, but both also invested time, energy and their considerable talents in defending Native American culture, its landscape and wildlife. In this respect they remain the two greatest Native Americans that never were.

Those impostors whose masquerades are discovered during their lifetimes may well envy those who, like Grey Owl, are in no position to face difficult questions by the time the truth emerges. Sioux Indian Chief, William Red Fox, almost made it to the end when his mask began to slip; he was 101 when his autobiography caused a serious publishing controversy in 1972. Red Fox's description of the massacre at Wounded Knee in 1890 was recognized as an almost verbatim plagiarism of an account by another author which had appeared in 1940. Despite the fact that this discovery cast doubt on the reliability of Red Fox's general testimony, the furore enhanced rather than harmed his career, and the centenarian became a chatshow star.

Red Fox was apparently 'not noticeably perturbed' by the storm whipped up by his book; part of his charm was his open acknowledgement that most of his life had been spent exploiting the white people's fascination with Indian culture and tales of the Wild West – he might then go on to describe to a goggle-eyed audience how to construct a fish-hook out of a fieldmouse's rib.

The concept of 'living memory' works powerfully on our emotions rather than our intellects; watching this ancient Indian on television, apparently remembering events which were already the stuff of history books, made a concrete link for viewers with a past which otherwise seemed decreasingly real. While they knew that Red Fox might not be authentic, he *seemed* real, and certainly more real than words on a page. He seemed a living link with a past that was already fantastic, and with the passing of this witness, audiences knew, the reality of that past would die a bit more. As it happened, one of the few aspects of his life story which was not disputed was his age. He died in Texas in 1976, 105 years old.

What does it mean to ask whether Red Fox's stories were true? Like Long Lance and Grey Owl he had not, on the whole, tampered with the historical facts, but had only misrepresented his relation to them. These racial impostors capitalized on the fact that, by and large, white people were fascinated by the concept of the noble savage: the little they knew of his history and culture was characterized by a nice blend of heroism and suffering. Above all, he remained a glamorous figure, faintly dangerous and never entirely knowable. It seems quite conceivable that this impression was what appealed not only to their public but to the men who became Long Lance, Grey Owl and Red Fox.

A Canadian woman who as a young graduate had assisted Grey Owl on his first British lecture tour wrote thirty-five years later on the delicate subject of honesty and imposture:

I still see and feel the almost magical impact his presence and message had on audiences, large and small, wherever he spoke. I literally saw him capture the attention and often the hearts of the very people he criticised and often scolded for their indifference or hostility . . .

In this his honour was above suspicion. Therefore it never occurred to me to doubt his statements about his father being a Scotsman and his mother a full-blooded Indian. Nor did I make any connection, then or since, between that detail and the authenticity of his being what he became and what he is remembered for.

If as later investigation showed he was not part Indian, well I for one am reluctant to describe him as an impostor, or put any pejorative label upon him. After all, an impostor is a hypocrite or a quack with devious ulterior motives, a person who misleads knowingly or is without qualification to advise. Certainly where his life and work were concerned he had earned the right to be respected and cleared of either epithet.

Long before pollution and the needless killing of wild-life began to worry the world as is today the case, Grey Owl strove to keep our Canadian Spring singing. In the end, that's what counts most, is it not?

Although these words speak specifically of Grey Owl, in a way they serve for all three of these 'Indian' histories. That these were all three magical voices is beyond question. The songs they sang were no less beautiful, nor any less true, for the fact that they were not their own.

Significantly, the Native American community took a generous view of their adoptive brothers. Native Americans who 'knew better' almost universally kept their counsel, accepting the spirit in which these men embraced their culture and stood up for their interests. Generally, of course, the principal problem with racial imposture is exposure by someone whose knowledge of the impostor's adopted heritage exceeds his own. How much better, then, to choose, like George Psalmanazar, to come from somewhere no one has been; better still, like Princess Caraboo, somewhere that does not even exist.

George Psalmanazar, self-declared Formosan prince, was launched on the London scene by the Revd William Innes, an army chaplain, who introduced him to Henry Compton, the Bishop of London, in 1704. The bishop, a leading light in the Society for the Propagation of the Gospel in Foreign Parts, encouraged the young Formosan, whom Innes had recently baptized as a Christian, to make a translation of the church catechism into Formosan.

Psalmanazar also quickly addressed the fact that hardly anything was known about Formosa (now Taiwan) in England by publishing *An Historical and Geographical Description of Formosa*. The book was an instant success, appealing both to minds hungry for accounts of foreign travel and culture and to those with less laudable interests. One excerpt will serve as illustration of the latter:

We also eat human Flesh . . . tho' we feed only upon our open Enemies, slain or made captive in the Field, or else upon Malefactors legally executed; the Flesh of the latter is our greatest dainty, and is four times dearer than other rare and delicious meat; we buy it of the Executioner, for the Bodies of all publick capital Offenders are his Fees; as soon as the Criminal is dead, he cuts the Body in pieces, squeezeth out the Blood, and makes his House a shambles for the Flesh of Men and Women, where all People that can afford it come and buy.

I remember, about ten Years ago, a tall, well complexion'd, pretty fat Virgin, about 19 Years of Age, and Tire-woman to the Queen, was found guilty of High Treason for designing to poison the King; and accordingly she was condemn'd to suffer the most cruel Death that could be invented . . . her sentence was, to be nailed to a Cross, there to be fed and kept alive as long as possible; the Sentence was put in execution, when she fainted with the cruel Torment, the Hang-man gave her Strong Liquors, etc. to revive her, the sixth day she died: Her Long-sufferings, Youth and good Constitution, made her Flesh so tender, delicious and valuable, that the Executioner sold it for above eight Taillos, for there was such thronging to this inhuman Market, that Men of great fashion thought themselves fortunate if they could purchase a pound or two of it.

The handsome and erudite Psalmanazar himself also became an object of excited curiosity. Although he had practised cannibalism in his own country, in England he contented himself with raw meat. (Formosan husbands, he also explained, were entitled to eat their adulterous wives. When told this was a 'barbarous' custom by an English noblewoman, he did admit it was a 'little unmannerly'.) The fascinating details of life in Formosa explored in his book ensured a second edition within the year; readers lapped up the accounts of 'the Impurity of Polygamy and other Uncleanness'. Polygamy was necessary due to the ritual slaughter of 18,000 baby boys per year, their hearts sacrificed to the elephant god, resulting in a constant shortage of males. Formosan justice was also satisfyingly bloody: murderers were hung upside-down and shot to death with arrows, while other offenders were torn to pieces by dogs.

At first, Psalmanazar had his believers and his doubters in equal measure. Although the likes of the Archbishop of Canterbury and academic Samuel Reynolds (father of the painter, Joshua) supported his claims, his more eminent challengers included Sir Isaac Newton and the astronomer Dr Edmund Halley of the Royal Society. His most disarming response to the suspicious was to point out that it would be impossible for an Englishman in Formosa to prove he was indeed English, so little did the two countries know about each other.

Bishop Compton, hoping that Psalmanazar would spread the Christian word on his return to his native country, arranged for him to study at Christ Church, Oxford, where he also reportedly lectured with a pet snake draped around his neck (the traditional Formosan method of keeping cool, apparently). Psalmanazar wrote to a friend of the damage his Oxford days wrought on his health; indeed, those who passed his lodging in the small hours noted that he worked round the clock – an observation confirmed by his chambermaids, who often found his bed had not been slept in.

Returning to London, following an acrimonious parting with his companion, the Revd Innes, Psalmanazar seemed to 'lose the plot' and became an increasingly ridiculous figure, unable to make his claims convincing. He gradually faded from public life and embarked on a second career as a serious academic writer. These were the days in which large-scale authoritative works, which ran into several volumes, were first being produced by collectives of writers (rather than a single author), to whom, individually, periods of history or subjects of study were parcelled out. This was often thankless and always laborious work, and Psalmanazar seems to have approached it as a kind of penance for his profligate past. He made substantial contributions to such daunting titles as *An Universal History from the Earliest Account of Time* (1736–50), in the light of which challenge it is perhaps not surprising that he took refuge in a nightly dose of 'ten to twelve drops of opium in a pint of punch'. To the encyclopaedic *Complete System of Geography* (1747) his offering included the section on Formosa, in which he took advantage of the opportunity to apologize for his earlier account while (without naming Innes), deflecting the blame on to:

. . . some few Persons, who for private Ends took Advantage of his youthful Vanity, to encourage him to an Imposture, which he might otherwise never had that thought, much less the Confidence to have carried on.

During a bout of serious illness, he had already confessed that he had never set foot on Formosa and had invented the saga so as to lead a life of 'shameless idleness, vanity and extravagance'. He also wrote (for posthumous publication, so none could charge him with a profit motive) his own, true, memoirs, giving a full confession of his imposture, but no hint of his true identity, place of origin or date of birth, which are still unknown. When he was sixteen, his mother had sent him on a 500 mile journey (on foot) to find his father in Germany, hoping that he would support the boy as she was unable to do so. George found his father was just as poor as his mother, and after a short career as a beggar he travelled to Holland, inventing *en route* a new identity for himself as a Japanese. Meeting the Revd Innes in Holland, the former challenged him to a translation test. Although Innes was not qualified to check the accuracy of the translation, by making the young man repeat the exercise he could see that the two versions differed substantially. Satisfied that Psalmanazar was an impostor, rather than expose him, Revd Innes collaborated in the deception, changing Psalmanazar's nationality to Formosan, which would be much more difficult to disprove, and taking him to London. Innes aimed to gain favour in the Bishop of London's eyes by having achieved the conversion to Christianity and baptism of this 'heathen'.

As for the selfless sacrifice of his health to his studies at Oxford, Psalmanazar admitted that he achieved this illusion by leaving a candle burning all night in his room and sleeping in a chair so as not to disturb the bedclothes. When he quitted his rooms, 'I went still limping about like an old gouty fellow, though no man could enjoy a better share of health and flow of spirits than I did all the time I staid there.'

In his latter years Psalmanazar of course really did work extremely hard, a fact which impressed Dr Samuel Johnson, who, while Psalmanazar lived, preferred the company of the reformed impostor to any other. He said of Psalmanazar that his 'piety, penitence and virtue exceeded almost what we read as wonderful even in the lives of the saints', and declared 'I should as soon have thought of contradicting a bishop.' Perhaps the harshest critic of his age, Johnson nevertheless named Psalmanazar as 'the best man I ever knew'.

Psalmanazar's success, while it lasted, depended largely on the attractiveness (or not) of his book on Formosa to various interest groups. The obvious fascination it held for the reader who loved to be shocked and appalled by the excesses of heretical foreigners has already been mentioned. There was also an impressive anti-Jesuitical streak running through the book, which went down well in a country in religious crisis, where many people still saw Jesuits as symbols of the Inquisition. On the other hand, the doubt cast on Psalmanazar's authenticity by the likes of Edmund Halley and others 'was generally imputed . . . to their supposed disregard for Christianity; the honour of which some thought, was not a little concerned in this notable conversion'. The eagerness of these men of science to expose Psalmanazar, a writer in the *Monthly Review* argued, only served 'to make others think the better of him, and to espouse his cause with the more zeal . . . It was, therefore, the luckiest thing that could have happened for George, that the

Free-thinkers were his first declared opposers.' The anti-Jesuit would be more likely to be pro-Psalmanazar; the anti-Psalmanazar was interpreted as anti-Christ. It was a complex and contradictory formula but one which neatly served a palpable prejudice. Psalmanazar's book, in short, was 'perfectly designed to appeal to the reading public in eighteenth century England'. As Richard Aldington summarized its attractions:

There was the appeal to ignorant wonder – he came from the almost unknown island of Formosa; the appeal to snobbery – he was the son of a King, and above all, the appeal to sectarian conceit – he had been sought after by Jesuits, Lutherans and Calvinists, but to this noble savage mind all had seemed wrong except the Church of England.

Psalmanazar is unusual among impostors in recapturing a large measure of respectability subsequent to his imposture being revealed. Frederic Foley, who wrote the definitive account of the Formosan impostor, concludes that Psalmanazar's reformation was 'complete and sincere' and that in his later years he was indeed 'a figure to inspire respect and admiration'. This is confirmed in a report which portrays the venerable Dr Johnson in an atypically cautious mode: 'So high did [Johnson] hold [Psalmanazar's] character in the latter part of his life' that when Johnson was asked 'whether he had ever mentioned Formosa to him, he said he was afraid to mention even China'.

In 1817 a pamphlet was published describing the arrival of a mysterious visitor to the West Country:

On Thursday evening the 3rd of April, 1817, the Overseer of the Poor of the parish of Almondsbury, in the county of Gloucester, called at Knole Park, the residence of Samuel Worrall, Esq., to inform that Gentleman and his Lady, that a young Female had entered a cottage in the village, and had made signs, that it was her wish to sleep under its roof; but not speaking a language, which its inhabitants or the Overseer understood, the officer thought it right to refer to Mr. Worrall, a Magistrate for the county, for his advice . . .

The female was in consequence ordered to be brought up to Knole Mansion, but to which removal she shewed signs of strong reluctance; and when there, refused for some time to enter its doors. After some entreaty, she was prevailed upon to go in, and was presented to Mr. and Mrs. Worrall; who . . . were unable to understand the language in which she addressed them; but intimated to her by signs, that they wished to ascertain whether or not she had any papers in her possession; upon which she took from her pocket a few halfpence, with a bad sixpence, and implied that she had nothing else.

She had a small bundle on her arm containing a very few necessaries, and a piece of soap pinned up in a bit of linen. Her dress consisted of a black stuff gown, with a muslin frill round the neck, and a black cotton shawl on her head, and a red and black shawl round her shoulders; both loosely and tastefully put on in imitation of the Asiatic costume; leather shoes and black worsted stockings. The general impression from her person and manners was attractive and prepossessing.

Mrs Worrall warmed to the young stranger and took it upon herself to 'keep her under her roof, till something satisfactory transpired concerning her'. During the days that followed, the young lady's behaviour provided some clues about her background. She appeared to recognize images of China which the local vicar had thoughtfully brought to show her, and said her name was Caraboo. As her fame spread, she received many visitors, several of them foreigners who hoped to be able to help identify her place of origin through language. All failed, and Mrs Worrall was beginning to suspect that her guest was imposing on her generous nature when 'a Portuguese from the Malay country; who happened to be in Bristol' succeeded in communicating with her in her own language. Following a long interview, Mrs Worrall was informed that she had a princess under her roof, from an island called Javasu in the East Indies, whence she had been abducted by pirates, brought to England and then abandoned. Delighted at this revelation, Mrs Worrall gave Princess Caraboo to understand that she should remain at Knole as her honoured guest for as long as she wished.

The exotic visitor, who had by now made herself a dress in her native style, cut a strange shape in the small rural community; however, the local tenants and farmers apparently 'grew very fond of her' and became accustomed to the unusual habits of their new neighbour:

Despite her stay she used to exercise herself with a bow and arrows, and made a stick answer to a sword on her right side, the bow and arrows slung on her left shoulder. She oftentimes carried a gong on her back, which she sounded in a very singular manner, and a tambourine in her hands, the sword by her side and a bow and arrows slung as usual, her head dressed with flowers and feathers, and thus she made it appear she was prepared for war . . .

Mrs. Worrall was one evening absent from Knole on the day of a wake in the parish, and on her return found her missing. The gardens were searched, and she was discovered sitting in a high tree, in which she explained herself to have climbed, because all the females in the house had gone into the village, and she feared contamination from the men.

However, the next time Caraboo disappeared, she was eventually found further afield. Within days word reached Mrs Worrall that her protégée was in Bath, where she tracked her down to the fashionable home of 'a lady of *haut ton*'. Mrs Worrall found Caraboo 'at the very pinnacle of her glory and ambition', enthroned in the drawing room, surrounded by well-heeled admirers of both sexes. Among these interested parties was one Dr Wilkinson, who regaled the Bath *Chronicle*'s fascinated readers with this account of the princess:

Her mode of diet seems to be Hindoostanic, as she lives principally on vegetables, and is very partial to curry; she will occasionally take fish, but no other animal food; water is her beverage; and she expresses great disgust at the appearance of wine, spirits, or of any intoxicating liquors: whatever she eats, she prepares herself. She is extremely neat in her attire; is very cautious in her conduct with respect to gentlemen; never allows them to take hold of her hand, and even if their clothes should casually come into contact with hers, she retires from them: when she takes leave of a gentleman, it is by the application of the right hand to the right side of the forehead, and, in like manner, on taking leave of a lady, it is with the left hand. She appears to be devout; and on a certain day in the week is anxious to go to the top of the house and there to pay adoration to the sun from the rising to the setting.

(These antics on the roof at Knole, incidentally, caused great concern to her hosts, as she ascended 'frequently at the imminent peril of her life'.)

Dr Wilkinson also went to some lengths to identify Caraboo's language, which she now wrote 'with great facility'. However, neither the search of a range of scholarly books on linguistics, nor the consultation of numerous experts in Oriental languages were able to throw any light on the matter.

Nevertheless, it was Dr Wilkinson who was largely responsible for the mystery being solved, although quite inadvertently. A Mrs Neale who ran a lodging house read his account in the *Chronicle* with more than ordinary interest, for in it she was reminded of a certain Mary Baker, who had lodged with her several months before. Mary had stuck in her mind because of her habit of telling preposterous stories; the landlady had privately considered the girl to be mentally unhinged. Brought before Caraboo, the landlady immediately identified her as her ex-lodger; Mary Baker burst into tears and confessed all. A servant girl from Devon, 'with a far from unblemished reputation', to whom, at other times, 'spirits and water were not quite so repugnant to her taste, as they had been at Knole', she had been motivated only by her own 'restless disposition' and had been roaming the countryside for some time before conceiving her new identity which, she reasoned, would enlist greater sympathy than that of an ordinary female vagrant.

Whereas Psalmanazar had generously provided a startling array of 'facts' about his homeland and even written a book about it, Caraboo's silence was in many ways more impressive – and less likely to get her into webs of deceit which might later trip her up. Unlike Psalmanazar, she had received only a very rudimentary education, and therefore her invented alphabet – which she furnished for academic scrutiny – was uncluttered with anything resembling known oriental characters. The fact that not a single piece of evidence – dress, language, customs, religion – could be pinned down to a particular place, transformed Mary Baker's ignorance into Caraboo's mystique. But this is not to say that what Baker did was simple.

As Baker listened to and watched those around her, she must have been perpetually concentrating on her 'part'. The housekeeper whose bed she shared at Knole 'never heard at any interval any other language or tone of voice than that which she first assumed'. Similarly, it was observed that 'she was always consistent and correct' in using her invented vocabulary of Javasu, always employing particular words 'in the same sense, meaning or object'. Before having her suspicions allayed by the Portuguese man who 'recognized' Caraboo's language, the kindly Mrs Worrall had taken Baker aside and warned her:

My good young woman, I very much fear that you are imposing upon me, and that you understand and can answer me in my own language; if so, and distress has driven you to this expedient, make a friend of me; I am a female as yourself, and can feel for you, and will give you money and clothes, and will put you on your journey, without disclosing your conduct to anyone; but it must be on condition that you speak the truth. If you deceive me, I think it right to inform you that Mr. Worrall is a magistrate, and has the power of sending you to prison, committing you to hard labour, and passing you as a vagrant to your own parish.

The presentation of such a real threat, accompanied with such a generous offer of assistance if she laid aside her mask must have at least given Baker pause for thought, yet we are informed that the mask did not even slip: 'During this address the countenance of the stranger evinced an ignorance of Mrs Worrall's intentions, at the same time making it apparent that she did not comprehend what Mrs Worrall had said to her; and she immediately addressed Mrs Worrall in her unknown tongue.' Moreover, she had always to be on her guard against those attempting to 'catch her out', as when a witty cleric aimed to flatter her into self-exposure:

He drew his chair close to her, looked steadily and smilingly in her face, and observed 'You are the most beautiful creature I ever beheld. You are an angel.' – Not a muscle of her face moved; no blush suffused her cheek; her countenance was motionless.

Many concluded, with Dr Wilkinson, that 'such is the general effect on all who behold her, that, if before suspected as an impostor, the sight of her removes all doubt.'

Her relentless self-control was only matched by her creativity in thinking up ways in which to enhance her alien status. It was not enough just to sit and 'be' Caraboo; Caraboo had to be constantly surprising. Whether she was climbing trees in order to escape contaminating males, sitting on the roof to worship the sun, banging gongs and tambourines, or practising with her bow and arrow, Caraboo had always to be conspicuously different, confounding expectations. Her invention of details from a strict diet to modes of salutation testifies to the sense in which she completely immersed herself in the role she played.

All of this begs the question: was Mary Baker unbalanced, as her late landlady suggested? To the extent that any impostor has crossed a line which the rest of us would not, the answer has to be 'yes'. Her father went further:

> . . . he really thought, she was not always right in her head. Ever since she was fifteen years old, in consequence of a rheumatic fever, which affected her head, he believed she was not right in her mind. At spring and fall she was particularly uneasy, always wishing to go abroad.

However, it is difficult to make a strong case for Baker being actually ill. As one gentleman acquainted with Caraboo wrote to Mrs Worrall:

> Can it be possible that she should be deranged in her mind, and yet have been enabled to carry on her deception so long and with such consistency? We have heard of the power of maniacs to conceal deep laid plans with the greatest subtlety, but I recollect no one being carried on so successfully, for so long a time, and under such a variety of circumstances.

Similarly, it seems unlikely that someone suffering from a mental illness could on the one hand construct such a meticulously consistent persona while on the other hand remaining sufficiently detached from it to immediately and completely lay it aside when detected. Baker was in no sense captivated by Caraboo, as, for example, Anna Anderson may have been by Anastasia. Yet in the end it has to be acknowledged that Mary Baker herself remains a greater enigma than Princess Caraboo.

Soon after her imposture was exposed, Mary Baker was prevailed upon to render a full account of her life prior to her arrival, as Caraboo, in the parish of Almondsbury. This proved to be a tale quite as fascinating as the purported history of the fictitious Caraboo.

She had been born Mary Wilcox, in Witheridge, Devon, in 1791, 'and received no education, being of a wild disposition'. Her father was a lame cobbler, and from the age of eight Mary undertook farmwork and spun wool. 'From her earliest years,' it was noted, 'she had always an ambition to excel her companions, whether at any particular game, playing at cricket, swimming in the water, or fishing, etc.' At the age of sixteen her parents secured her a position looking after a farmer's children, but she evidently found her duties insufficiently challenging (or inglorious) and 'often carried a sack of corn or apples on her back, endeavouring to do more than the labouring men'. She left this job because the pay was low, much to her parents' wrath and, feeling unwelcome at home, she set off for Exeter. After a brief sojourn in the family of a shoemaker ('As she was expected to wash, iron and cook, to which she was not accustomed, she only staid there two months'), she returned home. To her parents' disapproval Mary became 'very fond of finery', and it was their suspicion that she had procured her new clothes by compromising her honesty (from which can be inferred, her virtue). 'Knowing her innocence, and not enduring to hear this, she again decamped' and set off once more for Exeter.

Mary may have claimed the moral high ground, but in storming off had left both her clothes and money behind, and was reduced to a state of such extreme misery on the road to Exeter that she attempted to hang herself from a tree by her apron-strings. She was fortunately prevented from this desperate course by a disembodied voice which reminded her: 'Cursed are they that do murder, and sin against the Lord.'

Thereafter, Mary seems to have been buffeted from pillar to post by individuals and institutions both benign and malign. Her account gives an extremely vivid picture of a world now lost, where vagrancy was a primary – if not *the* primary – social problem. The vagrant represented a charge to the parish, and as such was continually being moved on. (It will be remembered that, on arriving at Almondsbury as Caraboo, Mary was immediately picked up by the Overseer of the Poor and taken to the nearest magistrate, Mr Worrall.) Before she hit on the Caraboo stratagem, as an ordinary vagrant she had travelled great distances, dodging the authorities along the way. One night, for example, begging on the road from

Bristol to London, she had the bad luck to knock at the door of the local constable, who immediately locked her in a room in his house, intending to take her to a JP in the morning, 'to swear her to her parish'. (Fortunately, 'when he went out for something in a yard behind the house, she made her escape through the window.') Yet the flipside of this relentless pursuit of the vagrant exposes a more sympathetic and charitable aspect to the period. Mary's story is punctuated by the kindness of strangers: whether it was a fellow traveller on the road who gave her five shillings, the Strangers' Friend Society at Bristol, who gave her four, or the poor women who, finding her weak and sick, ensured she got to St Giles's Hospital in London, thereby probably saving her life.

In London, after Mary recovered from a long and dangerous illness, a charitable trinity of matron, nurse and clergyman attached to St Giles's found the homeless and friendless girl a live-in job, where she at last found a measure of stability. She remained there for three years, during which time her mistress, a Mrs Matthews, taught her to read and write. But Mary's ship continued to pitch and toss; she left Mrs Matthews after a row over disobedience. She then made the extraordinary error of mistaking a home for fallen women for a convent:

She had often observed the Magdalen, in Blackfriars' Road, and conceiving it to be a nunnery, was resolved to get into it. She asked this woman about it, and she said that women went there the first Wednesday in a month. She called and knocked at the door at the appointed day, where there were many young women besides. As they entered the room, their bonnets and caps were taken off. They asked her, how long had she gone on in that way? How long had she been on the town? – the meaning of which she did not comprehend – she said she was sorry for her faults. They talked very seriously with her, and made her cry.

Mary spent six months at the Magdalen. When it was discovered that she was not an ex-prostitute, and therefore could not be reformed, she was reprimanded for falsehood, given a pound, and turned out. Intending to return home until she could find a place, but afraid of crossing Hounslow Heath ('on account of robberies, and murders, then prevalent'), she took the precaution of changing her own clothes for men's at a pawnbroker's. She recommenced her travels, looking 'very wicked', and on Salisbury Plain fell in with some highwaymen. Discovering her secret, they made her swear never to betray them and sent her on her way with a guinea and five shillings. She returned to female dress and a sequence of short-lived jobs followed, before Mary met and married a man of whom she seemed to know little more than that he was a foreigner.

The couple travelled for a while before pitching up in Brighton, at which point her husband 'gave her some money to take her to London; [he] proceeding to Dover, and from thence to Calais, promising to write and send for her, which he never did'. Returning to London, friendless and pregnant, Mary went into domestic service until her baby was born, taken to the Foundlings' Home, and died. Subsequently, Mary drifted with a band of gypsies, picking up their 'gibberish'. At Bristol she went to the quayside in search of a ship bound for America and a new start. Informed that one sailed in fifteen days' time and the cost of passage was £5, she resolved to find the money in the allotted time. Shortly afterwards, Princess Caraboo appeared.

It may be imagined with what combination of incredulity and compassion Mrs Worrall listened to this story. She wanted to help Mary, but her charity was strictly conditional on its object's honesty. Extensive inquiries were duly made to the employers Mary had mentioned, her parents and several other individuals whose paths she claimed to have crossed. Back came reports: apart from the incidents of the Magdalen home for repentant prostitutes and the nest of highwaymen (which were not, perhaps understandably, researched at all), Mary's story was comprehensively corroborated. Out of the goodness of her principled heart, Mrs Worrall paid Mary Baker's passage to America.

The story did not end as her ship sailed out of sight, however. Bath and Bristol continued to buzz with the affair. Those who had known Mary Baker before she became Caraboo came forward and gave their pennyworth. The family she had worked for immediately prior to the birth of her baby had been 'very partial to her' and recalled that she:

. . . told such odd unaccountable stories that she became proverbial amongst them for the marvellous; they were stories, however, which never did harm to anybody, but seemed to arise from the love of telling something extraordinary.

Mrs Matthews, her employer in London, related that 'Her behaviour was always strange and eccentric, and her ways so mysterious . . . that no one who did not know the girl would believe them, were she to relate what occurred.' Like all her other employers, she attested to Mary's goodness, trustworthiness and cleanliness. She also noted, as did others, that Mary very seldom went out. 'She would sometimes say, she should like to go and live in the woods; and sometimes she would not eat for days together, to shew how long she could live without food . . .'

Weeks later, the affair had still not died down, and an article appeared in *Felix Farley's Bristol Journal* which paid indirect homage to Baker's deception by testing the gullibility of its readers once more. The writer described how a mysterious young woman had pitched up on the island of St Helena, home of the exiled Napoleon:

Sir Hudson introduced her to Bonaparte under the name of Caraboo. She described herself as Princess of Caraboo, and related a tale of extraordinary interest, which seemed in a high degree to delight the captive chief. He embraced her with every demonstration of enthusiastic rapture, and besought Sir Hudson that she might be allowed an apartment in his house, declaring that she alone was an adequate source of solace in his captivity. Since the arrival of this lady, the countenance and figure of Bonaparte appear to be wholly altered. From being reserved and dejected, he has become gay and communicative. No more complaints are heard about the inconveniences at Longwood. He has intimated to Sir Hudson his determination to apply to the Pope for a dispensation to dissolve his marriage with Maria Louise, and to sanction his indissoluble union with the enchanting Caraboo.

Mary Baker would doubtless have enjoyed this fiction; as it happened, she was enjoying her real life even more. The Caraboo affair had made her so famous that she was obliged to travel to America under the name of Burgess, yet this ruse fooled nobody; as she wrote to a friend in Bristol, 'the Ladies and passengers called me nothing but Caraboo on the passage.' Landing in America after a nine-week voyage, far from leaving the past behind, Baker found the English newspapers had overtaken her across the ocean, with the result that 'there were hundreds of people on the wharf to look at me'. She quickly discovered the pressure of fame:

. . . the public curiosity was so great, that it prevented me from accepting many places that were offered to me, and I was not able to leave the House I lived in, without being followed by the people: as I could not therefore procure that employment and seclusion I wished for, I was induced by my friends here, to give a concert, which was managed for me by several English gentlemen and ladies. It was given at Washington Hall, the longest public building in this city. The room was splendidly lit, and the company was numerous, and if you had seen me handed on and off the Stage by two gentlemen you had thought I really was a Princess, as I really did at this time.

Setting aside, for a moment, her royal treatment, Baker shares with her girlfriend various chatty details, from the intriguing intimacy that on the vessel out 'the mate wanted me to marry him and because I would not, behaved very ill after my arrival here', through having been bought 'an American hat', to the observations that

Philadelphians are 'very distant' and 'everything is very dear here.' She also writes, somewhat wistfully:

Although I have the best of everything and live as I ought like a Princess, yet I hope one day or other to see old England again and those kind friends I left in it, as I can never forget the attention they shewed me.

Mary Baker was indeed to set foot in old England again, as the following newspaper account makes painfully plain:

In the year 1824, Caraboo having returned from America, took apartments in New Bond-Street, where she made a public exhibition of herself – admittance *one shilling* each person; but it does not appear that any great number went to see her.

10. The Impostor Within

Are we who we say we are? Do our clothes reflect who we really are or who we wish we were? We like to think, when we style our hair or put on make-up that we are simply 'making the best of ourselves'. If this is truly the case, why do we adjust our choice of appearance according to the occasion and the company? We can all come up with convincing and reassuring answers, but we also know, deep down, that we like to present different versions of ourselves at different times. Sometimes we want to fit in; at others we seek to stand out. Appearance, of course, is only part of the story. All aspects of the way we speak – accent, vocabulary and tone – are subtly modulated according to the context. Add 'body language' to all the above, and it is clear that we consciously contrive to *make our selves different*. Moreover, this is without taking into account *what* we say. The impostor, it could be argued, simply goes much further down a road that we are all of us already on.

Although we may acknowledge our own, minor, modifications of our selves, we nevertheless remain curiously trusting about each other. We place an unwarranted degree of faith in official-looking pieces of paper, even though we know that we could probably not detect a forgery. We have almost entirely abdicated the responsibility for checking these credentials and identities to other, faceless 'authorities'. We allow ourselves to be reassured by extremely unsophisticated factors such as dress, context and behaviour – all of which can be supplied to our satisfaction by the accomplished impostor. But perhaps most importantly, for a society which tends to cynicism, most people are astoundingly trusting. Despite the impression of our culture which could be gained from watching our inhumanity to each other nightly on the news, the truth is that we simply do not expect to be lied to. For all these reasons we find ourselves in the astonishing position where it does not occur to us to ask whether the masked figure poised with a knife over our unconscious naked body is really a doctor.

It is perhaps a measure of civilization that lies remain shocking. Valuing truth, then, why do we find tales of imposture attractive? The popular appetite for such stories is testified to by the fact that so many have been made into highly successful films. By and large, the public loves an impostor, thrilling – overtly or secretly – to this kind of taboo-breaking. It is precisely because one of the very first lessons we are taught as children is to tell the truth that when we learn that someone has pulled off a monumental lie our first reaction is excited interest. We generally admire the complex and the creative, tending to judge less harshly the audacious train-robber or the teenage computer-hacker because, as with impostors, we know intelligence and hard work have gone into perfecting the crime. If we do not admire the impostor, we at least marvel at him.

It is also the case that we associate disguise and dual identity with positive as well as negative images. Nerdy journalist Clark Kent moonlights as Superman; respectable millionaire Bruce Wayne transforms himself into Batman; from Spiderman to Zorro, from the Scarlet Pimpernel to the Lone Ranger, masked men transcend the constraints of everyday life, even bend the rules of nature, in order to change the world in a way which is inaccessible to them as ordinary mortals. Viewed in this light, the impostor is in the mould – albeit a rather warped one – of the archetypal popular hero, skilfully deploying wit, courage and deception on a world ignorant of his true identity.

We can also identify with the frustrations which might lead to imposture. Take for example the case of the disappearing magician. In the late 1980s Sophie Lloyd found herself facing a seemingly insurmountable problem. The impediment to her success was the Magic Circle, the professional association for magicians, membership of which was a basic prerequisite for a career in showbusiness.

It was not that she was not sufficiently talented to gain membership; she was simply the wrong sex. The Magic Circle, as a matter of policy, only included men. Lloyd had an ally in her anger, her agent Jenny Winstanley. Between them they cooked up a scheme which would expose the hypocrisy of the Magic Circle's archaic rule.

A little while later, Raymond, an amiable sixteen-year-old lad, appeared on the club circuit, performing magic tricks. Raymond was the product of meticulous research, preparation and attention to detail. With the employment of a wig, glasses, plumpers to fatten her face and theatrical padding to fill out her figure, Lloyd's appearance was transformed into that of a non-athletic male adolescent. The way Raymond moved, walked and talked also required work. While coaching Lloyd, Winstanley measured her progress by studying people's interaction with and reaction to Raymond in shops and pubs, on buses and trains; from walking up the street to downing a pint, Lloyd was groomed to 'pass' as Raymond. A life was also invented for him: family, friends and school – and a personality. Raymond, the women decided, should not be too much of a conversationalist (in fact, like many boys of that age, verging on the monosyllabic), and should be magic-mad: the showbiz equivalent of a trainspotter or computer nerd.

Over a year passed before, in 1989, the women were sufficiently confident of his success to enter Raymond as an applicant for membership of the Magic Circle. The examination was to be performed before an audience of two hundred people, after which (and actually more stressful under the circumstances) Raymond was obliged to mingle and chat informally with members of the Circle. He passed.

Months later, when the Magic Circle finally bowed to public pressure and changed its regulations in order to allow women to become members, Lloyd and Winstanley revealed their grand illusion. The Magic Circle responded by revoking Raymond's membership and refusing membership to Lloyd, whom they also threatened to sue. An anonymous late-night phonecall informed Lloyd and Winstanley that their careers were over and subsequently they experienced great difficulty getting bookings.

The moral of this story seems to be that imposture, even when eminently justifiable, remains an extremely hazardous strategy. This is because it is often the case that the controversy surrounding an imposture cloaks a greater clash of wider interests. In the 'Raymond' case, this social drama was obviously feminism versus male privilege. The case of the Tichborne claimant received much greater media attention and succeeded in polarizing public opinion, dividing the country along class lines. As Nick Yapp has written, 'The poor believed him: the rich didn't. Those who sneered at Orton and rejected his claim did so on the grounds that he looked coarse, that his hands were calloused, that he spoke with a common accent, and that he, therefore, couldn't be a gentleman.' Such was the anger aroused by the patronizing and mocking tone of several speeches made in court, which were widely reported by the newspapers, that prosecuting counsel required a police escort to and from the court to defend themselves from huge crowds which gathered to boo them. To lower and upper classes alike, the Tichborne claimant represented a threat to the status quo, and his cause was consequently respectively championed and vilified by them.

Many of the other cases mentioned here also reveal competing social and political interests, reminding us of ugly aspects of relations between social classes, men and women, black and white. Yet while an imposture may *illustrate* a social drama, it is often first and foremost the product of the idiosyncratic nature of the impostor, who is peculiarly emotionally and psychologically fit for such a role, enabling him or her to make a cognitive leap which would never occur to the majority of us. One characteristic shared by most of the other impostors we know is a breadth of imagination which most of us have edited out of our way of thinking by the time we reach adulthood. The impostor's worldview retains the same broad horizons characteristic of a child's. Any five-year-old will confidently tell you he or she is going to be a racing driver, a dinosaur-fossil hunter, an explorer. Ask them again at fifteen and they're already less sure; a recognized aspect of maturity is a sense of proportion, perspective, 'realism', an acceptance of our own limitations. The five-year-old's plan is cruelly exposed as a fantasy. But the impostor dares to dream the dreams of childhood, where the future is something you choose for yourself, where achievement proceeds logically from ambition.

The story of Raymond and the Magic Circle derives some of its appeal from its setting in the entertainment industry: it was a performance within a performance. A large proportion of the impostors in this book had connections with the theatre or cinema at some point in their lives. Wilhelm Voigt (the Captain of Köpernick), Harry Domela (the Kaiser's grandson) and female sailor Hannah Snell all performed in stage shows based on their real-life experiences; while Lady Newborough was an actress long before she began to pursue her claim to royalty, Mary Anne Talbot became an actress after her career as a sailor, and both Long Lance and Ferdinand Waldo Demara had brief stints as film actors. Even the lecturing careers of Deborah Sampson, Grey Owl and Louis de Rougemont, and Red Fox's appearances on television chatshows represent a kind of theatrical performance. Many also capitalized on the public interest in their cases by writing autobiographies. It seems likely that this creative or theatrical bent was closely linked to their capacity for imposture; as such, the step from playing the role in real life to playing a part upon the stage or screen was a short, natural and easy transition. One could even go so far as to suggest that, had many of these characters gone into showbusiness or become writers they might never have become impostors: the entertainer and the author are legitimate pretenders, their inventions are sanctioned, their imaginings celebrated in the sharing.

As is suggested at the beginning of this chapter, we do not have to look much further than our own, average behaviour to begin to understand the roots of imposture. However, for some people the *idea* of the impostor becomes intrusive and threatening. For example, it is not an uncommon phenomenon that people (those who are not impostors, that is) fear they will be 'found out' as impostors. Successful, well-qualified and experienced people, who really ought to know better, fear in the back of their minds that at some point someone will tap them on the shoulder and say: *Excuse me, but there's been a mistake. It's perfectly obvious that you aren't up to this job. It's a wonder you've got away with it so long.* People involved in the arts, where success is dependent on opinion or taste rather than more scientifically quantifiable standards, are particularly susceptible to this kind of gnawing self-doubt. We all suffer from it to an extent, but some people suffer extremely in an incapacitating way and actually become ill, believing themselves to be impostors. This condition has been labelled 'pseudocompetence' or the Achilles syndrome: it is only a matter of time, sufferers believe, before their weak spot is identified and their world falls apart. While this syndrome is an extreme manifestation of a condition which in most people never exceeds a sense of nagging anxiety, there is another mental illness associated with the idea of imposture which bears no relation to most people's experience and is fortunately extremely rare. Capgras's syndrome causes the sufferer to believe that someone close to them has been abducted or killed and replaced by an exact double, often with evil intentions.

In 1995 Alan and Christine Davies were both injured in a car accident. Both recovered physically, but Alan was convinced that his wife had been killed and that Christine Two, as he called her, was an impostor. Psychiatrist Sudad Jawad observed that whenever the couple came to see him, Alan 'never acted as though he was sitting next to a real person'. His wife and daughter described how Alan had changed from an outgoing, tactile, affectionate personality who discussed everything with his wife to a man who barely communicated with her and could 'not bear to touch her'. After two years of treating Alan, Dr Jawad reluctantly came to the conclusion that his delusion was fixed and incurable. The couple were still living together at the time of writing, although as Alan said, 'I have good days and bad days but I still believe my wife has died.'

The idea – and the reality – of the impostor strikes at the very core of our assumptions about identity. It makes us question the way we see the world, the assumptions we make about those who share it with us. But taking a closer look at some examples of imposture also reveals it as a liberating strategy and a force, in some cases, for good. At the very least, the impostor takes control of his or her life, utterly changing its direction, whether just for a single day or for a whole lifetime.

Most of the people whose stories are told in this book have failed: as was stated at its outset, the fact we know they are impostors *means* they failed. A successful impostor will never be known as such. The impostor does not occupy some cloak and dagger world apart from the rest of us but exists very much in the everyday, in the here and now. He or she may be about to take your temperature or hear your confession. Perhaps he or she is sitting next to you on the Tube or lying next to you in bed. Or even, maybe, reading this book.

Further Reading

Louis de Rougemont: 'A Sort of Wizard'

All quotations from de Rougemont's account of his travels are from the book version (which is easier to consult than the instalments in *Wide World* magazine): *The Adventures of Louis de Rougemont, as Told by Himself* (London: George Newnes, 1899).

All the correspondence and journalism cited appeared in the pages of the *Daily Chronicle* in the month of September 1898.

Geoffrey Maslen, *The Most Amazing Story a Man Ever Lived to Tell* (London: Angus & Robertson, 1977), contains both extracts from de Rougemont's account and details of the controversy.

VIPs; or, 'Guess Who's Coming to Dinner?'

Accounts of the impostor VIPs discussed here, and a range of other impostors, can be found among the following general titles:

Margaret Barton & Osbert Sitwell, *Sober Truths: A Collection of Nineteenth-Century Episodes, Fantastic, Grotesque and Mysterious* (London: MacDonald, 1944)

Derek Cooper, *The Gullibility Gap* (London: Routledge & Kegan Paul, 1974)

Horace W. Fuller, *Impostors and Adventurers* (Boston: Soule & Bugbee, 1882)

Stuart Gordon, *The Book of Hoaxes: An A–Z of Famous Fakes, Frauds and Cons* (London: Headline, 1995)

Hoaxes and Deceptions (Alexandria, Va: Time-Life Books, 1991)

Egon Larsen, *The Deceivers: Lives of the Great Impostors* (London: John Baker, 1966)

Richard Newnham, *The Guinness Book of Fakes, Frauds & Forgeries* (Enfield: Guinness, 1996)

Stanley B.-R. Poole, *Royal Mysteries and Pretenders* (London: Blandford Press, 1969)

Jeremy Potter, *Pretenders* (London: Constable, 1986)

Carl Sifakis, *Hoaxes and Scams: A Compendium of Deceptions, Ruses and Swindles* (London: Michael O'Hara, 1994)

Judge Gerald Sparrow, *The Great Impostors* (London: John Long, 1962)

Gordon Stein, *The Encyclopaedia of Hoaxes* (London: Gale Research, 1993)

Bram Stoker, *Famous Impostors* (London: Sidgwick & Jackson, 1910)

Colin Wilson, *World Famous Crimes* (London: Robinson, 1995)

Nick Yapp, *Hoaxers and Their Victims* (London: Robson, 1992)

Ferdinand Waldo Demara and Other Professional Types

For a full report of Brian MacKinnon's imposture, see:

Ian Parker, 'I was Brandon Lee', *Granta* 58, Summer 1998, pp. 115–45.

The two principal sources for the life of Ferdinand Waldo Demara are:

Robert Crichton, *The Great Impostor* (New York: Random House, 1959)

Joe McCarthy, 'The master impostor: an incredible tale', *Life*, 28 January 1952, pp. 79–89

'I Know Who I Am'

There are a great number of books about Anna Anderson ('Anastasia') and the Tichborne claimant. Far fewer have been written on the Martin Guerre affair, the most authoritative being by Natalie Zemon Davis, *The Return of Martin Guerre* (London: Penguin, 1977). Early writings on the psychology of imposture include:

Karl Abraham, 'The history of an impostor in the light of psychoanalytic knowledge', *Psychoanalytical Quarterly* 4 (1935), pp. 570–87.

Helene Deutsch, 'The Impostor: contribution to ego psychology of a type of psychopath', *Psychoanalytical Quaterly* 24 (1955), pp. 483–505.

Phyllis Greenacre, 'The Impostor', *Psychoanalytical Quarterly* 27 (1958), pp. 359–82 and 'The relation of the impostor to the artist', *Psychoanalytic Study of the Child* 13 (1958), pp. 521–40

Dr James Barry: 'A Gentleman Every Inch'

There are two full-length biographies of James Barry:

Isobel Rae, *The Strange Story of Dr James Barry* (London: Longmans, 1958)

June Rose, *The Perfect Gentleman* (London: Hutchinson, 1977)

Shorter pieces of interest include:

Brian Hurwitz and Ruth Richardson, 'Inspector General James Barry MD: putting the woman in her place', *British Medical Journal*, 1989, vol. 298, pp. 299–305

Anne Savage, 'The lord and the lady', *Journal of the Royal Society of Medicine*, 1998, vol. 91, pp. 279–82

Other Singular Gentlemen

General works on women passing for men include:

M. M. Dowie (ed.), *Women Adventurers* (London: T. Fisher Unwin, 1893)

O. P. Gilbert, *Women in Men's Guise* (London: John Lane, 1932)
Julie Wheelwright, *Amazons and Military Maids: Women who Dressed as Men in the Pursuit of Life, Liberty and Happiness* (London: Pandora, 1989)

For a wide-ranging discussion of cross-dressing see:
Marjorie Garber, *Vested Interests: Cross Dressing and Cultural Anxiety* (New York: Routledge, 1992)

Individual 'Lives':
Herman Mann, *The Female Review: Life of Deborah Sampson, the Female Soldier in the War of the Revolution* (Boston: J. K. Wiggin & W. P. Lunt, 1866)
The Life and Surprising Adventures of Mary Anne Talbot (London: R. S. Kirby, 1809)
The Female Soldier: or, the Surprising Life and Adventures of Hannah Snell (London: R. Walker, 1750)
Diane Wood Middlebrook, *Suits Me: The Double Life of Billy Tipton* (London: Virago, 1998)

Chief Buffalo Child Long Lance:
'One Hundred Per Cent American'

Sylvester Long's story, as he told it, is *Long Lance: The Autobiography of a Blackfoot Indian Chief* (London: Faber & Gwyer, 1928)

The only full-length account of Long's real and invented lives is by Donald B. Smith, *Long Lance: The True Story of an Impostor* (Toronto: Macmillan, 1982)

Other Foreign Bodies and Exotic Aliens

Two people who featured in the career of Archibald Belaney, his publisher and his wife, wrote books about him:

Anahareo, *Grey Owl and I* (London: Peter Davies, 1972)
Lovat Dickson, *Wilderness Man: The Strange Story of Grey Owl* (London: Macmillan, 1974)

George Psalmanazar has left us both his pretended account, *An Historical and Geographical Description of Formosa*, 2nd edn (London: M. Wootton, 1705) and his true story, published posthumously, *Memoirs of ★★★★, Commonly Known by the Name of George Psalmanazar*, 2nd edn (London: P. Wilson, 1765). A full analysis of the deception is given by Frederic J. Foley, *The Great Formosan Impostor* (Taipei: Mei Ya Publications, Inc., 1968)

The contemporary exposé of 'Princess Caraboo' was: *Caraboo: A Narrative of a Singular Imposition Practiced upon the Benevolence of a Lady Residing in the Vicinity of Bristol* (Bristol: J. M. Gutch, 1817)

This is not a complete bibliography, but a guide to the principal sources, and further reading.

Index